THE AFTERLIVES OF KATHLEEN COLLINS

STUDIES IN THE CINEMA OF THE BLACK DIASPORA
Michael T. Martin and David C. Wall, editors

THE AFTERLIVES OF KATHLEEN COLLINS

A Black Woman Filmmaker's Search for New Life

L. H. STALLINGS

INDIANA UNIVERSITY PRESS

This book is a publication of

Indiana University Press
Office of Scholarly Publishing
Herman B Wells Library 350
1320 East 10th Street
Bloomington, Indiana 47405 USA

iupress.org

Manufactured in the United States of America

First printing 2021

Cataloging information is available from the Library of Congress.

ISBN 978-0-253-05901-7 (hardback)
ISBN 978-0-253-05903-1 (paperback)
ISBN 978-0-253-05902-4 (web PDF)

CONTENTS

ACKNOWLEDGMENTS

THE BLACK FILM CENTER/ARCHIVE at Indiana University, and many of the administrative people connected with it were essential to this project. My early engagement with Collins was made possible because Phyllis Klotman, a professor of Black studies who was a passionate advocate for Black film studies, was enamored with Collins's work and recorded and archived pivotal materials about and from Collins. Later, the film scholar and critic John A. Williams would amass a personal research archive of Collins's films and plays that he contributed to BFC/A. Notably, Black independent filmmaker Haile Gerima gave me permission to view the Howard University film earlier than its release in 2016 on Vimeo and the DVD extras of *Losing Ground*—providing insights into how thoughtful peers can be of each other's works, especially when the works are underappreciated ones they believe in.

Collins's unpublished and unproduced short stories, screenplays, theatrical plays, letters, and journals have been preserved and cared for by her daughter, Nina Collins, in ways that exceed collective Black cultural memory and traditional archival functions. Nina granted me access to these materials in 2010. She also connected me to other important people in Collins's life, specifically former students: Ronald Gray, Susie Korda, and Rebecca Williams. All three were especially valuable in helping me understand details of pedagogy that archives are not equipped to incorporate. Alfred Prettyman, Collins's second husband, ensured the survival and publication of some of Collins's scripts through Alexander Street databases. I am grateful that he participated in interviews with me and provided a portrait of Collins that could not be extrapolated from any of the previously mentioned archives or interviews.

During my faculty tenure at Indiana University, Michael Martin was a consistent teacher and mentor who nurtured my research and study of Black film, and my very specific interest in Kathleen Collins. As an early supporter of this project, he served as a vital sounding board for transnational and Diasporic cinematic formations in the book. Former student and curator, critic, professor, and filmmaker Nzingha Kendall was a tremendously helpful interlocutor throughout this project. This is the third book of which my S.P.A.C.E. crew read an early version of the introduction, and the writing retreats we started a decade ago continue to feed me. So, thank you again.

THE
AFTERLIVES OF
KATHLEEN COLLINS

INTRODUCTION

—〰—

THE AFTERLIVES OF KATHLEEN COLLINS: OPENING SCENE

Long shot: The cutting room floor. Two people sit looking at a computer monitor trying to decide which images will be cut or rearranged. The editing software is malfunctioning and freezing up. They can't delete the scene of Kathleen Collins writing a letter. In frustration, they shut down the system before leaving the room.

Deep focus shot: The camera zooms in on the monitor, now black. The monitor's reflection shows a raised hand.

Dutch tilt: Slowly the hand moves and the camera pans down and across the computer monitor and video editing keyboard. Three seconds of stillness pass before the monitor turns on.

Close-up: Cut to frozen, blurred black-and-white image as it sharpens into a notebook page, a letter in cursive handwriting.

Close-up: Camera pans letter, and the flat words on the page shape-shift into three dimensions. They turn into ghostly writing that dissolves as viewers hear.

Kathleen Collins V.O. (voice-over):

Film plans, realization, and recognition (external recognition) still hasn't come my way. So I go about continuing my work and <u>know</u> that if I'm really good and really do have something unique to put out there, it'll happen when it's supposed to. And if I'm not, then I'll discover that before I get wrapped up in too many illusions and go about redefining my life accordingly.[1]

Camera zooms out. Fade to black.

1

Sometimes creative individuals provide the world with artifacts that exceed the limited cultural and political aims of their particular moment. But if an artist and her art are really good, she will wait for us to catch up and discover her beauty, truth, and meaning—even if it means doing so in an afterlife. Such is the case with Kathleen Collins and the films she left us—*The Cruz Brothers and Miss Malloy* (1980) and *Losing Ground* (1982)—the published and unpublished plays, the yet-to-be-produced screenplays, and the many short and long pieces of fiction as well as her productivity as a dramatist, with plays such as *In the Midnight Hour* (1981) and *The Brothers* (1982).[2] Despite the lack of recognition for her writing and filmmaking during her terrestrial life, Collins never stopped creatively producing the world she wanted to see; her visions provided new life and life-writing in which little Black girls and grown women would no longer have to defer their dreams.

In my dreams, I am not a late-forties academic failing at crafting a highly sophisticated but theoretically accessible scholarly biography of Kathleen Collins, Black woman filmmaker and writer—a biography that no one, save some Black feminist or avant-garde film and theater students will read. As her daughter, Nina Collins, once stated matter-of-factly about my early book proposal, "It seems very sciencey." Had I harbored any hopes of developing the ideas in that proposal, they would have been thwarted by that truth. Besides, in my dreams, I am a young independent filmmaker trying to finish shooting the opening scene from my first film, *The Afterlives of Kathleen Collins*, a cinematic biopic of the gone-too-soon intellectual, writer, and filmmaker. Sadly, twenty-first-century technology keeps failing me. The script and the actors are amazing. However, I cannot get the shot I want because the camera's depth of field does not register the ghosts from Collins's lives. Nor does it capture the resonances, which I can see, from future versions of Collins. Too often, grammar, structure, technology, and science fail me, as they do many Black women trying to capture their form of things unknown. I hope to work it out during the editing process, where, as Kathleen Collins theorized, I might better translate the grammar of my cinematic language. Someone needs to invent a new camera with a more expansive viewing system that accounts for nonlinear temporality and multitemporal narratives as well as rethinks spatiality and the built archives that currently govern the structures and strategies from which biographies and biopics tend to flow. Neither technology nor institutions do Collins, one of the earliest Black women to write and direct feature-length films, a damn bit of historical justice.

Still, the reality of our current era insists that I can, instead, offer something in lieu of a biography—or life-writing, as the genre has been called—for reasons other than failing at becoming a great biographer. I want to offer a concept of "afterlife-writing" and apply it to the work of Kathleen Collins, because, as I hope you will discover, she was dedicated to seeking out new lives and forms different than the biopolitical narrative imposed on her very existence and that of other Black women. As the phenomenally expressive writer and thinker Kevin Quashie has maintained, "But if we want to try to conceptualize aliveness, we have to begin somewhere else" (*Black Aliveness* 7). Quashie's elsewhere, his thesis of aliveness and aesthetics, is most relevant to my methodology, "aesthetics as a form-of-life, aesthetics as a schema for considering the aliveness of phenomena of aliveness . . ." (*Black Aliveness* 58). My elsewhere begins with queer methodologies and Black temporality where aesthetics have necessarily served as a form of life.

With regard to structure and approaches, this work is deeply influenced by a genealogy of queer methods that have served as interventions into Black life writing. Overall, this book emulates Audre Lorde's inventive genre of the biomythography and Rosamond King's audaciously transdisciplinary genre of critical biomythography. Individual chapters are a nod to Isaac Julien's poetic intervention into archives, Cheryl Dunye's satirical interruption of the realist documentary (Dunyementary), Rodney Evan's intergenerational homage to the Niggeratti, or Angela Robinson's speculative approach to domestic life and comic book creations. Black . . . Queer . . . filmmakers have demonstrated time and again that cinema can intervene on the historical and textual limitations placed on life writing of figures who, heterosexual or queer, spent much of their life defying their era's definition of normality and humanity. What, other than her sexuality, was heteronormative about Kathleen Collins—filmmaker? She, like the aforementioned cultural producers, imbued life writing about iconic cultural figures[3] with imaginative play around a thesis of afterlife so eloquently theorized by Audre Lorde: "But that that is the shape of where I am living and functioning . . . and that I am going onto something else the shape of which I have no idea. All I know is that it is going to be quite different. What I leave behind has a life of its own. I've said this about poetry; I've said it about children. Well, in a sense, I'm saying it about the very artifact of who I have been" (*A Litany for Survival: The Life and Work of Audre Lorde*).

This book, then, is about Kathleen Collins's life, but it is also about the life of what she has left behind. Audiences are only now beginning to understand the importance of her work—its absence and its recovered presence—to entire fields of knowledge as well as to political and artistic movements now and yet to come. I argue throughout this book that no life-writing could adequately demonstrate such an impact. I cannot naively accept that if Collins had lived beyond her forties that her work would be better known. There is ample evidence in the history of Black women filmmakers to suggest that it would not.

The implicit or explicit forgetting, erasing, and undervaluing of Collins's films and writings during her lifetime, and thereafter, was to ensure one future of Black filmmaking and film studies over another. That future is now our present. This type of passive-aggressive futurism to preserve whiteness and masculinity is something this project works to avoid in its critical engagement with Collins. Afterlife-writing speculates on multiple possible future engagements with an artist's creative output to underscore the importance of past art passed over as well as to understand its importance to shifting elements in the present toward any or all of those multiple futures.

Around the same time that Zora Neale Hurston was working at Paramount Studios as a writer and consultant in 1941, Collins was born in Jersey City, New Jersey, in 1942 to a father who was a well-respected educator (a principal) and politician and a stepmother who was a homemaker.[4] Though she was not immersed in film and cinema while growing up (due to strict religious beliefs), Collins learned early on from her family about the duty to work for racial uplift and equality. As a young woman, she was a Civil Rights activist and member of the Student Nonviolent Coordinating Committee, and she worked to ensure voter registration efforts in the South in the 1960s. She graduated from Skidmore College in 1963 with a bachelor's degree in philosophy and religion. She went on to earn a master's degree in French literature and cinema in 1966, studying André Breton and the surrealist movement. A French literature course on adapting literature to film provided her with early insight that she might enjoy telling stories through cinema. She also served as a translator for *Cahiers du Cinéma* in Paris from 1965 to 1967. She would return to the United States in 1969, briefly pursuing a doctorate in theology while also working as an editor for public television in New York City.[5] By 1971, Collins was deeply immersed in her less than ordinary life as a filmmaker and film professor. She would also work with John Carter on *Cotton Comes to Harlem*, in addition to work with Bill Jersey Productions, the BBC, Craven Films, John Carter Associates, and William Greaves Productions (Klotman and Cutler 1999, 109).

Ava DuVernay and Julie Dash, two of the most important Black women filmmakers in the contemporary era of Black filmmaking, have acknowledged Collins as a trailblazer who paved the way for their success.[6] Collins was a writer, a philosopher, and a harbinger of Black humanity. Because her work was set apart from the Blaxploitation, New Jack Cinema, and LA Rebellion movements, it might appear that Collins was an auteur without a movement. However, in this book I propose that she was a movement in and of herself, diligently self-determining a cultural insurgency that defies the periodization or national identity so typically attached to art or politics. Hers was a cultural revolution set to determine a new meaning of life: in the previously mentioned words of Audre Lorde, a something else to move onto—the shape of which would be determined later. Can a filmmaker change the definition of life, and the systems, structures, and institutions that produce that definition? This was the question, I argue, that Collins sought to answer en route to challenging the Eurocentric Western representations of Black life and living out her short existence of being human in the twentieth century.

Collins might be described as a filmmaker out of time and out of place—not simply because she was one of the few Black women filmmakers and film professors in the 1970s editing, producing, writing, and directing work outside the Hollywood studio system; she was out of time and place because she made films that questioned notions of realism and forms of humanism, films that insisted on understanding the construction of mythological and structurally oppressive arrangements of race, gender, class, and nation. She wrote fiction and plays that highlighted why external cultural and political circumstances or conditions should not contain and influence an interior self. This disjointed timing between the external world and the interior sense of self would become her trademark vision. It appears in *The Cruz Brothers and Miss Malloy*, her first film, about three Puerto Rican brothers as they try to make their way in the world guided by the constant presence of their father's ghost. And it appears in her second film, *Losing Ground*, about a Black woman philosophy professor in search of ecstasy that will not come via the domesticity of marriage.

The growing interest in Collins's work is not, then, because she was the first of a few. Rather, it reflects her gift as a filmmaker and the fact that her cinematic vision of quiet and animacy resonates with a new generation of Black, women, and queer filmmakers and audiences hungry for new ways of being and representing themselves. Collins's refusal to exist in one political or cultural arrangement of time is most evident in her having as active an afterlife as the ghost in her first film. Her films and her virtuosity are being discovered by a new generation of filmgoers, filmmakers, and film critics, as substantiated by major rereleases of her films on DVD, a run on Turner Classic Movies, and film screenings in the United States and abroad. The lessons that Collins has for audiences also far exceed filmmaking and film studies and are worthy of a well-produced critical biopic that questions the very meaning of Black life as it has been written. However, contemporary Black biopics, though visual, too often rely on written screenplays that incorporate tropes from a dominant form of life-writing (the biography) that contain philosophical conflicts about Blackness, gender, life, and what experiences or evolutions of humanity are worth representing—the charismatic and normative.

AFTER LIFE-WRITING: WRITING LIFE-FORMS IN AND FROM EVERY DIMENSION=AFTERLIFE WRITING

What comes after the life-writing seen in autobiographies and bio-pics is a query asked by one major Black writer more than four decades ago: the iconic James Baldwin wrote *The Devil Finds Work* (1976) to intervene on Hollywood's incessant dehumanization of people of color on-screen. To say that Baldwin was pissed with Hollywood in his critiques of *Lawrence of Arabia, Guess Who's Coming to Dinner,* and *In the Heat of the Night* would be an understatement, but he saved his most virulent and passionate critique for the biopic of his beloved Billie Holiday. He insists of director Sidney J. Furie and writers Chris Clark and Suzanne De Passe's representation of Holiday in *Lady Sings the Blues,* "The film leaves us with the impression, and this is a matter of choices coldly and deliberately made, that a gifted, but weak and self-indulgent woman, brought about the murder of her devoted Piano Man [a character largely the film's invention] because she was not equal, either to her gifts, or to the society which had made her a star, and, as the closing sequence [sepia stills, applause, etc.] proves, adored her" (Baldwin 1976, 116). Baldwin's concerns about the biopic seem even more relevant given the recent bio-pic *The United States vs. Billie Holiday* (2021) that contains phenomenal acting in spite of its unimaginative nationalistic approach to representing a small facet of Holiday. This representation fails to convey the practice of aliveness that her voice and performance makes possible for herself (first) and others (second).

Certainly, the biopic as constructed by Hollywood is faulty, but so is the written genre of biography. Tom Brown and Belén Vidal's *The Biopic in Contemporary Film Culture* insists that "the time is ripe for a reconsideration of the biopic's significance in contemporary film culture" (Brown and Vidal 2013, 2). As Brown and Vidal's edited collection delves into the form's international movement, hybrid forms, narratives, and politics, its broad scope finds little space to discuss *Black* biopics. Nevertheless, their statement appears especially relevant to Black film studies—that is, the time is ripe for a consideration of the function of biopics in contemporary Black film culture. Yet, rather than focus entirely on the form, I provide a case study of Kathleen Collins as confirmation that, for some Black subjects, the linear recounting of a biological and social life in one form or medium is not enough. Rather, we must accept Lorde's theory of any artist's afterlife, consideration of their art in a future distinct from their own historical era, and present an imagined portrait of that person's afterlives using the very aesthetics and philosophies of life they championed. In doing so, we fundamentally gain clear insights about the creation of new life-forms they made and make possible, as opposed to recovering and contextualizing them as noteworthy for a singular life-form or artistic period. This afterlife writing, then, can be essential to ensuring that the artist or her work are never overwritten by the very forms of life she was attempting to write herself out of during her own era.

Collins herself traced her interests in interiority to life-writing, claiming in one diary entry, "I have always liked to read memoirs, autobiographies, biographies, always been interested in the inner life" (Collins 2019, 42). Though she would then conclude, "It is true that with age this habit is diminishing—as if, with age, my life is sufficient material unto itself and doesn't require any further comparison with other lives" (42). Collins was discovering, as she aged, many lives within her own being that she could mine not only for plotlines centered on the individual and society but also for the voices of characters and the genres they played through. Of her note-taking and journaling, she explained, "When I go back to that entry and the others that surround it, I can pick up the flavor of a new beginning. I recall when I first realized that I might have inside me the capacity to reap a great deal on my own" (42). A biography, a memoir, or an autobiography might make it difficult for a student, a scholar, or an artist to comprehend and translate the simultaneity and plurality of many lives where one could pick up a new beginning. Afterlife-writing, as I theorize throughout this book, is a critique of the singularity of life in biopolitical narratives such as biography, autobiography, biopic, and biological sciences. It also disturbs the temporalities of Blackness in artistic and political movements, and their historical and present possibilities. The form of things unknown, then, remains particularly relevant to this critical study of Kathleen Collins's art and life.

The recent access to Collins's unpublished writings and films make a typical biography wholly possible as they provide evidence of being that is missing for early Black writers and filmmakers. In "Writing Early American Lives as Biography," scholar Annette Gordon-Reed asks, "How does one write a good story with limited documentary evidence, while maintaining the standards of scholarship? In other words, how do we make a biography read like a novel without allowing parts of the work to become one?" (2014, 498). Documentary evidence, as outlined by Gordon-Reed, would be archives containing copies of work, newspapers, interviews, reviews, etc. Documentary evidence would be recognition that she and the work mattered to someone. The standards of scholarship (impartial evidence), however, does little for marginalized artists working during Jim and Jane Crow and after in the informal de facto system of segregation. There is no archive that could hold all the writings and films of failed and unrecognized writers who could not carry, keep, and maintain their imaginations and dreams until an end to apartheid. Who and how can their life stories be rendered via the standards of scholarship. Fortunately, there is some documentary evidence tracking Collins's life and life's work to provide us with some standards of scholarship. None of which duly explains how and why she kept writing, why the work is saved by self and family, or its eventual afterlife. Clearly, Collins possessed a definition of life that documentary evidence and the standards of scholarship cannot account for. Perhaps this attention to method and temporality can.

"How can narrative embody life in words and at the same time respect what we cannot know?" Saidiya Hartman asks as she clarifies her theoretical intervention on methodology—critical fabulation—in "Venus in Two Acts" (Hartman 2008, 3). Hartman renders the past with counterhistories of slavery and understands the archive of slavery as mortuary. Her narrative interventions challenge the discipline of history, but they also challenge one of literary studies' greatest narrative modes, life-writing, especially when the life being written about is a Black woman's. Her method provides an example of the innovation that is necessary to write about a forgotten or underrecognized figure. If this were a biography of Collins, critical fabulation, especially its critical reading of the archive and the building blocks of narrative, would be enough. However, this book engages what Collins left behind, which have lives of their own: the very spontaneous invention and unordered reinvention of lives with no truth or histories, only possible futures.

For these reasons, in my examination of what Collins leaves behind, I propose a methodology that integrates Black critical theory, philosophy, and the creative aesthetics and devices of literary and cinematic arts. Afterlife-writing seeks not only to reorient Collins into film landscape but also to intervene on the methods and discourses that make her recovery necessary. Through an examination of the work of Kathleen Collins, this book also becomes a study of Black literary forms, Black cinematic narrative and genre, and Black intellectual performance that contests life-writing and the biopolitical and geopolitical discovery of life-forms in the Americas. The emphasis on truth over fiction proposed by Gordon-Reed is a superficially imposed false dichotomy perpetuated by other narratives that write—that is, represent—life and life-forms. These are some narrative forms whose function is to write human life:

- Biology: a discipline in which scientific cellular description/ coding is used to denote the origins and parameters of cellular existence and transformation on earth
- Biography: a third-person, detailed, factual account of events in an individual's life

- Autobiography: a first-person or self-authored narrative of an individual's significant and lived experiences
- Biomythography: a combination of equally valuing myth, memoir, and history in the textual representation of someone's life
- Critical biomythography: hybrid text that uses radical interdisciplinarity (scholarship and creative arts) to narrate an individual's life
- Biopic: a cinematic rendering of a person's life or period in their life

Benedict Anderson's *Imagined Communities: Reflections on the Origin and Spread of Nationalism* notes the temporal contradictions and ironies involved when one form of life-writing is compared with another: "Against biology's demonstration that every single cell in a human body is replaced over seven years, the narratives of autobiography and biography flood print-capitalism's markets year by year" (2006, 204). In each mode, the writing is never a reproduction or replication of a life, but an interpretation from what is already externally known and imposed. Biographies and biopics are interpretations of an individual's life, which is already an interpretation of life itself, a reiteration of biopower and biopolitics. What is externally known also implicitly incorporates colonizing judgment about what constitutes a reliable archive or truthful history, who is a worthy subject of life-writing, or what persons appear to be necessary to political and national identity or artistic movements. These forms, then, produce literacy privileging specific genres of humans and their ways of life. They always make humankind an extraordinary subject, and they tend to present a challenge to those deemed not human, resulting in further mythologization. Despite the emphasis on myth in biomythography, myth remains present in every other form of writing for Black people, whether they are being written about or are writing themselves into being human. The difference between biomythography and other life-writing is that biomythography does not purport to be completely authorized by institutional records deemed rational, empirical, and historically linear. Moreover, those other forms of life-writing organize life around discourses of ethics regulated by citizenship and discourses of rights established by settlers who have mythologized their form of life in juridical practices that erase other definitions of life.

As scholars note, biopics have been linked with national identity since the silent film era. William Epstein's "Introduction: Biopics and American National Identity" explains that "the generic plot . . . 'Biopics and American National Identity' comes to life with *The Birth of a Nation* and the emergence of narrative film itself in the formative years of the silent era" (2011, 10). Ian Christie, another critic, claims that, "in every national cinema, and especially in the supranational Hollywood cinema, 'life-stories' became a major genre" (2002, 290). The genre of biopic, and any study therein, as it relates to Black people must find a way to engage the issue of how the form translates and incorporates the sociological narratives of race and national identity in lieu of being subsumed by the pathological weight and trajectory of each. But how?

Eugenics, Black Codes, and segregation were scientific theories and laws, but they also mythologized Blackness and Black life as differently monstrous, a lifeform that requires segregated living space. Segregation exemplified life-writing that could narrate life-forms and introduce racialized contours into modes of storytelling. Certainly, this would explain the initial erasure of early Black filmmakers such as Oscar Micheaux, William Foster, and Noble Johnson, who successfully produced a number of films and orchestrated an entire movement and industry outside of Hollywood, only to have their works lost and legacies forgotten. According to Richard Grupenhoff's "The Rediscovery of Oscar Micheaux, Black Film Pioneer," "No full-length biography of Micheaux ha[d] been published . . . and little was known about his family background, the disposition of his records and estate, or his filmmaking methods and techniques" (1988, 40). Many years later, several of his films have been restored and numerous biographies containing extensive research have been written, but there has been no biopic. Indeed, to tell Micheaux's impactful story on-screen would go against the grain of Hollywood biopics and their incorporation of white national identity, since Hollywood is still trying to ensure a national cinema steeped in white supremacy. Too many Black biopics on figures living in the era before segregation recoup and recover figures into a narrative of American national identity.

Gordon-Reed provides some reasons for this, explaining that "biography, of course, is the ultimate form of storytelling in that a life comes with an easily discernible beginning, middle, and end—if the subject is dead" (2014, 507). I might add integrated, converted, or assimilated, in the case of Black biography. Moreover, even if the biological subject is dead, the subjects of racism and white supremacy live on, hinting that the linearity of biography cannot do Black life on-screen justice. Such reflections on the form do not account for communities of people written as savages or as chattel, or for their descendants. According to *The Oxford Companion to African American Literature*, biography, "a word derived from the Greek words for 'life' and 'writing,' has been a significant part of literary production in Western culture. Among African Americans, for a variety of reasons, its place historically has been less prominent and in some ways even controversial. Nevertheless, the genre is of increasing importance, and the publishing of full-length biographies of writers and other leading figures has become a growing feature of African American literature in recent years" (Andrews, Foster, and Harris 1997, 65).

This attention to biography as a genre intends to highlight the mythologizing of Black life that happens not only in the fiction of Harriet Beecher Stowe or the Uncle Remus folktales recorded by Joel Chandler Harris but in the very act of constructing narratives in which one human life is manifestly destined for exceptionalism and another for bondage and servitude. Though illiteracy might provide a reason that the genre was not initially prominent for Black authors, the function of the genre and form as conveying a moral and scientific advantage (destiny and survival) would dissuade any white author not interested in abolition from making any non-white person the subject of the narrative form. Finally, early American controversy in the writing of Black life occurs because "the truth" of any fugitive Black subject's life would place an individual or her community in danger and at odds with escape and freedom dreams. Thus, the truth could not always be historically and judicially corroborated with a paper trail, believable (white) sources, one's own handwriting and thoughts, or a legal and decriminalized possession of literacy/education.

William L. Andrews continues, "For two centuries, however, biography has been a poor relation of Black autobiography. Biography typically involves academic training in historical methods, a sustained effort at research, and the freedom to reflect on and write the life story in question. With these demands, it has attracted and held far fewer writers than the fields of autobiography, poetry, or fiction, for example. The vigorous recent growth of black biography has coincided, not surprisingly, with the widespread acceptance in the national academic community, and especially in research-oriented universities, of African American literature and history as challenging fields of study" (Andrews, Foster, and Harris 1997, 65). As Andrews notes, training as a scholar on how to research a Black person's life, as well as freedom to pursue the search for life, is entirely structured by a system of knowledge invested in producing and reproducing one hierarchical, anthropocentric form of life—Man and any of its overrepresentations.

Since the slave narrative's inauguration of an African American literary tradition, autobiography and biography have been tied to heroic figures and narratives of freedom that sought to translate the African into the Negro and render that being as human and worthy of emancipation. Readers peruse pages of translation upon translation of an othered human, in which the myth of the Negro is still intact in converted salvation, emancipation, segregation, and integration, as opposed to encountering what freedom and liberation proposed: new life and new forms of living. Thus, we find ourselves fully equipped with the scientific and technological tools that make individuals capable of writing about external social or material life—biography or biology. And in biography we often assume the dominance of an external life over the production and output of an inner life. However, to conceive of methodology, archive, and theory that could write of a human's interior life and what it leaves behind, we must rely on the creative, imaginative, and intuitive. Perhaps Collins's afterlives reveal how to make legible this option.

With this background in mind, to write a typically linear, historical, and critical biography of Collins would mean turning away both new life and new narratives about those new forms of life. Academic and popular biographies are written as if the subject has only impacted a knowable past and present, with little exploration of the unknown future. As shown in this book, Collins's greatest gift as a writer and filmmaker was highlighting the role of dimensionality and foresight in making visible multiple lives and ways of being. Audre Lorde's words about the form of things unknown, living, and survival can be taken as an applicable intervention into the writing of Black life—the writers propose to pursue both a form of life and a line of inquiry in which humanness and humanity are not foundational. As examined in each chapter here, Collins's films, plays, and short stories were preoccupied with finding a solution to a question she once asked: "How do we divest ourselves from the need to make ourselves extraordinary?" She followed up that question with this response: "The problem of narrative for us [Black people] is the process of demythologizing ourselves" (Collins 1984). Yet this question and problem are not simply about racial scripts; they are about the meaning and definition of human life and the way life is written in European, American, and Western science, culture, and religions. Thus, I examine her search for new life using filmmaking, and I name my task in representing that search for new life afterlife-writing and methodology.

In film and writing, Collins encountered and took to other forms of life. Her ability to represent those forms and experiences in their full complexity meant that she moved between the biographical, theoretical, philosophical, critical, and creative registers of cinematic, theatrical, and discursive texts in many of her writings and films. In doing so, she ensured that any attempts to write about her or her works would need to strategically and deliberately intervene on life-writing in American and African American traditions in a similar fashion. That means intervening on research methods and narrative approaches to how life and life-forms are narrated. Certainly, late twentieth-century critics that valued Collins's filmmaking comprised a small eclectic group who provided brief but amorous engagement with Collins's films: Phyllis Klotman, Gloria Gibson-Hudson, Toni Cade Bambara, Mark Reid, David Nicholson, and John A. Williams.

Geetha Ramanathan has provided the most sustained examination of Collins's films, first in one chapter from *Feminist Auteurs* (2006) and then in her recent monograph *Kathleen Collins: The Black Essai* (2019), the first book-length study of Collins's films. Even fewer institutions discerned the significance of Collins's entire collection of work. Certainly, there are traditional archives that preserved her films. The New York Public Library and the Black Film Center/ Archive (Indiana University Bloomington) housed her film reels and videos for decades, and the Schomburg Center for Black Culture was recently charged with keeping her papers. The process of recovering the significant legacy of Collins might be easy if it were simply a process of combing through libraries teeming with protected manuscripts, dusty books, and film reels. However, the whole of Collins's legacy both mirrors and differs from the combination of biographical elements found in Zora Neale Hurston's, Lorraine Hansberry's, and Oscar Micheaux's lives. The places, or rather the people, that enable the survival of her work are shaped by intimacies that the archives can never produce or hold in place. Her work survives not because the work itself had an impact on so many individuals or political or artistic movements—with little to no distribution and few audience encounters, it did not—but because Collins still lives alongside the people responsible for holding on to her legacy: family, friends, students, collaborators, and peers.

Collins's films, short stories, and plays were not only about changing the negative representations of Black people; they were also about interrogating the systems of knowledge that produced the social constructs of race, gender, sexuality, class, or nation and the institutions that sustained them. Deliberately, then, she developed more than an approach to filmmaking; she developed an approach to knowledge production less reliant on historical materialism and an approach to revolution less concerned with the exterior social world, more attuned to the interior world, and more psychically capable of highlighting the anteriority of Black audiovisuality. We cannot understand her aesthetics as a filmmaker without a reconsideration of temporality, biology, and spatiality. That is, we cannot understand her if we remain bound to singular forms of reading and comprehension that demand a separation of the creative from the critical, the theoretical, the visual, or the haptic.

Life-writing is about representation, but the many possible futures of afterlife-writing hinge on what may or may not be seen in representation. Collins knew as much. In a published excerpt from her unfinished novel *Lollie: A Suburban Tale*, one of the narrators—the psychic Janice—tells her husband, Andrew: "I turned on the camera in search of some picture that would show me myself. Nothing.... Oh, God I've got no future" (Collins 1993–94, 114). The camera referred to is the gift of psychic vision—an interesting concept for film that I take up in chapter 3—but the sentiment of seeing or not seeing oneself in an image constructed by one's own mind remains relevant to the discovery of new life-forms. Psychics are unauthorized biographers who do not have to adhere to these false boundaries that stretch out space between intimacy and objectivity or between distance and admiration. Taking a cue from Collins, I propose that the dynamic elements most associated with the biopic genre, poetry, and speculative fiction—all of them joined in their discontent with sociological narrative and realism—can present an alternative methodology to intervene on the mythologization of race, gender, and national identity in biography and its form of human life. Because the Black biopic, unlike the slave narrative, has not so readily been linked to the abolition of slavery or the end of segregation, even as it may be a post-integration form, there is still time to theorize it not as evidence of humanity or human life-form but as something more: afterlife-writing.

AFTERLIFE-WRITING: DECOLONIZING
BLACK BIOGRAPHY AND BIOPICS

According to film scholar Belén Vidal, "The term 'biopic' is used to refer to a fiction film that deals with a figure whose existence is documented in history, and whose claims to fame or notoriety warrant the uniqueness of his or her story" (Brown and Vidal 2013, 3). Vidal's definition unveils historical fact as a type of representation that can be fictionalized as well as the implicit judgment calls that determine worth in history (documented) and in filmmaking genres (notoriety or fame). I argue, via my creative-critical examination of Collins's work, that filmmaking exceeds the function of representation and becomes a tool to locate new life-forms, with interiority serving as a directional force of where to go or look.

Michael Boyce Gillespie's theorization of "film blackness" crystallizes why such an approach would be useful for Black biopics in general and for an afterlife-writing of a filmmaker like Collins. He claims that film Blackness "is meant to demonstrate a methodological prerogative to incite a discrepant engagement with the idea of black film. . . . Film blackness targets the idea of black film with a motivation concentrated on aesthetic, historiographic and cultural consequence" (2016, 6–7). In the case of afterlife-writing, my discrepant engagement is with a specific genre within Black film—Black biopics. Representation has been a major topic in Black film studies, and when contextualized with other themes such as visuality, spectacle, and authenticity, the process of demythologizing cannot be initiated. Recent scholarship in Black film studies has showcased that studies of Black Diasporic films do not have to emulate European and American film studies, especially when the films being analyzed and interrogated may exceed, usurp, or criticize thematic, artistic, and genealogical traditions within the artistic periods and movements of those geographical locations.

While the basic questions of race and representation, gender and gaze, independent versus Hollywood, audience, production, and psychoanalysis remain, recent scholarship contains more complex conversations about ontology, being, humanism, new technologies, cultural geographies, and methodologies. This work includes Frank Wilderson's *Red, White, and Black: Cinema and the Structure of U.S. Antagonisms* (2010), Miriam J. Petty's *Stealing the Show: African American Performers and Audiences in 1930s Hollywood* (2016), Amy Abugo Ongiri's *Spectacular Blackness: The Cultural Politics of the Black Power Movement and the Search for a Black Aesthetic* (2009), Jacqueline N. Stewart's *Migrating to the Movies: Cinema and Black Urban Modernity* (2005), Peter Jones's *Teaching Black Cinema* (2006), and Keith Harris's *Boys, Boyz, Bois: An Ethics of Black Masculinity in Film and Popular Media* (2006), in addition to *Black Camera's* special issues on "Fugitivity and Filmic Imagination" and "Black Film and Black Visual Culture" (Ford 2015; Harris 2016).

Moreover, several contemporary examinations of film and Black visuality demonstrate how and why filmmaking enacts a form of world-making: Deborah Willis's oeuvre, Akin Adesokan's *Postcolonial Artists and Global Aesthetics* (2011), Racquel J. Gates's *Double Negative: The Black Image and Popular Culture* (2018), Nicole Fleetwood's *Troubling Vision: Performance, Visuality, and Blackness* (2010), Olivier Barlet's *African Cinemas: Decolonizing the Gaze* (2000), Kameelah Martin's *Envisioning Black Feminist Voodoo Aesthetics: African Spirituality in American Cinema* (2016), and Allyson Field, Jan-Christopher Horak, and Najuma Stewart's *L.A. Rebellion: Creating a New Black Cinema* (2015). In this world-making, the camera, as a vessel that allows for exploration, does not have to become a cultural vehicle for a traumatic Middle Passage to a New World. It is not constrained to repeat the 1492 Western worldview of exploration, in which the world is flat and without other life, or the Hollywood worldview in which studios whitewash both narratives and the significance of representation. Both of those paths lead to the expansion also known as colonization and assimilation, and ultimately to the erasure of entire beings. Helmed and steered by a decolonial mindset, however, the camera-as-vessel can become a tool of cooperation, peace, and cultural exchange in its furthering of the idea that the world is round. The biopic remains an understudied form of world-making and the creation of new life-forms.

Studies such as George Frederic Custen's *Bio/Pics: How Hollywood Constructed Public History* (1992), Doris Berger's *Projected Art History: Biopics,*

Celebrity Culture, and the Popularizing of American Art (2014), and William H. Epstein and R. Barton Palmer's *Invented Lives, Imagined Communities: The Biopic and American National Identity* (2017) all see the biopic as what Hayden White defines as "historiophoty," or "the representation of history and our thought about it in visual images and filmic discourse" (1988, 1193). Biopics serve as a more accessible form that maintains the original function of the biography: to present a history, national identity, and fixed representation.

Nevertheless, the film genre's radicalness comes in its hypothetical disruption of traditional public spheres that accept monolithic versions of events. The biopic has the potential, like the psychic in Collins's fiction, to discover new life-forms. It can show us future lives since it does not have to stay bound to historical linear time, which insists on a beginning, middle, and end. Dennis Bingham's *Whose Lives Are They Anyway? The Biopic as Contemporary Film Genre* proposes, "The biopic is by no means a simple recounting of the facts of someone's life. It is an attempt to discover biographical truth, in this case gathered through scores of interviews" (2010, 7). Nevertheless, the very idea that a biographical truth exists depends on an acceptance of particular modes of living and valuation. Bingham continues, "The biopic is a genuine, dynamic genre and an important one. The biopic narrates, exhibits, and celebrates the life of a subject in order to demonstrate, investigate, or question his or her importance in the world" (10). Bingham's understanding of world does not mention the social and cinematic segregation of worlds, or that what is deemed important can change. Should the role of biographies and biopics that attempt to narrate the life of an African American artist, musician, or writer be to convey history or biographical truth alone? Can we instead recognize such sentiment as prioritizing a type of knowledge production that undoes their feats of genius, or their miracle of shifting communities' entire worldviews, and therefore use the form to do as they did? That is, can we imagine and create new worlds and new forms of life, instead of solely recounting past worlds and relics of life?

Film and television biographies of African Americans have made biopics the one cinematic genre that has fostered tremendous growth in African American representation on-screen. Black and non-Black filmmakers inside and outside the Hollywood studio system have been especially enamored with the life of Black musicians and athletes as well as maids and butlers. Only recently have biographies and autobiographies stretched beyond an interest in Black performance and entertainers. Audiences have filled theaters to see the lives of Black male political figures in *12 Years a Slave, Mandela: Long Walk to Freedom, Lumumba, Malcolm X, The Great Debaters, Hotel Rwanda, Selma,* and *Harriet.* Independent flicks such as *Basquiat* and *I Am Not Your Negro* provide a glimpse of strategies for artist and intellectual biopics. Black film biography has become a profitable genre, but it has seldom been an artistically expansive genre. Films such as Don Cheadle's *Miles Ahead* fulfill the potential of the genre as articulated by Bingham: "The biopic is a form that itself is about self-identification and self-invention, but it is also about identification with others" (2010, 378). So much of African American social life stresses communality, but many Black biopics present individual triumphs that do not take enough note of gender, sexuality, or class.[7] This is a problem of both genre and gender as the exalting of Black masculinity in these films seeks to overwrite myths of Black men's inhumanity. Cheadle's unconventional take on the biopic succeeded as an artistic exploration that exposes violent conflicts about race and gender rather than being a strict historical accounting of Miles Davis's singular life as a great jazz musician, because it meditated on the futurity of Davis and his work as opposed to making a visual case for his humanity.

In examining the international life of the biopic, Vidal confirms that the "biographical picture, biopic, is a troublesome genre" (2013, 1), and this statement is doubly true of biopics about Black women from across the Diaspora. Notably, when Black women's stories make it to the screen, they are conveyed in a manner that privileges White narratives of success, citizenship, and capitalism—the very elements that tend to lessen both the impact of Black women's lives and the representation of those lives on-screen. Despite the early commercial success of films such as *Lady Sings the Blues* and *I Know Why the Caged Bird Sings*, Black women's biopics continue to have a race and gender problem that cannot or will not be solved with a docudrama approach. Most recently, realists approaches have also failed. The documentary *Tina* (2021), which was centrally conceived to give the iconic Tina Turner the final say on the representation of her life in books, film, and theater authored by others for over three decades. Even with that intent, the realist function and filmic devices of the latter's documentary genre are never able to fully release the subject from the form of life and living repetitiously authored by others—product of dysfunctional family and survivor of domestic violence.

In general, scholars have correctly noted that "biopics of women . . . are weighted down by myths of suffering, victimization, and failure perpetuated by a culture whose films reveal an acute fear of women in the public realm. Female biopics can be made empowering only by a conscious and deliberate application of a feminist point of view" (Bingham 2010, 10). Yet feminist points of view that do not incorporate a deep perspective of intersectionality can also pose problems that lead to controversy, as was the case with Cynthia Mort's *Nina*. Documentaries such as *What Happened, Miss Simone?* or *A Litany for*

Survival can, when taken together, offer multiple approaches to Black women's lives, correcting limited visions that do not account for intersectional living.

The directing, acting, and cinematography in films such as *The United States vs. Billie Holiday, Bessie, What's Love Got to Do with It, Black Venus, The Josephine Baker Story*, and *Introducing Dorothy Dandridge* are outstanding, and thus critically acclaimed, but the biopic form still fails its subjects in many ways. As Bingham perceptively asks, "Once one averts the melodramatic plot structure, the downward trajectory, the aesthetic of victimization, and the male gaze and outside scrutiny, what's left? The question itself is sexist" (2010, 350). The on-screen adaptation of Black women's lives, particularly those who are not entertainers or victims, seldom happens without white authorial/savior intrusions on the narrative. *Belle, Hidden Figures, Loving,* and *The Immortal Life of Henrietta Lacks* are notable films that rely on white authority to compel empathy for Black lives. Small-screen depictions of Black women's lives by the Lifetime and BET networks have been less concerned with aesthetics and production value and more invested in melodrama, cheap production, and quick ratings. They fail to translate and capture the futurity of their subjects, and "as we look into the future at the beginning of the twenty-first century's second decade, the prospects for the female biopic are murky" (Bingham 2010, 348).

Now, then, is the perfect time to engage with the emerging innovative approaches to Black film studies. I want to insist on speculative ways to broach the lives of Black women, specifically Black filmmakers in film studies scholarship. I use this approach to ensure that the past, present, and future theories of Kathleen Collins—filmmaker, writer, and teacher—are valued as significant in multiple fields. Collins stands as an exemplary case of why shifts must occur in biography, biopics, and Black film studies if they are to include such an enigmatic figure. In not writing a standard biography of Collins, but in imagining and thinking through the concept of afterlives as a methodological approach, I can delve into what history has thus far disallowed: complex poly-recognition and new forms.

Afterlife-writing and methodology can be classified as a de-Westernizing gesture, as outlined in the important edited collection *De-Westernizing Film Studies*. Editors Saër Maty Bâ and Will Higbee, taking up John Akomfrah's (2012) call, define the gesture or process as

> a method of rethinking a binary or Eurocentric approach to film studies
> in particular in relation to the west and the rest in cinema (as the term
> "world cinema" has tended to suggest) in order to propose new method-
> ologies that will lead to an alternative "un-centered" version of knowledge

that gives credit to multiple viewpoints in order to arrive at original and innovative ways of studying film history, theory and practice in a globalized context. Above all, this notion of emergent methods requires, on the one hand, a flexibility to methodological approach.... A variety of (nonacademic) writing styles and forms of expression have been incorporated ... and we would claim this itself as a form of de-Westernizing. (Bâ and Higbee 2012, 13)

Afterlives methodology asks that we consider history and archive as unable to hold and preserve evidence of Black women's living, as well as their search for new life. As actor Hattie McDaniel's life and death make clear, the problem is also one of industry and institution. Hollywood's refusal of McDaniel in segregated America leads to a body made absent in awards ceremonies, cemeteries, and walks of fame, as well as the loss of an artifact (her Oscar) befitting of any film archive, should archives of Hollywood ever be integrated.[8] Posthumous efforts for McDaniel such as a commemorative postage stamp, induction into the Hollywood Walk of Fame and Black Filmmakers Hall of Fame and late star treatment do not halt the narrative of life-writing nor the forms that made such treatment possible. Afterlife-writing asks us to confront the tools of empire and capitalism that silence, erase, and misplace the living: commodification, distribution, control through private/public binaries, lack of ownership, and copyright—all of which undermine collaboration, recognition, and the sharing of Black women's living.

Afterlife-writing is a genre intervention on methodology fetish in disciplinary and artistic practices, and it is also a spiritual interruption of genres of the human. Understanding, as Michael Gillespie has theorized, that "black film is always a question, never an answer" (2016, 16), each chapter in this volume begins with a possible afterlife-form of writing that serves as a question about what artistic genre Collins is using to undo a specific genre of the human. The genre question enables us to see the importance of Collins presently, historically, and futuristically to political and artistic movements such as Black Lives Matter, Black feminist genealogies, narrative medicine, and Black film, theater, and fiction traditions. These creative openings/interpretations of Collins's life are based on her papers. I then provide critical close reading and analyses of specific films, screenplays, and fiction by Collins as well as theorize about their importance to particular film genres, feminist theories, political movements, and aesthetic philosophies.

My approach is not about inventing a figure that does not exist, as biopics are sometimes said to do. Rather, it is about creating a space where anteriority of

Black film can serve as the answer to a question that will be infinitely embedded in the study and production of Black film. What is the future of cinemas of the Black Diaspora? This is a question that innovator John Akomfrah has taken up in his films, and in his own theories of cinema and film studies, in which he stresses that there could "be a way in which one could reconfigure a history of cinema without mentioning Méliès or Godard but still be just as legitimate, because the questions this new history would raise would be just as pertinent and just as real" (2012, 28). Akomfrah's comments hint at an anteriority for Black film, and it is also the very factor that could provide a platform for the visionary work of Collins. Several chapters here highlight the global Blackness of Collins's intellectual canon and demonstrate how adept she was at locating an anteriority of global Black visuality simultaneously rooted in sacred non-Western visual aesthetics and the quotidian and ordinary experiences of telling stories. How might anteriority of Black film and visuality shift the ways in which Black films are critiqued, analyzed, and archived? How can such studies shift the ways in which we think about the artistic labor of Black filmmakers and their daily lives? How can such studies create seismic shifts in the production of knowledge about Black film studies? Afterlife-writing and methodology may offer answers to these questions.

This book honors the philosophy and processes that Collins held deeply: freedom and demythologization. It honors the aesthetics and techniques of alternative modes of visualization. As I propose throughout, this dilemma—how to bypass rather than internalize an external white colonial gaze that dehumanizes—can be resolved with genre innovation that borrows from non-Western regimes of visualization. My faith in Collins's earlier words, that she put something unique in the world, emboldens my approach and the themes of each chapter. What are the afterlives of her failures to make films, her successes at making films, her translations of a Haitian medical text, her theories of technology, her nondisclosure of illness and dying, her tarot readings, and her mothering?

In chapter 1, I explore how Collins's calling as a writer, her philosophical approach to adaptation, and her attention to experimental aesthetics helped her develop and refine a unique cinematic inner vision that precedes the constructed applications of the human gaze that reproduce themselves in film studies and scopic technology. Close readings of her focus on Haitian cosmologies in her first film script, *Women, Sisters, and Friends,* her deconstructing of exteriority and interiority in her short stories, and her attention to Black material culture (quilt making) demonstrate how her writing becomes a ritual practice that allows her to explore Black embodied audiovisuality as anterior to Hollywood filmmaking and visuality.

Chapter 2 investigates Collins's critique of romantic narratives of love with a focus on non-Western visual aesthetics and the ideals of the ecstatic and mysticism in *Losing Ground* (film), "Losing Ground" (short story), and *Only the Sky Is Free*. These works serve as the foundation for my thesis of afterlife-writing and her revision of romantic love in her final screenplay, *But Then She's Madame Flor*. I begin with Collins's experience of translating Louis Mars's *The Crisis of Possession in Voodoo* (1977) as a way to read her philosophy about the roles love and ecstasy occupy in women's lives. I then demonstrate Collins's methods in representing love as a challenge to Hollywood genres of action film and narratives of love story that do not account for the necessity of revolution and rebellion based on race and gender.

Chapter 3 dissects Collins's film pedagogy, alongside analysis of her experience of being an editor for public television, to showcase Collins as a futurist and progenitor of a fifth dimension cinema. Chapter 4 argues that Collins's first film, an adaptation of a novel, provides a blueprint for how other filmmakers might think about countering a cinema of policing and the carceral imagination with what I theorize as Collins's cinematic marronage. Contrasting Collins's *The Cruz Brothers and Miss Malloy* with Black films and television programs explicitly about police brutality, I argue that Collins's film is just as relevant as those critical and political darlings for the ways that it addresses concerns of the current Black Lives Matter movement, the prison abolitionist movement, and the surveillance technologies being deployed by carceral states.

Chapter 5 addresses Collins's death from stage-4 breast cancer, and outlines the difficult labor Collins undertook in her personal writing and unpublished/unproduced plays during her years of dealing with cancer. I place Collins's writing in conversation with other Black women writers who wrote about illness, Western medicine, and alternative healing traditions. I submit that Collins's writings about her cancer experience exemplify what Denise Ferreira da Silva defined as a Black feminist poethics grounded in the poethics of blackness, which consequently challenges the coloniality of reparative narratives and the medicalization of cancer that seldom accounts for other ideologies of living, healing, and dying. My conclusion attends to the evolution of Black feminist theory and cultural production in the twenty-first century. I call for a continuation of earlier Black feminist innovation in film scholarship in terms of genealogy, methods, and recovery to unveil the rich tradition of Black women filmmakers and writers still understudied.

During a lecture at Howard University in 1984, Collins closed her oratorical manifesto referencing the early beginnings of the script for what she hoped would be her third feature-length film, *Only the Sky Is Free*, a screenplay about

Bessie Coleman, the first Black woman aviator. Collins discusses her approach to the narrative of the story, calling it a refusal to mythologize Coleman as *the first*. She states, "It is not the heroics of her as the first . . . because when she is the first she is a saint for God's sake. What I am interested in is why in the hell does this woman want to fly?" (Collins 1984). In this work, I am interested in Collins, but not as one of the earliest African American woman filmmakers to make feature length-films and teach in film schools. I am interested in why the hell this woman wanted to make films, write fiction, develop plays, and teach others to do the same.

ANTERIOR LIFE

Kathleen was really about story. . . . It was easier for her on the page
. . . more delightful for her.[1]

CHAPTER ONE

⸺ ∿ ⸺

SHE LIKED WRITING

AT DUKE UNIVERSITY'S BLACK WOMEN Writers at Work symposium in September 2019, inspired by Claudia Tate's important 1983 collection *Black Women Writers at Work*, I attentively listened to Farah Jasmine Griffith, Beverly Guy-Sheftall, Deborah McDowell, Cheryl Wall, Thadious Davis, Carole Boyce Davies, Hazel Carby, and Mary Helen Washington reflect on the significance of Black women writers to the fields of Black studies and Black feminist studies. They discussed brilliant Black women novelists, poets, playwrights, and activists of the Harlem Renaissance and the Black women's literary renaissance of the 1970s and 1980s. Some reminded the audience of how Toni Morrison, as an editor at Random House, shepherded the works of Angela Davis, Toni Cade Bambara, Gayl Jones, and many others. Some recalled establishing important book series dedicated to publishing out-of-print works by Black women writers or collaborating on important anthologies and journal issues. Others discussed past and present experiences with archival materials on or from the previously mentioned writers. Many described how they were told that the very fields they helped foster were not possible because there was no tradition of Black women's writing that was worth studying.

Many of the talks from the symposium brought me back to a question I have been unable to answer since I first encountered the massive unpublished material of Kathleen Collins in 2010: How did someone who wrote as much and as imaginatively as Collins did about Black women during and immediately after the Black women's renaissance become such an obscure figure? Several of her works were published in anthologies before the flurry of publishing initiated by her daughter after Collins's death in 1988. *The Brothers* and *In the Midnight*

25

Hour are two plays anthologized in important collections about Black women playwrights. However, the majority of Collins's fiction, plays, and screenplays remained unpublished or unproduced in what has been noted as the late twentieth-century era of Black women writers at work.

Nevertheless, Collins kept writing—and writing, and writing. She seemed to know throughout one life, and during her transition into another life, that her words would find anyone who needed them whenever they needed them. None of this changes the predicament that arises in past celebrations of Black women writers at work—that something in the structure and foundation of the groundbreaking impeded support and development of Kathleen Collins's work.

Collins's screenwriting, playwriting, and print writing certainly engaged some of the same themes as several of those writers, but in very different ways. Hazel Carby's reflection in "Where Are We Going (and Why)?" provides insights that might be useful to understanding the illegibility of Collins's oeuvre to that time period. Carby discusses her own positioning in late twentieth-century Black studies, explaining that she was vested in

> challenging and interrogating dominant forms of knowledge production ... [and that] while militantly protesting our exclusion or marginalization I also saw our work to be a profound intellectual analysis of representations of our presence in racialized capitalism[,]... exposing how knowledge has been historically and culturally constructed, institutionalized, and fettered to disciplines which also have to be transformed. Perhaps in the celebratory moments of half a century of African American studies it is time to interrogate the edifice of what we have built and, in the words of student movements from Europe to South Africa, decolonize our curriculum from American nationalism. (Carby 2019)

Carby deliberates on her disappointment at the lack of growth in transnational perspectives in Black studies, decades after she contributed significant critical and historical treatises on its importance. She further admonishes the role of US nationalism and exceptionalism in Black studies and institutions dedicated to Black studies, stating quite explicitly that "US exceptionalism distorts, not defines, the representation of Black history" (Carby 2019). Whereas Carby demands recognition of the plural geopolitics of the Americas as shaping Black histories, cultures, and politics, as well as developments of Black thought outside the United States, I believe her words also provide an opportunity to recognize how plural geopolitics can inform approaches to forms and aesthetics with regard to subjects and theories of race, gender, class, and sexuality. They provide an imperative to interrogate how and why the privileging of particular forms of storytelling and resistance valued in the twentieth-century Black United States—novels, poetry, theater, and journalism—replicate US nationalism and exceptionalism and how these ideologies align with particular art forms. Such a question becomes especially germane when examining the work of Black intellectuals and writers who may have been from the United States but whose training outside the country made possible their writing in forms seen as unavailable to and depoliticized by US Black writers and artistic movements of the time—specifically film and television.

NO HEAVEN OR HELL: JUST AN ALTAR OF SPACE, AND LIGHT

"Once she started making this altar she stopped altogether going to church with us on Sunday," says an anonymous woman and secondary character in *Women, Sisters, and Friends* (1971)—Collins's first original screenplay that she wanted to make into a feature film. The script arguably establishes film as a new type of altar for spiritual cosmologies previously threatened by colonial spiritual systems that enforced conversion and assimilation. *Women, Sisters, and Friends* was a revering of Haitian worship and Vodou cosmologies. Well before Julie Dash's cinematic and literary African Diasporic masterpiece, *Daughters of the Dust*, or Kasi Lemmons's beautifully told *Eve's Bayou*, there was Collins's unproduced script about three Black bourgeois women on a beach vacation who encounter African Diasporic spirits consorting with the living.[2] Unsurprisingly, producers at the time seemed unable to grasp the transnational themes and feminist implications of the script. Or maybe they did and deemed it unworthy. To make films as a Black woman in the early 1970s, and to make the type of films that Collins wanted to make during that era, meant creating a new world and a belief system to support that world. She did so, but the society she lived in knew nothing of that unseen dimension.

By Collins's own admission and critics' biographical appraisal of her influences, surrealism and André Breton were subjects of study for Collins. However, if we follow up on the specifics of those influences in her work, it becomes clear that Collins was enamored with a very specific focus of Breton and surrealism: Haitian visuality, myth, and culture as expressed in Vodou.[3] Like Breton, who appreciated the work of Haitian artist and Vodou practitioner Hector Hyppolite, Collins drew upon visual techniques from the religion to guide her imagery and storytelling in *Women, Sisters, and Friends*. However, unlike Zora Neale Hurston and Katherine Dunham, who came to Vodou through a stated appreciation of folk and vernacular modes of knowledge production they could highlight via methods in anthropology and ethnography, Collins's immersion would come via a surrealist focus on aesthetic syncretism. If Hurston sought to highlight the folk complexities of Vodou and Katherine Dunham the embodied movements of rites and rituals for dance, then Collins's study was one of how ritualized uses of space and light could be oriented toward a practice of abolishing the necessity of representational politics in the creation of Black life, living, and worlds. She would draw from metaphors, symbols, and objects of Vodou to depict the other realm of possibilities. Consequently, though Collins never explicitly claims a study of Vodou, as she does of André Breton and Lorraine Hansberry, many of her characters in writing and film serve as proxies who learn from and cavort with Ezili.

Collins spent most of 1971 trying to raise money to make *Women, Sisters, and Friends* into a feature film. Of that experience she noted, "Nobody would give money to a black woman to direct a film" (Campbell 1983, 58). It wasn't just that Collins was a Black woman wanting to direct a film; she was a Black woman wanting to make a film that centered on women, their relationships with one another, and the invention of a self not steeped in concepts of Blackness underwritten by the nationalist biopolitics of race in the United States. As the script shows, she wanted to make a film about Black women that addressed American exceptionalism and Black nationalism.[4]

In several interviews about the films she was able to make, critics challenged Collins about whether her cinematic stories qualified as Black films and whether she considered herself a Black filmmaker. For example, when discussing *The Cruz Brothers and Miss Malloy*, interviewer Oliver Franklin twice insists, "Let's talk about politics. You have such an individualistic approach to what a film should say. Do you think of yourself as a black filmmaker?" He later asks, "How do you see politics functioning within your cinematic creations? Many filmmakers who believe in the dominance of 'external social reality' would disagree with your intensely personal aesthetics" (Franklin 2015, 34). Today, Black literary theory challenges such ideology. As Quashie advises, "attempts to segregate aesthetics from politics misunderstand the mutual conditions between lived life and art; such attempts also misappreciate the philosophical bearing of representational practices" (*Black Aliveness*, 57). Certainly, Collins's writing and filmmaking demonstrate the truth of such statements. Ironically, what Franklin reads as intensely personal aesthetics might also be classified as themes of metaphysics shaped by Vodou's ritualization of aesthetic possibilities to ensure her filmmaking as sacred practice. To use film to uphold the dimensionality of words (as worlds) in an art form said to be about representation and capture is the Blackest and most decolonial practice that Collins could undertake. To use light and space to counter the logics of Black social life that slavery introduced or the biological definitions of race that eugenics sustained was visionary.

As Stan Brakhage suggests in "Metaphors on Vision," the artist "imagines an eye unruled by man-made laws of perspective, an eye unprejudiced by compositional logic, an eye which does not respond to the nature of everything but which must know each object encountered in life through an adventure of perception" (2014, 62). Collins offers such an eye for our current era. Rather than attempting to translate the written word onto screen, she wishes to produce her own signature (cinematic) language for her vision of Black worlds.

The script for *Women, Sisters, and Friends* is short, but Collins's vision is oceanically deep in what it wants viewers to see and feel. It is an un-American spiritual story and an African Diasporic visitation love story centered on three Black women characters—friends Sylvia, Marita, and Lillie. The women are vacationing in a beach town and become intrigued by a mysterious man who resides in a nearby house. Based on script details concerning shooting angles, location times, and scene descriptions, Collins was using light, space, and shadow to narrate a film about spiritual exchanges that do not have to be violent, horrific, or extreme. Most important, they do not have to rely on Christian myths and tropes of sin and salvation. The opening is described as follows:

> A man, naked to the waist, wearing white pants . . . his back is to the camera. We start from a MS [medium shot] slowly pulling back as he walks away from the camera down a long stretch of deserted beach. It is early morning. Some night light remains in the sky, among the foggy, misty atmosphere. He walks near the water's edge. He is singing a refrain over and over with an almost mocking laughter in his voice.
>
> MAN
> "Oh, fix me; fix me Jesus fix me."
>
> We follow him until he disappears into the fog.

Collins's attention to space and light are not simply aesthetic choices; they are also choices to counter Western metaphysics of body, blood, and human suffering. Though we do not know why the man is mocking the well-known Black spiritual, we do know, based on the lyrics of the hymn, that spiritual salvation, death, and resurrection are being critiqued. Collins later reveals that the man singing is a ghost. Collins, like the ghosts she brings to the screen, has a belief system. Perhaps this spirit mocks the hymn because it has not forgotten that one spiritual practice has overwritten another.

James Baldwin's earlier critique of the Hollywood film industry, and specifically the failure of film adaptations of Black autobiography, remains pertinent for this chapter's focus on sacredness in filmmaking and Collins's quest for a cinematic language. Baldwin writes,

> Now, obviously, the only way to translate the written word to the cinema involves doing considerable violence to the written word, to the extent, indeed, of forgetting the written word. A film is meant to be seen, and, ideally, the less a film talks, the better. The cinematic translation, nevertheless, however great and necessary the violence it is compelled to use on the original form, is obliged to remain faithful to the intention, and the vision of the original form. The necessary violence of the translation involves making subtle and difficult choices. The root motive of the choices made can be gauged by the effect of these choices: and the effect of these deliberate choices, deliberately made, must be considered as resulting in a willed and deliberate act—that is, the film which we are seeing is the film we are intended to see. Why? What do the filmmakers wish us to learn? (1976, 107)

Baldwin's appraisal of film, and his prioritizing the written word over the visual, does not engage the epistemic violence that occurs in Black life-writing—the writing of oneself into being—which is why a different question must be and has been asked by Black women filmmakers.

Notably, Baldwin's insistence on film as the translation of the written word undermines the artistry of the filmmaker as well as the dimensionality of language and its capacity to exist in different mediums and forms. The answer to Baldwin's question might be that the white filmmakers whom he critiques wish us to accept subjugation and inferiority. But another important question that might be posed is, What do films by marginalized filmmakers want us to unlearn? Collins, unlike Baldwin, believed that film did not have to be the devil finding work, and most likely she would not accept the macabre nature of his religious analogy. While Baldwin may have been exceptionally accurate in his assessment of Hollywood's white supremacist gaze, his inattention to Black cinematic traditions of directing, cinematography, or musical scoring is surprising in its shortsightedness. Moreover, his faith in biography and the written word over cinematic language is troubling, because it points to a faith in an order of knowledge understood but not necessarily shared or embraced by Collins and other Black filmmakers—Christian world-making and human being. As Michael Gillespie attests, "Black film operates as a visual negotiation, if not tension, between film as art and race as a constitutive, cultural fiction"

(2016, 2). In the absence of a theory of anteriority, ontological positionality in space and time can be overwritten by humanism's imposed split subject who must navigate exteriority and interiority fixed in space and time. To tell her story and devise her cinematic language, the Black filmmaker must seek out a visuality that precedes the cultural fiction of race in aesthetic philosophies.

"If any of you have seen my work, you know I'm only interested in telling stories," Collins once admitted to Howard University students (Collins 1984). Collins consistently defines herself as a writer, but as her output demonstrates, she did not think that meant that her stories would be confined to a singular form or formulaic aesthetics. Collins did not grow up wanting to be a filmmaker, or even going to the movies on a regular basis. She was interested in telling stories, but what that meant for her was the search for multiple languages that would allow her to avoid inflicting violence on the genres of human being she was creating for her world. The use of light and space became that language. Filmmaking is storytelling, and Collins had a rich tradition of storytelling from which to erect her tradition of Black filmmaking. As she would write in a letter to her good friend Bluette L. Dammond, "I want to make a film about shadows, shadows which cross a person's face—something that's true, elusive, real—detached from the flux—that can be found only in a look, a gesture, an arc of light."[5] What stories use light as a language? There are many, but Collins turns to sacred African diasporic stories that rely on light and dark. In the script, this particular spirit appears only during the moments of dusk and dawn, never fully in day or at night.

Art critic Dana Rush notes, "In Vodun thought, the seemingly contradictory ideas of the ephemeral (impermanent, fleeting, short-lived) and the unfinished (ongoing, enduring, never-ending) merge in a dialectics that maintains the requisite tension between the two" ("Ephemerality and the Unfinished in Vodun Aesthetics," 60). Collins's use of fog and mist and natural visualization of transition as a beginning and end throughout the script act as visual choice meant to challenge the assumed corporeal difference between the living and the dead. Instead, as Collins's narrative unfolds, physics—that is, matter, energy, and force—provides an alternative definition of living beings: these meetings are simply visitations between two different types of beings. From the very beginning, Collins makes it clear that whatever we are to learn about friendship, love, community, life, or death will be conveyed with a language whose grammar and rules are arcs of light, ephemeral forms of matter, and vibrational shifts in space.

Though all the characters in the script are rooted by this rule, Lillie becomes the character who is open to visitations from the mystery man. Collins takes her time unveiling why, but she does provide some hints. More than Marita or Sylvia, Lillie spends most of her time in the water and on the beach. When

the women take out a small boat, Lillie swims alongside rather than riding in
the boat. Like the description and shot directions for the man, scenes for Lillie
stress her positioning based on sunlight and against the shoreline. In one scene,
as Lillie stands drying herself after a swim, a woman comes along and talks to
her. The woman says that Lillie reminds her of her younger sister, who had died
two years ago. The woman explains,

> You know, she was strange. She had this hobby of making things out of
> broken bottles, you know, like old Coke bottles, even beer bottles. She'd
> mash them together into funny shapes and paint them different colors. . . .
> She'd make these glass things that would hang from pieces of thread and
> suspend them and when the wind blew they would make sounds. . . .
>
> Then one day she started building this altar. I think she was real su-
> perstitious. I mean she was religious. . . . It was all made of glass of course
> and she even made statues for it from little tiny bits of cracked glass all
> glued together and bright colors—so bright they glowed in the dark. . . . I
> think she really wanted the altar down here by the water instead of in our
> backyard. That would have been something . . . with the glass reflecting
> off the water at night and her coming out of the water all naked and going
> inside it to pray.

Spiritualties sustain their own cultural practices of visuality through rites and
rituals, and they can also enable practitioners to develop material objects as
technologies that can sustain those practices. The younger sister is both religious practitioner and artist. Collins uses this exchange to tell a story within a
story. In addition, she establishes the interplay of glass and light as a language
for narrating how the natural landscape of the beach serves as a significant
replacement for the written word (the Bible) and as a space of worship for the
woman's sister. Such recognition acknowledges the importance of change and
fluidity, as the message delivered in such a church will never be the same, depending on the light. At the end of the story, Lillie learns that the younger sister
had fallen in love with a young Haitian man before she died. The older woman
describes how the couple would go out every night and swim before making
love in front of the altar as she and her husband would voyeuristically listen
to their lovemaking as a type of foreplay to their own pleasures. The woman
provides a tale about spiritual worship and prayer in which the broken bottles
do not need to be fixed and made whole again, but rather can be used to create
something new, more vivid ways of seeing and being in the world. By the end of
the woman's story, we know why the man was mockingly singing "fix me Jesus"
at the beginning of the script.

In a later scene, Collins returns to the man who appeared at the beginning of the script: "From the edge of the lawn we hold a long shot of the house, dark and silent. Behind us, a shadow made by a tall man. He moves up the steps close behind us and begins to walk towards the house, talking to himself." As the unnamed woman did, the man now tells a story, this one about a biracial girl who trusted no one, and whom no one else trusted: "And so, one day, having nowhere to turn, she, who had always given faithful allegiance to Agwe, God of the Sea, got into her boat and rowed out to meet him." Up until this point, Vodou has subtly been providing the foundation for much of the script. The mention of this specific *loa* symbolically linked with the sea, however, makes the connection more obvious. Given the representations of Black women, ghosts, Black Christians, and Vodou in Hollywood in the 1970s and 1980s, the chances of Collins's first film ever being produced were slim to none. Nevertheless, this was the script she needed to write to make a space for herself and what she would do next. Ironically, there is no violent crisis or upheaval involving demons or the devil for the Black women in the screenplay, just the meandering crisis of a colonized spirit struggling to be free from capitalism. That is what a vacation or holiday is, is it not? As Baldwin pointed out in his critique of *The Exorcist*, "The Western world pivots on the infantile, and, in action, criminal delusions of possession, and of property" (1976, 120). In Collins's script, Lillie's confessions about falling in love with a man with money, who becomes her husband, showcase her as someone originally vested in material possessions.

Nevertheless, in Collins's script some characters exist in a reality in which humans still talk to gods without an intermediary, and these interactions become the basis of stories about spiritual possession that counter structures their lives. When Lillie encounters the mystery man, he listens to Lillie talk about her marriage and the man she may or may not have loved. The stranger's response to her tale is one of the only instances of affective explosion, though it is still quiet:

His voice a husky, too husky whisper
    MAN
"You a jive, jive chick. . . . Somebody's been messin' with your mind
(Chill laughter): but you <u>do</u> be one of us."

A revelation has been made about Lillie, and the script calls for her to appear stunned and frightened, but there is no dialogue from her in response to the man. Instead, Collins provides a descriptive sequence in which the camera pans up a dark stairway and into a white room, where Lillie sits surrounded by lush, green plants as sunlight streams in. Though it won't be obvious until later, these visuals signify the beginning process of decolonization of a spirit. The sequence then cuts away to Lillie getting back into a boat.

Much of the screenplay is quiet and without excitement in plot and dialogue. The external world of the characters remains as (un)eventful as the interior world of each character. In close quarters, the women make an intimate world among themselves and share their life experiences with one another. They speak of the men in their lives (Lillie tells of the first man she fell in love with), they reveal sexual ineptness to each other during makeover sessions (Marita confesses that she has never had an orgasm), and they share fears about abuse and death (Marita analyzes emotions awakened at an uncle's funeral). However, descriptions, stage notes, and character monologues require director and filmmaker to push visual boundaries in terms of color, angles, landscape, and motion. Collins meant for the dimensional definition and context, as well as the translation, of her words to be taken up in shot selection, costume design, casting choices, timing, and staging.

If the script were to be justly rendered as a film, then the last scene—in which Lillie, like the younger sister in the woman's story and the girl in the man's story, is converted from her colonized self into a new being—would force any savvy director or cinematographer to produce a deliberate vision of an altar that displaces symbolic crosses or baptismal water imagery and conversion. This natural "edifice" made out of space and light would enable viewers to grasp Lillie's actions as evidence of spiritual conversion as opposed to unwilling possession or insanity: "Night. Lillie alone on the front lawn. The moon is high. She sits with her legs under her. She is breaking glass into minute fragments and containing the smashed pieces in a box. . . . She scatters the fragments of glass on the glue, pressing the pieces down, then she begins to paint them." This is both spiritual ritual and art. The scene fades out, and the script declares "the end" on the last page. Lillie, if we believe the man, was a god capable of invention and reinvention of self. She only needed another perspective on space and light. As René Depestre would write, "Voodoo, a product of Franco-African syncretism, is an example of religious surrealism. The behavior of the voodoo gods is supremely surrealist."[6] Though Collins's script was never turned into a produced film, what Collins accomplished was an exploration of and introduction to alternative modes of visual excess. What she wanted to do with shadows and light—reordering them through Haitian cosmologies as well as women's lives—was remarkable in expressing the anteriority of global Black visuality and Black film technologies. The need to tell stories would propel her forward from the disappointments dealt to her by the film industry.

ANTERIORITY AND VISUAL STORYTELLING

Writing was another altar for Kathleen Collins, a ritualized arrangement of fragments, words, and images to worship and be worshipped. As *Women, Sisters, and Friends* demonstrated, Collins was a prodigious fabler of African Diasporic tales. This was also evident in the other narrative forms she took to throughout her life—short stories. Descendants of ancient cosmological narrative forms, short stories are nonmechanized technological devices of the mind—time machines. Like equations in physics, short stories are qualitative formulas used to solve specific problems within numerous universes. In the hands of Collins, short fiction becomes film theory, not simply because of its adaptation to cinematic possibilities but because it provides a way to theorize the configuration of LIGHT . . . SPACE . . . TIME . . . SPACE-TIME . . . NARRATIVE. Historians disremember that time is as much of a narrative device as it is an allegory or a red herring. Storytellers do not. Short stories have always been lively pedagogical tools capable of teaching nuanced and complex lessons.

Because some of Collins's short stories contain no dates and others have specific dates, the remainder of this chapter does not project a linear or comparative timeline of writing and production that connects Collins's short stories to her films. Even though doing so might illuminate one aspect of her creative process—for example, how editing techniques in narrative cinema were impacting her long- and short-form print writing—producing such a timeline might obscure the ways we comprehend the radicalness of her decisive ability to simultaneously create in multiple artistic forms. Aesthetic techniques from short fiction writing heavily influenced her scriptwriting and directorial vision. To understand her as doing all these at the same time is to recognize her preoccupation with how the life forms she sought to represent required a dimensionality that only multiple and simultaneous creation could provide. Such radical simultaneity also demonstrates a desire to avoid Western settler preoccupations with arrangements of space and time that support a manifest destiny as well as Western capitalist ideologies that discipline creative expression into forms and rules for the purpose of property rights and ownership— that is, who can claim to be most significant or first.

These cultural microcosms of colonialism and capitalism come undone when the boundaries of form are transgressed, when Collins does not stay in one place. Consequently, I highlight the importance of adaptation of and experimentation with form to her skill as a storyteller, and note that Collins believed that play with form could be a strategy that ensured the survival of global Black aesthetics, forms, and techniques that might otherwise be sub-sumed by a single country's representational politics, universal narratives, and exceptionalism.

Like her first film, and perhaps because it was never produced, several of Collins's writings went unpublished. The nonpublication of Collins's fiction compels me to interrogate the edifice of what has been billed as Black women's writings. Whose fault is this? Hers, for not being diligent and dogmatic about pursuing publication as she also sought film production and distribution. Save correspondences from Alice Walker and Toni Morrison, there is little evidence of overwhelming support from publishers or agents for her submissions.[7] She certainly discloses such rejection of her filmmaking. Whose fault is it? The white corporate entities of the publishing, film, and theater industries, for being unable to foster and groom artists capable of transdisciplinary and imaginative art and writing that intertwines filmmaking with literary writing with stage work. Whose fault is it? The Black publics and counterpublics whose failure of imagination regarding form and whose prioritizing of publicness in Black social and political life left no way to value the quiet intimacy of Black interiority and Collins's temporal and spatial defiance of Black social life. Whose fault is it? Definitively, it is not the fault of Black women writers at work simultaneously uncovering and recovering works as they theorized and built a field, a movement, and an enterprising future for Black women writers who would follow. Certainly, it is not the fault of Black women writers at work who died young and who, before their early deaths, began to notice and comment on the erroneous omission of Collins from the literary and cultural history of Black women writers at work.

The writer who most exemplified the last of these categories was Toni Cade Bambara, who, like Collins, critiqued US exceptionalism throughout much of her life's work. It was Bambara who expressed, in an interview with Kalamu Ya Salaam, that "we will have to invent, in addition to new forms, new modes and new idioms" (Holmes and Wall 2007, 58). Bambara the writer and filmmaker and Collins the filmmaker and writer executed their art through experimentation with multiple art forms, theorizing the cinematic through the short-story form.

Bambara notably tried to tell everyone about the brilliance of Collins. Having seen one of the few early screenings of *Losing Ground*, the illustrious Bambara wrote, "The late pioneer black woman filmmaker Kathy Collins Prettyman was a liberating sign" (Bambara 1996, 128). Years earlier, Bambara had attended to the pathologization of Black people in white filmmaking in her phenomenal short story "Blues Ain't No Mockingbird" (1971). This was sixteen years before she theorized the function of Black independent cinema in the biting essay

"Why Black Cinema" (1987), in which she insists that "people can awaken, people can change, and in changing enable each other. We can be concerned with something larger than ourselves. We CAN rise above our training. We can think better than we're taught" (Holmes and Wall 2007, 205). The allusions to Kathleen Collins in the essay are clear, as Bambara mentions the will to change what is supposedly known about Blackness and Black art and culture: "It occurred in the '70s when bloods trained in films schools like Yale got out of there and hooked up and trained with people who trained at City College in New York" (204). Collins was one of the figures who trained the bloods. Once an instructor at City College herself, Bambara was acknowledging another Black woman writer at work in a tradition different from those she began with in her writing career.

Bambara found something of value in an ignored tradition of Black filmmaking, and saw it exemplified by Collins, whose evolution hinged on decolonial approaches and a rejection of US exceptionalism and empire.[8] Speaking on Black cinema, Bambara would exclaim, "We may not know the exact moment when there was a sense among these filmmakers that launching a movement, that moment when they recognized the necessity for institutionalizing and internationalizing. But by the 1980s, potentially powerful links had been forged between African filmmakers in the US, the UK, in Europe, and on the Continent" (Holmes and Wall 2007, 204). Collins was part of the international cohort of the Black independent film movement and was drawn, late in life, to a Black woman writer who precedes a late twentieth-century tradition of Black women writers at work.[9] As has been documented, Collins credits Haile Gerima, an African Diasporic filmmaker, with introducing her to the work of Lorraine Hansberry. Collins drew numerous comparisons between herself and Hansberry as a result of their shared critiques of Black middle-class aspirations and commitment to theatrical writing traditions. Hansberry thus became a literary bridge between Collins, Gerima, and Bambara. That bridge spans time and roles: as Hansberry's work was for Collins, so Collins's work was for Bambara, so Bambara's legacy and Collins's afterlife are for contemporary filmmakers and future writers and filmmakers. The search for new forms connects these artists beyond their development as filmmakers, reaching toward their function as storytellers. Turning now to Collins's foray into short fiction, I exalt it as her transdisciplinary method, both playful and erotic, for handling the exterior spectacle of sexuality and body on-screen while alluding to the interior labor of decolonizing the self.

The Cambridge Introduction to the American Short Story insists, "It could be argued, indeed, that around the 1820s and 1830s, the [white] Americans virtually invented what has come to be called 'the short story,' in its modern literary sense" (Scofield 2006, 1). The volume later mentions European and Middle Eastern predecessors and accounts for trickster tales in Koasati and other Native American oral traditions that may have played "some part in the mental formations that gave rise to the literary short story" (3). Short stories have been serious endeavors since long before they were serious business for the nineteenth-century American magazine literary marketplace, which capitalized off an audience or reading public motivated by the design of Edgar Allen Poe (1966) or Alexis de Tocqueville (1968, 608–9). The gatekeepers of form measure, as men do with dicks, and counting words instead of inches, how many words dictate a short story. They offer a critical rehearsal of the importance of difference and diversity made possible by the form: "The genre speaks in a host of different voices—as we shall see, the sense of 'voice,' the closeness to the scene of an oral narrator is a strong strand in the web of the American short story—and has the freedom to tackle an immense variety of subjects in almost as many different modes. An approach to it cannot be centered on any one mode (romantic 'tale,' realist story, 'tall tale,' anecdote, sketch, or parable) but must take account of them all" (Scofield 2006, 9). Even after such caveats, the *Cambridge Introduction*'s one chapter on African American short story up until 1965 tends to Charles Chesnutt, Richard Wright, and James Baldwin, as if there were no Pauline Hopkins, Zora N. Hurston, or Ann Petry. As Sylvia Wynter (1971) has written, there are numerous genres of the human just as there are many genres of literature and music. *The Cambridge Introduction to the American Short Story* uses the words of Raymond Carver to outline the prescriptions of the American writer and the short story genre: "It could be taken as one motto for the American short story writer: 'Get in, get out. Don't linger. Go on'" (Scofield 2006, 9). However, such a motto could never account for the immersive, affective depth made possible by short stories in the African American women's literary tradition. Eroticism, desire, or lust, while sustained and persistent throughout any one life, have been astonishingly represented in short-form narrative where figuration can change and shift in accord with approaches to embodiment and liminal genders and sexualities.

NEW FORMS, NEW MODES, NEW IDIOMS:
LIGHTS, CAMERA, ACTION

In addition to being about strategic uses of light, visual culture depends upon the manipulation of space and composition to orient viewers into a filmmaker's perception and storytelling. If the storyteller/filmmaker's sensorium has not been fully colonized, then the other components of perception that comprise visuality might become the basis on new forms, modes, and idioms. Depending on what traditions they are from, short stories contain modes of visuality that prove useful to decolonizing film. She mixes fiction with the cinematic and the theatrical to shape movements between interior monologue, prose narrative, humor, and irony. Her characters' voices and the tone of the stories use humor, irony, and, wit, resembling the work of Langston Hughes and Bambara. In some of these stories, Collins establishes how to use space and light to create a dimensionality that can convey the depths of interiority. Writers and film scholars such as Geetha Ramanathan (2006, 2020), Hayley O'Malley (2019), Terri Francis (2018), and Elizabeth Alexander (1994) have all provided critical analysis about why Collins was enamored with representing women's interior life on film and page. Thus, I move on to delineate how the need to translate interiority in multiple forms taught Collins to employ transvisual approaches to body, embodiment, eroticism, and sexuality.

David Trottier's *The Screenwriter's Bible* explains that camera placement, time of day, and location serve as the basis for a scene. There is also rhythm or pace, according to Collins, who understands the cinematographer's role as arranger. A cinematographer or cameraperson, though her presence may not be evident in a scene, addresses embodiment for actors and the audience by introducing, keeping, or producing rhythmic spatialization for scenes. The cinematographer, or the cameraperson, shows up as a character in Collins's short fiction several times. Collins's decision to construct characters as cinematographers as opposed to directors seems to answer some of her questions about which forms and methods are best for representing interiority while also dealing with the exterior of racial or gender discourse. In the posthumous collection, *Whatever Happened to Interracial Love*, two short pieces, "Exterior" and "Interior," mark what might be noted as Collins's signature "out-of-love" scenes, as opposed to love scenes. Collins understands Western anatomies of a scene, but she approaches them from an embodied multisensory perspective of technology as opposed to one of disembodied technology and the colonized sensorium.

In "Exteriors," the main character is an ungendered narrator who is shooting a film scene about a young couple. What moves the story forward is the narrator's main concern with light, and Collins writes this via the character's discussion of location: "Okay, it's a sixth floor walk up, three rooms in the front . . . roaches on the wall . . . with a stained glass window. The light? They've got light up the butt!" (Collins 2017, 1). Throughout the short piece,

Collins demonstrates the central tenet of good scene building and storytelling: showing instead of telling. The narrator, focused on exterior surroundings, describes the light and how to light rooms and bodies for a scene: there are spotlights, lights "up the butt," soft gel, and backlight. The exteriors show what kind of movie might be being made—low-budget, independent—and what kind of lovemaking scene is being directed—artistic, soft-core pornography. We understand that the "exteriors" of the title concern light and its reflection, but in the telling there is also showing that invokes tactility. There is no dialogue between the couple being filmed; the narrator informs us how light operates. Light not only reflects; when it radiates, it also touches: "Then fade him to black and leave her in the shadow while she looks for the feelings that lit up the room" (3). The climax of the narrator's filmed scene is the dramatic ending of the man leaving the woman, but the climax of "Exteriors" itself comes from a recognition or revelation that the room and the light served as a metaphor for what was occurring in the body: a depth of heartbreak that spoken dialogue alone might fail to capture. Here, Collins devises a narrator looking out and through a lens to bring viewers inside a room, a woman, and the end of a relationship. Although the scene is about a quest to showcase and locate exteriors, it is also simultaneously about the interior.

"Interiors," on the other hand, uses rhythm, ellipsis, and voice to show rather than tell. In the short story, a male narrator, a husband, who is a musician, describes falling out of love with his wife, a violinist. She, then, recounts her thoughts on the end of their marriage. The man begins, ". . . It's a long improvisation, my life . . ." (Collins 2017, 5). The ellipses indicate a stream of consciousness as the husband recalls childhood memories, first meetings with two women, and events that offer a glimpse into the world of someone who has the privilege of not being bound by time or place, in the form of possession. The woman, on the other hand, begins her stream of consciousness with ". . . The first time my husband left me, I took a small cabin in the woods" (9). Collins writes the two musicians as a duet collaboration. As the husband explains that "no woman living has ever been a part of my dreams," a composition about domesticity and art emerges (6). Just as light produces narrative about tactile affect in "Exteriors," Collins invokes speech and musical rhythm in "Interiors" to signify abruptness, harshness, and cutting—but ellipses are also about space. They emulate textual manspreading/mansplaining to visually exemplify what Collins imagines as the interior tone of narcissism. The ellipses in the wife's narration appear later in the story, and when they are used, they are literally shorter—two or three periods versus four or more for the husband, who also uses them early and often. For Collins, masculinity exists as a gendered technology of visuality and cinema in a way that far exceeds Laura Mulvey's "male gaze" (Mulvey 1975). Visual technology of gender operates as a spatial orientation device whose function is to accumulate or occupy external space, and the technology repeats itself throughout much of her writing and filmmaking. For example, in "Interiors," the narrator equates moneymaking with "replacing the magic potion I used to find in my dick" (Collins 2017, 6). When Collins switches into women's perspectives, the reverse is true, as seen in another short piece, "Treatment for a Story."

In film and television, a *treatment* is supposed to be a dynamic summary or overview of a film, pitched to studios. However, the term *treatment* outside the entertainment industry connotes a healing aid. As Collins clarifies in "Treatment for a Story," another prose piece included in the posthumous collection *Whatever Happened to Interracial Love?*, treatments are also portals into the interior worlds of those attempting to create or speculate about alternative realities. In "Treatment for a Story," a woman visits her male lover, who happens to be a writer. The anonymous woman understands her presence as pulling him from a world she cannot see. Alone in his apartment, she "pulls the dirty sheets over her and starts to doze . . . Starts to doze until the room pulls her awake, overpowers her with its clutter, its scrawled notebooks and poems and letters to himself . . . Himself . . . The odor of his conversations gets under her skin, keeps her awake. As if she did not belong there" (Collins 2017, 84).

As the story proceeds, Collins uses the woman's point of view to describe sensory perceptions of the room, the man, the couple's lovemaking, and their physical interactions. The woman's explicit focus on what occurs in the external world they share—the taste of perspiration or smoke on skin, the feel of heat from one body to another, the smell of flowers and wet dirt (84)—is in stark contrast to what she perceives as her denied access to another world: "Pounding the wet typewriter keys. Himself. Scribbling interminable notes. Himself" (85). By the end of the piece, we understand that the man, unlike his lover, exists in and moves between multiple worlds. One of them is an interior world, to which the other will never be granted access. In these three pages of prose, Collins demonstrates how *treatment* can be both a teaching tool and a healing aid for students and teachers more concerned with what interiority can do than with whether external factors will find value in the internal world. "Interiors," "Exteriors," and "Treatment for a Story" demonstrate how Collins used her knowledge of filmmaking to dimensionalize the short narrative form beyond text and word count to provide depth as it relates to perception and orientation, and to disorient ideas of the camera as a technological extension of an eye that gazes rather than looks in and seeks out.

ONCE UPON A TIME SHE LIKED WRITING . . . SEX: VISUALITY AND EMBODIED TECHNOLOGY

In her filmmaking and her prose writing, Collins positions the body as a mode of technology. The depictions of the body as simultaneously an expression and a technology, in both film and prose, derive from her pointed use of space and light. In another short story, "Documentary Style," Collins reveals that the camera can be an extension of any body part, or of the whole body. The story is about the "best goddamn black cameraman to hit New York," who has aspirations to be a filmmaker (Collins 2017, 115). From the beginning, Collins details sensory experiences beyond the eye. The unnamed narrator says, "My body was tight from years of karate and I could handhold a camera, pan, tilt, track, like a motherfuckin' dancer. I knew I knew more about filmmaking than most of the dudes coming out of the films schools and I was gonna make me some films" (115). Whether Collins's short story is a fictional rendering of her own experience or of one of her Black male film students such as Ronald Gray is not important. What is pivotal about this opening sequence is how Collins uses the idea of dance to center her suggestion of filmmaking as visual art that is not static and disembodied, but physical, rhythmic, and choreographed. As such she uses short fiction to invent innovative kinesthetic approaches to her characters and themes.

Later in the story, heat between subjects, in addition to the cameraman's footwork and rhythm, become markers of stylistic difference between the Black protagonist and a white cameraman during shooting and editing (116–17). What Collins gains with such an approach is an inclusion of full-body perceptions of the filming process, both exterior and interior, that are outside scopic visuality. She highlights the elements of rhythm and footwork underlying the visual rendering of a director/cinematographer's vision. The gaze is not simply a gaze. Collins insists on recognition of the multiple dimensions involved in visualization. In other stories, she manipulates elements of fictional form to ensure that the characters and telling are not flat, producing auditory experiences of the visual through a strategic use of voice and tone.

Though she did not theorize the narrative form of the short story or one-act plays as other writers had, in practice Collins proved that short-form writing could provide entrée into sophisticated film theories and film production notes. Collins's cinematic approach to representing race, gender, and class in her short stories in which sexuality, eroticism, or ecstasy are major elements of the plot seems remarkably different from short stories in which she takes on themes of race and gender alone in plots. As she makes obvious in the philosophical dialogue of her second film, *Losing Ground* (1982), specifically in conversations between protagonist Sara and Sara's mother, Collins was very critical of Black middle-class sensibilities around the body, eroticism, and sexuality. Elsewhere, I have referred to this critique as redemptive softness (Stallings 2011). Collins's concerted effort to do more than screen sex can be seen in her short fiction, in which sex scenes appear to be choreographed for a film in which the actors' bodies may or may not be in rhythm with a director's rhythm or a reader's expectations and wishes (Stallings 2011).

Collins's short fiction, then, is important to Black sexuality studies and film studies because of the way it interrogates audiovisual embodiment and sexuality, and the role of actor, director, and cinematographer in translating a character's embodiment or sexuality to the screen. What is the camera person's/the director's/the actor's relationship to their body? What, if any, is their philosophy on embodiment and how might that philosophy, or lack thereof shape individual scenes in a film and thus the overall film project? Collins positions the entire body and its sensorial processes as modes of technology for motion picture. Such a strategy is less about homing in on directing an actor to do a sex scene but rather facilitating a performance of embodiment that emphasizes what affect and cultural moorings design any character's desire and lust. In her filmmaking and her prose writing, Collins used adaptation as a method from which to map out and theorize her directorial vision for bodies and sex on screen: specifically, a short story becomes a film theory, or vice versa, in which the moral prescriptions undergirding the acting and the directing of sex scenes are challenged along with the normative models of gender and sexuality, and the privileging of perspectives based on race, gender, and sexuality.

In the short story "Nina Simone," Collins offers a momentary glimpse into the possible start of one romance and the end of another, beginning with a shared interest in jazz great Nina Simone. As a masterful musician and storyteller, Simone serves as inspiration for how Collins can approach the theme of monogamy from multiple perspectives. Like "Interiors," "Nina Simone" entails shifting points of view. The first narrator is a Black man and jazz session musician who begins in the body—or rather, begins by describing the physical appearance—of the second narrator, a married Black woman freelance writer: "She came in while I was recording and asked to listen to every Nina Simone album in the house.... Her in a page boy with bangs. Light skinned. Nice eyes" (Collins 2019, 11). The Black woman narrator begins, "My husband and I had been together almost a year" (12). The third character, the white husband of the freelance writer, insists at the beginning of his recounting, "I didn't like being married but I was happy with her" (13). Whereas the previous stories utilized shifting perspectives that centered on sight and the visual, here Collins relies on Black musical tradition to establish the shifting perspective and then attends to the depth of the tone she establishes.

The story does more telling than showing in its narrative development, and Collins's technique of shifting points of view becomes the action. Plot, in this case, does not simply move forward; it expands. And the expansion is acoustic. The first narrator, a musician, serves as the opening chord. He establishes the rhythm and temporal setting when he alludes to Herbie Hancock's song "Maiden Voyage," saying, "which puts us around 1965" (11). This reference, combined with the title, sets the story in a year when Simone released two studio albums: *Pastel Blues* and *I Put a Spell on You*.

Pastel Blues had Simone field hollering and pleading on "Be My Husband" and conveying bluesy longing on "Tell Me More and More and Then Some." In *I Put a Spell on You*, Simone's versatile interpretations of pop standards included feigned youthfulness and sarcasm on "Marriage Is for Old Folks," beautiful malevolence on "I Put a Spell on You," loving passion on the thunderous "Feeling Good," and sad and languid forlornness on "Ne Me Quitte Pas." These songs about relationships contain themes about longing, love, desperation, loyalty, and desire. Subsequently, it is no coincidence that the tone of this short story is Simonesque, setting a mood that alternates between these emotions through each character's point of view.

Each of the three characters provides a different take on the same plot points and events, but the overall subject concerns what happens when desire is ignited. After the musician describes his early interactions with the writer, it seems as if he is nearing the end of his account when he says, "She drove me home and I asked her to come in" (12). Readers do not immediately learn from the first narrator whether a one-night stand occurred. As one person's narrative unfolds, Collins interrupts it with another person's. The woman recounts her time with the musician, and eventually she reveals, "When I drove him home he asked me to come in" (13). Yet the story, or the song, does not end there. The wife's account is interrupted by the husband's: "Then one night she came home looking odd and jumpy" (13). The story's structure allows Collins to build tension around felt desire in three different bodies, which is voiced differently in the diction, syntax, and tone of each character: "And I wanted her so bad. It came down on me like that" (14), or "I *couldn't* be feeling this for someone else. I wanted him really bad. My insides hurt" (14). This singular moment, described by each character, becomes not only the basis of an internal or external conflict that must be resolved but also the bridge from one perspective to another. Collins avoids nonsensical abruption by employing techniques from musical arrangements. There is repetition and revision in the phrasing of common experiences that reaches a crescendo that is not all that satisfying. Simone's power as a storyteller is in her delivery of the tale, but inevitably, no matter how climactic and sonically powerful the Simone songs are, they offer no absolute resolution. In Collins's "Nina Simone," while there may be resolution for at least one of the characters, such resolution could be ambivalent depending on whose perspective a reader is most invested in.

The experiential gains Collins makes from her exploration of embodiment, interiors, and exteriors, both in cinematic technique and formalistic qualities of short fiction, result in another unique short story, "Raschida" (2019). With "Raschida" Collins offers a fun and fantastic representation of what it might mean for a woman to direct and choreograph a sex scene, or to create a love quilt as Collins would write it.[10] As Jennifer Nash's *The Black Body in Ecstasy* explains in its attention to Black feminist ideologies and the pornotroping of Black women's bodies, "If dominant representation injures, resistance and recovery are possible only when black women act as authors of their own images, taking the site of violence—the visual field—and making it a space for performing their wholeness" (Nash 2014, 147). Throughout "Raschida," Collins avoids the moral panics of 1980s sex wars that pitted feminist anti-pornographers against sex-positive pro-porn feminists to better engage the larger question of western embodiment and how it might negatively influence filmmaking. There is no evidence that Collins ever dabbled in pornographic filmmaking. However, "Raschida" demonstrates that she was theorizing what it might look like for her to direct sex scenes. Consequently, "Raschida" is a story whose plot provides a prescient and welcome commentary about the lack of training filmmakers receive about representing eroticism and sexuality, Hollywood studio's appropriation of the Me-Too movement, and the industry's sweeping implementation of intimacy directors on set in response to sexual harassment and exploitation in the industry.

Remarkably, Collins's intervention on the audiovisual presentation of bodies and sexuality in her short fiction writing allowed her to demonstrate how the folk art of quilt making provided an anterior to the visual regime of filmmaking and modernity's motion pictures industry. Collins's uses of the erotic and her philosophies of embodiment matter for film directors, the presentation of sexuality on screen or stage, and for undoing the colonial truth of sexuality.

In "Raschida," an unnamed narrator protagonist remarks on her nineteen-year-old friend Raschida, who lives in a Brooklyn apartment making quilts and cooking, and Gerard, a male prospect whom the narrator intends to bed. The unnamed protagonist develops a scene, frame by frame, in which Raschida and

Gerard will have sex with each other. This unnamed character is one of Collins's female narrators who gets to construct a scene around desire and direct and build a climax. Both the anonymous narrator and Raschida are depicted as women fully in their bodies. Raschida enjoys cooking, quilting, and lovemaking, and the narrator enjoys eating and lovemaking on Raschida's quilts.

Before the lovemaking scene, our narrator conveys that Raschida has gone shopping for a new outfit and that she has a new hairstyle, highlighting that Raschida relishes texture, dimension, and color. In contrast, the unnamed narrator relishes in spectacle and soft vulgarity, as in the very beginning when she describes Raschida's bed—or more specifically, the quilts on the bed, which serve as backdrop for her lovemaking: "This was your tenth quilt in a year. . . . And I've used every one of them," she says, laughing (Collins 2019, 19). The narrator not only describes the images and color of the "blue-black maroon quilt" (17); she ascribes the quilt to a season, as "the winter one," and considers its texture and temperature, referring to "all the snow and the little fireplaces in velvet" (19). She understands the quilt not just as a visual art form but also as functional materiality and erotic stimulation. The material culture of quilts precedes camera technology as a form of storytelling capable of narrating a tale about bodies.

Quilt making is, as Carolyn Mazloomi's and Faith Ringgold's artistic examples convey, a great storytelling tradition:

> African people weren't allowed to read and write here, so it was an easy transition from that oral African history to a pictorial history. . . . So what better way than to say it in a narrative quilt? We're always telling stories, you know. We're always celebrating the ancestor stories and we continue to follow that oral tradition. It's just—it's a preference, you know, it's a preference of African-Americans for these pictorial quilts. But I find the trend changing a little bit, but that's another story.[11]

The folk-art tradition has been associated with transmitting secret messages about the underground railroad, telling children's stories, recording family traditions and events, conveying spiritual practices and rites, and recording astronomical histories. Quilt making also dabbles in eroticism. Quilts touch bodies that engage in lovemaking on top of or in between them. Quilts have stories to tell about sex. Quilt making also precedes the scene making and construction of film frames that require editing. According to Faith Ringgold, quilt making's visual creation is a frame by frame process: "And that's the same thing I do with the quilts. I know exactly how many frames I have to write: it's six at the top and six at the bottom. I know it's six frames, I know how deep the frames are—six twelve-inch-by-three-inch blocks—then I find out how many words I can fit in there. It's very technical" (Graulich & Witzling 1994, 9).

As the narrator directs Raschida and Gerard to the bedroom, where she takes quilts from the closet to show off Raschida's skills, she insists, "Lie down on this one, Raschida. See how it matches your blouses. Lie down next to Raschida, Gerard." Then she becomes more direct about what she intends: "Why don't you make a love quilt, Raschida? Show her how to make a love quilt, Gerard. Take your thing out and show her how to make a love quilt" (19). Despite her coaxing tone, the narrator is directing both Raschida and Gerard's movements. The reader learns that Raschida has little rosebud-like nipples and that Gerard has a huge penis, and that the narrator is excited by both. A love quilt becomes an alternative mode of understanding what a sex scene could be beyond the "frenzy of the visible" discussed in Linda Williams's work on pornography (2008).

Collins's short story belies assumptions critic Linda Williams has made about pornography—namely, that "Black female viewing pleasure, it would seem, is the least well served by these newly racialized, noisy confessions of pleasure" (Williams 2004, 302–3). During the first part of the short story, the narrator nervously laughs as she instigates erotic play; however, as she begins issuing more direct instructions, her laughter is replaced with farting. Certainly, this could be indigestion or nervousness, but the point Collins makes is that there can be no disembodiment for the actors or the director. After the narrator has issued her first direction, she exclaims, "What was that noise? Did I fart again? I farted? I'm sorry" (19). As she continues guiding Raschida and Gerard through their love quilting, her excitement grows. Gerard hardens, Raschida gets wet, and their rhythm is established and maintained in accord with her voice and will. At no point do the narrator's directions, excitement, or farting lessen: "Don't stop, Raschida. Take him. Oh God, I'm farting. Excuse me. . . . Oh God, take him woman. . . . Oh Jesus, Gerard, I'm coming with you" (20).

What do we make of the humorous detail of farting in this scene direction? Laughing and farting are a far cry from the moans and climatic shrieks of the pornographic imagination produced by white male filmmakers. How does one direct or edit the wet hapticality of a love quilt. How does one ignore arousal, nervousness, of those being directed and she who is directing. If our narrator or Raschida is a substitute for a director, then Collins conveys that artistic direction, creation, and process entail physical and interior arousal. Something physically happening in the director, as it would be for actors. Rather than shy away from that, Collins offers something other than a mediator of Hollywood studios.

The love quilt being made by Gerard, Raschida, and the narrator accepts a particular world order that is neither pornographic or post-porn modernist. This is what Raschida conveys. A deep reading of Collins's decision to name this as making a love quilt beckons us to understand the erotics of quilt making, its mode of communality, and its visual markers. A western pornographic perspective might insist that the narrator/protagonist alone is directing a sex scene, but a Black world perspective about quilt making might reveal, as the title of the story implies, that Raschida the quiltmaker was always simultaneously acting and directing this scene via a different visual register.

The signs of sex for the quiltmaker can be haptic and do not require a unified whole form. Texture/fabric invokes memory and feeling and ideas. Raschida can rely upon haptic aesthetics to move her fellow actors into her story or fantasy quilt by quilt. Quiltmakers know that stiches provide motion, just as light and optical manipulation does so for film. Color of thread for a stitch, types of stitches, binding, and materials used contribute to dimensionality, as well as narrates the story being told and characters being constructed.

Quilt making, Ringgold tells us, was a communal art practice that built and sustained community.

> You can make your quilts, you can make them out of rags, you can use old clothes, you can use your friends, you can sit around and commune with your friends and have some dinner. You can make a social event; the slaves did it. After working in the fields all day, they would have a quilting bee, and it was like a party. And they could actually make something that they could give to somebody: they could pass something on. They couldn't enjoy the luxury of an object. they were cut off from the drum, they were cut off from the mask. But they weren't cut off from those skills of sewing and appliqueing and piecing things together. And when they were sitting there they were talking and respecting each other because the best way to learn to respect another person is to work with them. . . . Now, that hasn't been talked about a lot, but it should be. The visual art tradition of black people has been seriously cut off. (Graulich and Witzling 1994, 17)

Collins theorizes that a director's production of a sex scene can draw from this visual art tradition of Black people. With Raschida's love quilt, Collins performs what John Akomfrah labels "de-westernizing as double move" (Bâ and Higbee 2012, 13). She de-westernizes the colonization of senses in the visual regime and she theorizes communal and equitable depictions of constructing a sex scene in an alternatively Black visual regime. The quiltmaker and her love quilt challenges Hollywood studio's new proliferation of intimacy coordinators, and confirms them more or less as a new model of setter colonial sexuality.

This chapter assesses other forms and mediums—sacred tales and short stories—to highlight the significance of Collins's entire canon to the future of Black filmmaking and film studies. Some time ago, African American literary critic Kenneth Warren (2011) created a notable controversy in his announcement of the premature end of African American literature. As many readers will have already assessed, African American literature continues to be relevant and necessary. Certainly, the production, distribution, and creation of what constitutes African American literature continue to be important to African American freedom, resistance, revolution, and decolonization. African American literature and drama, however, remains underutilized in Black filmmaking despite the box office or critical success of films such as *A Raisin in the Sun*, *Native Son*, *The Color Purple*, *A Soldier's Story*, *Roots*, *Waiting to Exhale*, *How Stella Got Her Groove Back*, *Devil in a Blue Dress*, and *Miracle of St. Ana*. More recently, we have seen the failures of Black literary adaptations to film with *Beloved*, *Precious*, *Their Eyes Were Watching God*, and *For Colored Girls*, followed by successful ventures such as *Queen Sugar*, *Fences*, *The Hate You Give*, and *If Beale Street Could Talk*. This chapter, then, is a call to remember early Black independent filmmakers' opposition to the cinematic colonization that Hollywood studios continue to offer in their remakes, illogical casting choices, and acquisition of Star Wars and Marvel entities. It issues a call to adapt existing and original globally Black stories and narratives, to translate Black literary forms and audiovisual structures for the screen from a foundation of love.

LOVE LIFE

Revolution is the word: Establishing Shot

and the word is revolution . . . : Wide Shot

Revolution spelled backwards is NO IT U LOV ER: Cut to POV Over
the Shoulder

Know it you love her . . . : Low Angle, Medium Long Shot

NO IT U LOV ER: Close-up

Revolution is about love, revolution is about her: Cut Away

Know it, know her, know love when you see it: Reaction Shot

Backward and forward: Zoom

Revolution is a rotation, a cyclic motion, a turn, an orbit: Pan

and its axis is love . . . is love . . . is: Dissolve

no it u lov er: Fade to black.

LOVE, A CRISIS OF POSSESSION

God! the revolutions we live! . . . the outer shell goes on about its tasks
And the world for the most part, is none the wiser. Yet inside! Inside!
what revolutions are possible!

KATHLEEN COLLINS, "LETTER TO PEGGY DAMMOND," DATE UNKNOWN

When we fail to re-establish a synthesis of our inclinations—will,
ideas, sentiments, and beliefs—when one of these physical elements
begins to act independently, we lose possession of ourselves.

LOUIS MARS, *CRISIS OF POSSESSION IN VOODOO*

For more than a century, in silent film, in black and white, in color, and in 3D, from storyboard to final cut, Hollywood has reproduced the same representation of love, even when filmmakers delve into nonheteronormative expressions of it. Love is a noun: an object that must be given and received. In Hollywood stories about love, depictions of women's relationships and lives are domesticated under the genre of romance. These domestic narratives are significantly marginalized in comparison to nationalist films in multiple genres. In Hollywood, when filmmakers tell stories about revolutions, they are classified as historical dramas, action and adventure, war stories, or spy thrillers. Nationalism serves as the basis for a butched-up romance genre, specifically depicting love stories gendered for men in which love of country means more than romantic or familial love. The conflict of these two genres is that women cannot be revolutionary in love stories, and that any cinematic rendering of women in revolutions requires concepts of love antithetical to most nationalist discourses.

Black Hollywood is no different. After *Mahogany* and *A Warm December,* but before *Love Jones, Love and Basketball,* and *Sylvie's Love,* Collins created screenplays that should have been important interruptions of heterosexual love stories produced by Hollywood and Black Hollywood. Her screenplays provide some of the earliest takes on revolutionary love, revolution of self-love, for Black women ever conceived. In her filmic representation of Black women and love, Black women are not primarily choosing between self and a man's love or between self and a nation's love: They are choosing between different versions of themselves and the forms of relationality that can express those selves. Collins's depictions offer something more than love, they provide what Kevin Quashie would highlight as an "engagement of liminality [which] is, as a practice, synonymous with finding god in oneself, a self-divinity that is a key aesthetic principle in the African Diaspora" (2004, 83). Her aesthetic principles were guided by her lived experiences.

In another letter to her friend Bluette, Collins mentions the ineptness of the word *love* to denote the emotions she experiences—she calls it lifeless.[1] She implies that love is both a dead word and a mediocre emotion. Since she was a writer and translator, turning to how she eulogizes the word to give birth to something new reminds us to employ an ethics of care for ourselves when we attempt to disentangle love from object (possession) to actionable interior movement (revolution). The static version of love presented in Hollywood films cannot justly represent Black cosmologies that outline human emotion as interior movement, as action—revolution, revolutionary love.

Kathleen Collins loved men. She loved a diverse range of men who became lovers, husbands, and co-creators: Douglas Collins, Henry Roth, Gilbert Moses, Carl Weathers, Ronald Gray, and Alfred Prettyman. She attempted to love them as equals, and some of them would do the same. Collins loved women. She loved various women as sisters, friends, and co-creators: Peggy Dammond, Bluette L. Dammond, Carole Cole, and Seret Scott. She also deeply loved her children Nina and Emilio. Her epistolary prose details all these sides of her love life. Her letters rival the romance narratives embedded in the sonnets of Western canonical writers like Philip Sidney and Edmund Spenser or the Victorian novels of the Bronte sisters. Writing from Woodstock, Collins tells a college friend, Ellen:

> And when I think of you sometimes it makes me cry. Because I have been
> so blessed by the people that have come my way.... And each I want to

hug close to me and say thank you for showing me what I hadn't seen
before me. And when we parted I was able to look at some part of me I
didn't know was there. Or find the answer to a question I didn't know I
was asking. . . .

But there is the painting that we made together . . . and it hangs somewhere. . . . And it is a fine and lovely thing.[2]

That Collins epically writes about her experiences of platonic and familial love
against and in relationship to her erotic love with men and her creative art, all
with the same depth and intensity, is why she can never be classified as a fool
in love. Collins uses the experience of creating a painting with her friend as a
metaphor for the ways in which individuals' relationships, and the emotions experienced with different people therein, can produce or unlock creative energy
that provides a new, maybe shared, vision of what lives can be possible. If Collins's journals and letters were the only way to understand how she processed
love, then she could easily be read as a romantic, a fool for love.

In a diary entry to her second husband, Alfred Prettyman, Collins writes
of her love for him, "I have been head over heels in love with you, staggeringly,
romantically in love with you as I have not allowed myself to be since we met"
(November 16, 1985). Yet Collins was the opposite of a fool in love. In the same
diary entry, she pronounces that she has learned something important from
her early failed relationships: "Because I understand now what romance is: it
is an indulgent dream of the self projected upon the other. It is the desire to
forget one's self entirely, ones separateness, one's loneliness, the rigorous self-
watching that growth requires. It is a need/desire/longing for annihilation in
and through another. It is fucking that doesn't end. The inside of it is delusional,
the core of it shallow." Collins does not ignore the way romantic love has influenced her relationships with men. Her dedicated diary entries to Prettyman
lay bare the way in which confessional writing about love threatens to undo
its function of privately exploring one's interiority. She asks, "Is this record
only for you and me, or does it participate, as all recording does, in belonging
beyond both of us?" (September 1, 1985). Nevertheless, she continues writing,
and the diary's confessional tone cannot escape the generic entanglements with
romantic love and epistolary sentiments.

However, in her creative cultural production, Collins charts a path to an
alternative space where romantic love, and therefore romantic comedy, is dis-
placed. In these endeavors, she was a love genius, a virtuoso of love, a prodigy
of eros, because she consorted with her daemons of love. None of this hy-
perbole means that she never experienced complicated, problematic, or failed

relationships. She did. Nevertheless, for Collins, love was a cosmic metaphysical puzzle that needed to be pieced together. Herein lies the uniqueness of her perspective, audaciously believing that love needed completion. Rather than accepting the rhetoric of love as a means of completion and wholeness for humans, she theorizes it as being incomplete without resistance or revolution. The piece that could complete it, she suggests, was a metaphysical and spiritual act of resistance or revolt. Collins knew that women—hetero-, homo-, bi-, and asexual, cis- and transgender—needed to author new narratives of love. Over the course of three film scripts, she would provide narratives on the incompleteness of love and reinvent the action film around love as a crisis of possession. Her point of origin was Vodou.

While the Louis Mars's quote at the beginning of this chapter advises on the crisis of possession in Vodou, his words are relevant to questions about love that, I argue, Collins was working to answer throughout her films and screenplays: Is there a crisis of possession in love, and if so, what must be done about it? Is love itself a crisis of possession? Can it be resolved in the same way that one would resolve a *loa* crisis? Collins would turn to her intellectual engagement with spiritual traditions and philosophy to answer these questions, but she would decenter Western Christian humanism in her exploration. A cursory appraisal of Collins's films might not reveal her comprehension of the power and significance of Vodou to Black women's love lives. However, in this chapter, instigated by Omise'eke Natasha Tinsley's statement that "Vodou also preserves *istwa* (stories/histories) . . . of gender and sexual creativity that are also mythohistoric records of slavery and revolution" (Tinsley 2018, 24), close readings of Collins's films and screenplays reveal how she would turn to Vodou time and again when attempting to represent mythohistoric records of Black women, revolution, and love. Vodou, building upon Tinsley's words, preserves *istwas* of love that are also mythohistoric records of revolution and rebellion, as opposed to submission and compromise.

Years before William Greaves gave Collins an opportunity to work with him as a production assistant on *Symbiopsychotaxiplasm*, he had been sent to Dakar in 1966 to shoot a five-minute film on the first World Festival of Negro Arts/ Festival mondial des arts nègres (FESMAN), a month-long Pan-Africanist arts and culture festival organized by Léopold Senghor. Greaves immediately knew the event deserved more than a perfunctory clip, and so he shot and edited footage taken over several days into a forty-minute documentary highlighting the joy and hope FESMAN enacted. The festival is reported to have had over two thousand participants, many of whom were African Diasporic historians, intellectuals, artists, musicians, writers, dancers, and filmmakers from across the world. It included numerous cultural producers influenced by the history and culture of Haiti, specifically those who had developed a circum-Caribbean culture of Vodou.[3]

One of the participants was Jean Price-Mars, renowned Haitian writer, doctor, ambassador, and ethnologist. Price-Mars was a student of the Négritude movement and a defender of Vodou in Haiti during a time when it was being threatened by laws and amendments such as the 1935 decree outlawing superstitious practices. He was adamant that Vodou be considered a religion, understanding it as a vital part of Haitian culture. Price-Mars was also the father of Louis Mars, the ethnopsychiatrist who would build on his father's legacy of decolonizing medical and anthropological knowledge in the groundbreaking work *The Crisis of Possession in Voodoo*. Mars argued the importance of his feat by reminding readers of his father's own words: "As Price-Mars has said, Voodoo mysticism is still waiting for its Plotinus, a great historian of Voodoo mysticism who would be at the same time a fervent practitioner" (Mars 1977, 17). Originally published in 1946 by a Port-au-Prince company, *The Crisis of Possession in Voodoo* was hailed as initiating a new stage in the history of Haitian sciences, since the book was classified as comparative psychiatry, in which Mars provides an examination of the mysticism in Vodou and performs "psychoanalysis of cases of possession" (21). Between 1976 and 1977, Kathleen Collins would translate Mars's study into English, setting the stage for what Greaves might certainly define as symbiopsychotaxiplasm. His definition begins with

> "symbiotaxiplasm," coined by the American social philosopher Arthur Bentley in his book *An Inquiry into Inquiries* [1954]. The term is an attempt to express all of the elements and aspects of the cosmos which interact, affect each other, and in which life—particularly humankind—is functionally interrelated.
>
> I [Greaves] was bold enough to insert "psycho" into the middle of the term to achieve the new word, "symbiopsychotaxiplasm," which … affirms more aggressively the role that human psychology and creativity play in shaping the total environment—while at the same time, these very environmental factors continually affect and determine human psychology and creativity. (MacDonald 1995, 47)

Both the spiritual system of Vodou and its importance in African Diasporic culture shaped Collins's philosophies, psyche, and creativity. Collins's translation of Mars's book was published by Ishmael Reed's cofounded independent press, Reed, Cannon, and Johnson Publishing, which had a devout mission to publish books on Black arts and culture that refused the colonization of African Diasporic life and culture. The first book from that press was a work of fiction by actor Alison Mills, who was married to Afro-Cuban director Francisco Newman. The press also published Faith Mitchell's *Hoodoo Medicine* (1978). Reed had a long-term interest in ensuring that critical writing on Vodou made its way to the masses, and as his decades-long collaborative friendship with filmmaker Bill Gunn showcased, that vision did not exist in print alone. These configurations of practices and individuals are not coincidences, but symbiopsychotaxiplasm.

Translation serves as a bridge between worlds or states, but it also becomes an occasion for linkages that might go unnoticed otherwise. These are the very transnational ways in which Collins fits into a global Black Arts Movement. Film and translation work signifies this most of all. In translating *Crisis of Possession in Voodoo*, Collins had to translate the mechanics of language and research, but she had to do it in a way that honored the value systems of Vodou and Haiti, both of which Mars worked to maintain and elevate. She would need to ensure that her decisions about words and contexts for meaning honored the work of both Mars and Price-Mars, son and father, who aimed to bring greater understanding of Vodou to people in the Americas, and to Black people across the globe. What survives in translation is often a reflection of the translator's perspective regarding the vital foundations of a culture, or of the translator's dismissal of a communities' values. Collins read Mars, but she also clearly read other works on Vodou. As chapter 1's assessment of her first unproduced script, *Women, Sisters, and Friends*, demonstrated, she had already expressed an interest in Haitian culture and cosmologies by the time she came to translate Mars. She comprehended the significance of the spiritual practice beyond the demonization of it by Western empires. As Kameelah Martin's *Envisioning Black Feminist Voodoo Aesthetics* observed, "For women of African descent, the feminine divine reflects the place and import of women within a black transnational cosmology" (2016, xvi).

This symbiopsychotaxiplasm shaped Collins's exploration and representation of the crisis of possession in love and of love as a crisis of possession in her film scripts. While Mars attended to the crisis of possession in Vodou, I use some of his analysis to demonstrate how Collins's translation work with Mars, as well as her personal reflections on love, allowed her to use her films and screenplays to explore love as a crisis of possession for women specifically. Collins interrogated different ideologies of love, using Mars's approach to the study of Vodou to create her own philosophies and theories about love and Black women. Throughout this chapter, I propose that her translation of Mars's work provided her with a way to think about the question of romantic love and its place in the lives of Black women, especially those who might experience something more powerful than romantic love. Notably, ideas from *Crisis of Possession* make their way into Collins's second film, *Losing Ground*. Moreover, the *loa* crisis becomes the foundational framework through which she explores Black women's lives in her screenplays *Only the Sky Is Free* ([1985] 2002) and *But Then She's Madame Flor* (1986). Had the last two been produced and developed as motion pictures, they would have joined her second film in ushering in a genre innovation in filmmaking: love stories cemented in polytheism and ecstasy as opposed to romance and monotheism.

TRANSLATING ANOTHER LANGUAGE OF/ FOR LOVE: POSSESSION

Love is a crisis of possession, even if it is not a *loa* crisis in the manner outlined by Mars in his documentation of particular symptoms: borrowing of a Haitian god's name, changes in voice and facial features, motor excitement, glossomania, sensibilities difficulties, and amnesia (Mars 1977, 24). Love is a crisis of possession. The inability to fully translate the polymorphic codes of love into a system or order that does not unravel the power dynamics of social customs, institutions, or notions of community, family, or nation as well as the notion of a fixed and unified self creates the crisis. For such a crisis to be translated, never resolved, requires someone who is fluent in multiple expressions of the languages that have created the very concept, idea, or practice of love as well as someone who can surrender to any or all of them simultaneously. Such an endeavor demands a translator who can convey the interior cadences and silences of eros as well as the syntax and grammars of ecstasy as presented by a metaphysics not colonized by Western religion. Collins was capable of performing this type of translation in various mediums and forms.

Folklore, anthropology, and ethnography have all contributed to knowledge about Haitian Vodou. Methodologies from each field have also led critics to think about the way in which the creative and critical merge in producing new knowledge that is ethical in regard to Indigenous communities. Collins's example provides a way to think about how translation of research on Vodou might become a horse for any particular *loa* to ride. Mars's examination of Vodou in *Crisis of Possession* reckons with colonial sciences' failure to translate and understand the psychological and philosophical logic of the spiritual system and practice: "If, as someone has said, science is a well-constructed language, then it is necessary to classify the clinical facts gathered on possession, to extract from the Proteus-like hysteria the secrets of some of the bio-psychological phenomena that it covers with its shadow, and to label them in the light of recent developments in psychopathology" (Mars 1977, 17). Mars's approach to the *loa* crisis and possession provides some evidence of how the act of translation might feed into Collins's interests in religion and philosophy as well as shift her away from her traditional Judeo-Christian background in her writings.

Translation cannot be classified as an emotive-kinetic act in the same way that dance in Vodou is said to create a collective excitement that allows possession. Yet translation might well provide a less physically visible emotive function of arousing "psychological states preparatory to a split in the personality" (Mars 1977, 15) in which a crisis of possession could occur. Whereas other artists and writers became students of Haiti because of their embodied participation in and study of folk culture, dance, and spirituality—that is, of the emotive-kinetic—Collins was guided by the psychological and philosophical aspect of her creative endeavors. Collins would join the likes of Zora Neale Hurston, Katherine Dunham, W.E.B. Du Bois, and Langston Hughes (who translated the novel of Jacques Roumain from French) as Black Americans changed by their experiences with Haitian life and culture. Though not a research trip based in ethnographic study of the nation and its people, the act of translating Mars's book was no less epic in its call to Collins to enter the circle of Haitian Vodou and its metaphysics. Placing Mars's text in conversation with Collins's scripts, I argue that Collins's translation of Vodou's crisis of possession allowed her to create a film genre that would very much counter every romantic drama, comedy, and tragedy in Hollywood and Black independent filmmaking while also rewriting Vodou and ghost stories away from horror.

ONLY THE SKY IS FREE: IS LOVE A CRISIS OF
POSSESSION? IS LOVE A *LOA* CRISIS?

Collins was an astute critic of Hollywood film genres, noting, "In American films, the motif of adventure is one of the many storytelling devices."[4] She also recognized the ways that gender and race could shape genre films, explaining, "In American film terms, the notion of adventure has certainly undergone a Black metamorphosis. Yet, how sad that in the end, we are still left with stagnant female souls hovering aimlessly around the male universe. How limiting is the idea that only men despair; Women can only comfort."[5] In *Only the Sky Is Free*, a fictional screen rendering of the Black aviator Bessie Coleman and her blues singer niece, Eloise, Collins quite simply reinvented the bio pic, action film, and love story via an articulation of revolutionary love as a *loa* crisis. In sum, she practiced afterlife-writing. With *Only the Sky Is Free*, Collins used her cinematic imagination to do away with Western narratives of the Roman and Greek gods of Eros and Cupid. As opposed to perpetuating myths of gods shooting arrows from afar, Collins introduces a question asked by Mars about the gods of Vodou: "And how do the gods manifest themselves? They become incarnate in the body of their servants. They eat, drink, speak, and dance in the person of their medium. They are gods who become men throughout the day" (Mars 1977, 19).

Only the Sky Is Free, which spans from the early 1900s to the 1950s, is both a love story and the rebirth story of a god who Collins believes should be significant to the history and culture of Black women and their ideas of love: Bessie Coleman. It might also be described as a revolution story anagramming as a love story without a couple, since it is about Coleman's love of flying. As this cinematic rendering reveals, Collins clearly found flight to be similar to her own love of writing and filmmaking. In her own life, Collins reflected on women's role in creating revolutionary change, when discussing her first husband and the rhetoric of revolution in the United States when she was at school in France: "The other day I said to Douglass . . . it is possible that there might be a real revolution in the United States. . . . And me . . . what will I do during a revolution . . . continue to do the dishes . . . to look after you . . . to love you . . . does any of this make sense?" (letter to Bluette, 8/28/67).

Because *Only the Sky Is Free* asks the same question, but is set during an era of Jim Crow and immediately after women's suffrage, it stands as a period piece unlike anything ever made about Black women. Collins relies on Bessie Coleman's life to juxtapose race work against revolution, and then discerns the nature of love in each. Though Coleman received some attention in the late twentieth century, she remains little known. The historical details of the script were possible because, according to Collins, one arts organization believed in the potential of the film project: "One lovely surprise is a sizeable grant from the New York State Arts Council for my Bessie Coleman project which will allow me to complete the research and travel around doing my interviews, etc."[6] The screenplay is one of the best scripts that Collins ever wrote, and she knew it. *Only the Sky Is Free* tells the story of a dark-skinned blues singer named Eloise and her lifelong spiritual connection to her deceased, light-skinned aunt, Bessie Coleman. Texas native Elizabeth "Bessie" Coleman, also known as Queen Bess, endured the harsh conditions of racism and segregation to become the first Black woman aviator. After being refused admittance to flight training schools, Coleman traveled to France and received training there. She was an aviator and stunt flier in barnstorming exhibitions and air shows until her death in 1927. Coleman was also supposed to be a part of early African American filmmaking. She was offered a starring role in a film titled *Shadow and Sunshine* that was being financed by the African American Seminole Film Producing Company. After reading the script, she refused the role because she thought it was too stereotypical. Despite her accomplishments, mainstream aviation reports from her time and later ignore or minimize her contribution.

In the screenplay, Collins constructs this erasure of Coleman's legacy as a crisis of possession for her descendants; their deep feelings for Coleman seem to exceed romantic narratives of love. Onstage one night during a drunken performance, Eloise angrily yells at her audience: "You tell me who's walking around in your head . . . somebody is, somebody who won't die, somebody you keep alive like it was yesterday, because they deserve it. They deserved it in life, even though nobody was looking. And they died irritated" (6).

Eloise has spent much her adult life telling Bessie's story, despite many people not believing that a Black woman had ever flown airplanes. As a kid, Eloise's teachers accused her of spinning tall tales, chiding her, "You're talking trash, girl," or more spitefully, "Now you know, Eloise, there isn't any such thing in this day and time as a colored woman who can fly" (3). These naysayers create a crisis in young Eloise, not simply because they refuse to believe in Bessie Coleman's existence or to honor her accomplishments but because in denying Bessie, they also deny the existence of Eloise, a little girl whose future was shaped by a belief in an aunt who could fly. Her god. In turn, Eloise becomes susceptible to Bessie's lingering presence because her faith in Bessie is constantly being challenged, and in rising to the challenge, she opens herself up to an experience.

According to Mars, "The loa crisis is at the center of complex problems. First of all, it poses in a new way, the question of the rapport between the soul and the body, of the incorrect delineation of the physical and the moral. Following that, what are the reasons that one category of human beings undergoes the crisis more easily than others?" (Mars 1977, 62). Though Mars does not reference the two constructs of race and gender specifically, Collins does explicitly explain that race and gender are complex problems. Mars left it to a "future metapsychology" to answer his questions, and Collins used her representations of Bessie's pursuit of flight and Eloise's use of blues to render Bessie's afterlife as that future metapsychology. Eloise's *loa* crisis is at the center of *Only the Sky Is Free*.

In *Only the Sky Is Free*, Collins uses flashbacks to document Bessie's life. She takes inspiration from the Harlem Renaissance, American modernism, and aviation history and early dreams of flight to tell the intersecting stories of Bessie Coleman and Harlem Renaissance novelist Jessie Redmon Fauset. These two very different women's experiences with race and colorism allow Collins to bring their art and lives together and create a cinematic representation of love, eros, and ecstasy. In the fictional world created by Collins, a young, dark-skinned Eloise becomes a sign of Blackness for the light-skinned Bessie, who wanted to ensure that she would be counted as a credit to the Black race:

> **Eloise:** . . . they used to joke about it, she and Momma, Aunt Nebbie, Uncle Nells, they used to say that when she got in a pinch she took me along to make sure they knew who she was. . . . "Come on, Eloise," she'd say, "I want you to go downtown with me today." She'd dress me up. (9)

If, as I have posited, child-Eloise constructs Bessie as a god, then Bessie positions her young niece, very early in her life, as a vessel for her to take possession of, from which she can engage the world of men. In doing so, Bessie burdens Eloise with a type of racial duty that she never asked her niece if she wanted to carry—that is, if she wished to be a symbol for racial progress. She does to her niece essentially what she despised others for doing to her.

The script calls for time shifts and juxtapositions that blur Eloise's life with Bessie's life, using the stage and dressing room of a nightclub as well as old newsreel film footage (the script directs that the latter should be in sepia tone) and newscasts of Bessie Coleman interviews. It is a love story devoid of the romantic narrative of US films, but it contains a narrative about ecstasy and freedom through the metaphor of flight. Eloise uses the blues to create a history and memory of Coleman, singing from the stage, "SLIP OVER A CLOUD DROP DOWN, UP, UNDER SO THAT'S WHAT IT MEANS COME RAIN, COME THUNDER THERE'S NO ONE BUT YOU YOU'RE LIGHT AS A FEATHER HOLD ON TO THE GLOW THE STARS AND THE WEATHER SLIP OVER A CLOUD DROP DOWN, UP, UNDER" (4). Eloise's song captures the range of emotions of aspiring beyond human limitations and pursuing spiritual freedom. Further, Collins's script chronicles Bessie Coleman's life, with biographical revisions of her time as a barbershop manicurist grooming the nails of World War I soldiers (being told as they flirted with her that she would have to change her anatomy to become a pilot) to her time as part of a novelty act in aerial shows in the North as well as the on-the-ground dangers of race-based violence and the minstrelsy of barnstorming in the Jim Crow South. Yet Collins cuts these harsh moments with tender childhood memories of Bessie lovingly combing and braiding Eloise's hair in a nightly ritual, or scenes of Eloise's mother and sister laughing over Bessie's audacity to be in the sky. Notably, Bessie was not the only fearless Coleman woman. At one point, Eloise remarks of all the women in her family, "They all had it, my Momma, Aunt Lou, Aunt Nebbie, a stubborn thing against being black . . . held-down black, I mean . . . instead of racey and free" (25).

Collins's script soon reveals why blues music became the best genre for Eloise to convey the affective pain and disappointment of Bessie's life. Collins characterizes Bessie as someone committed to the rhetoric of racial uplift, but also someone whose interior is very much changed by the experience of flying. Early on, Bessie tells a schoolroom of children who want to know what her life is like now that she has been in the sky:

> **Bessie:** (in an odd voice) When you come back down, you're not the same . . . they don't know that, but you do. (28)

Bessie grapples with the aftereffects that come from the ecstatic experience of flying. In speaking to the ecstatic experience, Mars explains, "It is not sufficient to fast or to dance in order to become a god, or even contemplate a god. One must give the form of a god to the confused excitement that comes from the fast or the dance, and that does not happen unless the spirit has hold of the form already. As a result of long work, one manages to impose one's self over the shadows that the orgy has called into being; and the form and the matter unite more rapidly in a conscience well prepared for this synthesis" (1977, 16).

Collins beautifully renders flight as a creative, erotic expression of interior being. In a later scene that is tied to what Bessie might mean to a future generation, Collins introduces dance as the corporeal metaphor for the mechanical innovation of flight:

> *DISSOLVE to: OPEN FIELD*
> *MEDIUM WIDE SHOT: A DANCER*
> *Alone, in an open field, A DANCER executes a dance evocative of FLIGHT.*
> *Powerful, intense movements*
> *carefully choreographed with the camera*
> *SUPERIMPOSED over the dance are the following shots:*
> –Bessie's airplane taking off into the sky
> –the plane executing a figure eight
> –CU BESSIE, waving
> –the plane doing a flip
> –the plane nose diving and righting itself
> –the plane doing a looping motion
> –the plane coming down to land
> *As the DANCE draws to a close, we watch BESSIE land and get out of the plane.*
> *SUPERIMPOSITION ends.* (54)

While traditional cinematic tropes might compose a montage of flight scenes alone, or insist on extended imagery of a plane with spectacular visual effects accompanied by a dramatic score, Collins's script requires viewers to understand flight as more than a technological and mechanical innovation while highlighting the embodied performance that may be happening for its raced and gendered pilot as she defies gravity and social mores. Bessie's freedom is constantly being interrupted by the race and gender work that Black women feel obligated to take up—work that does not necessarily align with Black women's love of self and search for a new form of life.

Throughout the script, Eloise and Bessie are confronted with questions about whether Bessie had been in love or had taken secret lovers. Bessie is also confronted with questions about whether her ambitions around flight are relevant to the politics of Black America. Her family also questions her about the longevity of her dream as it relates to being a woman. History reveals that Coleman and Fauset both attended the second Pan-African Congress in Paris in 1921, during which Black intellectuals, artists, and politicians outlined the goals and objectives for Black people across the globe. Flying was not a priority at the time, but as Collins reimagines Bessie's historical commitment to flight, she underscores what a Black woman aviator might have been up against. Though Bessie's feats were featured in several Black newspapers, they were often seen as lacking significant impact on the goal of Black political uplift. As T. Sharpley-Whiting notes in *Bricktop Paris*, Fauset failed to include Bessie Coleman in her first *Crisis* article, "Impressions of the Second Pan African Congress" (Fauset 1921), but she did include Coleman in the second write-up, "What Europe Thought of the Pan-African Congress" (December 1921), as a way to challenge ideas of Negro inferiority. Fauset noted Coleman's achievements, calling her "that charming young woman who was the first colored aviatrix of America" (Sharpley-Whiting 2015, 79). It seems, however, that Collins's research led her to interpret Fauset's earlier lack of inclusion as a critique of Coleman's ideology of aviation and flight as a vital part of Negro racial uplift. In one scene, Collins invents an interview between a news reporter and Fauset:

> **Interviewer:** And what do you feel about members of your Race learning to fly, as Mlle Coleman is deeply committed to this goal . . .
>
> **Jessie Fauset:** It's rather a novelty, isn't it . . .
>
> **Interviewer:** Isn't what . . .
>
> **Jessie Fauset:** . . . going up in the air and flying around . . .
>
> **Interviewer:** You mean you don't find it serious . . .
>
> **Jessie Fauset:** Well there's so much to be done right here on earth.
>
> **Interviewer:** Then you would discourage . . . flying around . . . as you put it. . . .
>
> **Jessie Fauset:** I'm sure that Miss Coleman is an admirable young lady, and every achievement, of course, is a victory for the Race. (36)

In the screenplay, Fauset might describe flight as a foolish pursuit, but for Bessie it stands as a radical occasion to love herself and an internal revolt or revolution. When a white reporter interviews Bessie and asks why she flies, Bessie states:

> **Bessie:** I can't talk for anyone else . . . for me flying is a reprieve . . . you must take into account the harshness of Negro life . . . that it is earth-bound in an extreme way . . . heavy . . . then suddenly, I leave it, it's like dropping an enormous weight. I feel like I'm living from within . . . and that what surrounds me—the sky, the clouds, the light, it's impossible to describe the brightness, even on a cloudy day—that that is life, not this dreadful pushing and shoving. (32)

Bessie's response echoes Eloise's earlier sentiments about the women in her family having "a thing against" being held down because they were Black.

The dialogue Collins writes for Bessie exposes the kinship that Collins must have felt with the icon's pursuit of flying. There is no doubt that Collins's aspiration to be a filmmaker was regarded as frivolous compared with the political race work and cultural work of radical and respectable Black men of the era. The script is Collins imagining love away from romance narratives in which someone has to be grounded (buried) in order for another (individual, race, or country) to be lifted up. One anagram of *revolution* is *love I run to*, another *violent our*, another *vie lorn out* ("lorn out" life, lonely and abandoned life). Collins captures the feeling of love as revolution and its many anagrams, proclaiming to Peggy Dammond in one letter, "Yet inside! What revolutions are possible! So many people are born inside us while others are sent away, often to their death."[7] *Revolution* is the word that reveals the word *love* as incomplete, or lifeless, as Collins stated earlier.

Collins returns to this type of revolutionary love in another letter: "The more I find myself, the more I discover how people I love imprison me and how, each departure, each separation, allows me to reclaim myself, to integrate myself afresh. This seems to come from a fact I have recently uncovered; which is that I see people not as they are but rather as they are capable of becoming."[8] In a later scene from the script, Collins underscores how Coleman may have grown tired and defensive about the dismissal of her dream by the race men and women of the time. In Collins's depiction, Coleman sees the ecstatic experience of flight as exceeding her own identity, and as a mode of becoming:

> **Bessie:** I know it's hard to put aviation beside all the pressing needs of our Race for employment, a decent home . . . I understand all those needs, but if we're to survive as a people, we must also put down roots

in the future, that matters a great deal, too. My school will be a symbol
of Race progress, Race vision . . . even if I have to begin it with only one
plane. (54)

Bessie's dialogue perfectly exposes the issue of temporality and Black social life, how the externalized present produces an inability to envision some people as possessing simultaneity and multiplicity. For Bessie, and Collins in turn, the imposition of distance on the future is an external premise. Each experiences the future as existing inside herself, outside of external time arranged by others. Understanding flight as a means of putting roots down in the future is not far-fetched if we accept a cosmological metaphor of stars as seeds that take root in space, not unlike tree roots in earth. For Collins, Bessie's race vision does not have to be rooted in the terrestrial since she has mastered the skies.

At the end of the script, as Bessie talks with her friend Ginger, the audience finally finds out the truth about whom Bessie may have loved during her lifetime:

> **Bessie:** Besides, it's too late with me for a man . . .
> **Ginger:** *(realizing it)* I never could find love connected to you . . .
> *THEY laugh.*
> **Bessie:** I'm a little bit in love when I fly, or at least I used to be . . . or in a
> daze . . . something strange happens . . . I feel like I take off my color and
> can finally run around free . . . *Laughter* . . .
> *HOLD . . . On the TWO OF THEM. Laughing gleefully.*
> *FADE-OUT* (86)

If viewers remain solely committed to an inept idea of love as a psychic/emotional possession that can be given or received, or as an incomplete experience of spiritual conversion that depends on an external force, then the meaning of Bessie's words about the future and race vision can be seen as frivolous. However, if the crisis of possession is our divine point of origin, then Bessie's statement about it being too late for her with a man can be seen as a concern about dimensionality and space as opposed to time and a failure to find love. She has, instead, seen a truth before she could ever accept a falsehood. Throughout the script, Collins ensures her audience, through a cosmic rendering of Eloise's and Bessie's lives, that it is not these women's inability to love and be loved that makes their lives tragic; it is society's inability to accept that they have already found something more powerful than romantic love in themselves. Bessie is in love with an experience, flying—an act in which she loses herself to herself. This act of ecstasy does not require dispossession. In Collins's writing of Bessie

Coleman's story, the geographical ideals of race and space, and terra/terrestrial notions of ground and roots as stable, solid, and foundational to identity politics, are replaced or placed in relationship to temporal ideals of race and space and to celestial ideals of the universe and stars. Collins addressed the conflict in another screenplay that did make it onto a film reel, and in that vision she underscores love as a crisis of possession.

LOSING GROUND: THERE IS A CRISIS OF POSSESSION IN ROMANTIC LOVE

Be it love of self, love of gods, or love of others, nothing about love is rational. It defies rationality even as humans attempt to define and contour it toward function, purpose, symbolism, and idealism. The enslaved, colonized, segregated, and poor, however, are burdened with ethics and morals of love that attempt to rationalize who and how they should love self and others. Women know that harm occurs when love is coupled with rationalization of power and inequality as well as when idealization of it requires it to be a superpower that can allow individuals to overcome harsh circumstances. Therefore, Black cinematic representations of love should, but often do not, challenge the discourses that attempt to rationalize love. Collins's *Losing Ground* remains one of the few African American women's films to not only challenge the romance narrative of love but also interrogate the racialized and gendered concept of humanity facilitated by Christian humanist thought.

Before *Losing Ground* the film, there was "Losing Ground" the four-page short story—an interior monologue that ruminates on the psychic toll that love takes on a woman. The narrator moves from remembering an unimpressive first meeting with her beloved, to the development of attraction and feelings for her male lover, to the intensity of losing oneself in another: "Later she would try and figure out when it shifted. When she began losing ground. Somewhere . . . But why? When all along she knew him to be a silly boy who hadn't found himself. Why was it she who had lost ground?"[9] None of these words made their way into Collins's first full-length original film. Yet the very premise of a woman who knows herself and is grounded in her truth before losing herself to a man who holds no fear of ever losing himself in someone, because he is a man, haunts Collins's cinematic oeuvre. The questioning "she" in the story demonstrates how Collins was keenly aware of how power dynamics in relationships are shaped by gender hierarchies and inequities that being in love cannot fix, repair, or reorder. She says as much in personal letters to friends in which she details some of the joy and pain of her relationships with male lovers, partners, and husbands throughout her life.

For example, Collins's first marriage, to Doug Collins, was the subject of many of her letters to Bluette L. Dammond. Collins's first husband was a failed filmmaker, businessman, and a philanderer. In journals and letters to friends, Collins lays out the torrid and torturous love they shared before divorcing. The marriage made Collins confront whether her own self-worth should be so singularly linked to a man, not out of choice but out of gendered roles and responsibility of women in society. In one letter, Collins details other women's interactions around her and her husband, and the ways that coupledom and the confines of traditional womanhood could lessen one's individual identity: "And neither do I like the situation of being 'a woman with her man' in relation to two single women. It makes me really feel like the 'wife' and this seems to create an abyss. . . . I loathe that, or any kind of manifestation of possession."[10] Collins crystallizes the predicament outside this group dynamic in another letter to B. Dammond: "I am finding more and more, except for those rare moments I have to hide away with my journal, my own work, and even everything I transform into the written word—that the 'self' is taken over by others—to live out their way of seeing the world, to measure thyself by their rhythm . . . to play the games that I think they like . . . and perhaps even, all this is not even me but the woman in me."[11] How does a woman in love maintain possession of herself with a being written in too many social and cultural narratives as greater than she? Collins's question in the short story, and in her life, becomes the central conflict of the film *Losing Ground*. Collins would try to make sense of the conflict between love, romance, and eros by displacing Christian humanism with African spiritual practices encoded in Black art and performance. As Tinsley observed, "Vodou . . . as epistemology . . . as a way of knowing that counters Enlightenment rationality" (2018, 22) can be a way to make sense of the world.

Losing Ground is about Sara (played by Seret Scott), a professor of philosophy, and her husband, Victor (played by Bill Gunn), a painter. The film provides a glimpse of a middle-class Black married couple that, from the outside, appears to be a good match between a respectable Black woman and her bohemian husband. They are, however, headed toward the dissolution of their marriage due in large part to the husband's narcissism and cheating. In the film, Victor has won a fellowship that will enable the couple to leave their home and travel to another city while he works. While there would be much to occupy Victor in that new life, Sara would be isolated and away from her family and work. As Victor pursues his artistic dreams, Sara contemplates her life, the role intellect plays in it, and the divide between her intellect and body.

The beauty and genius of Collins's work lies in her courage as a filmmaker to look beyond what most of white America and Black America of the prior decade wished to see of Black women and men. White America may have wanted to position Black women strictly within the jezebel, mammy, or bitch archetypes, but Black America's cinematic craving for superbad and sexy Blaxploitation icons like Foxy Brown, Coffy, or Cleopatra Jones; humble and respectable figures like Rebecca Morgan and Vivian Perry; tragic biopic figures like Miss Jane Pittman or Billie Holiday; or urbane divas like Tracy Chambers did not necessarily include Collins's cinematic protagonist—a philosophy professor at odds with herself and her Black artist husband. Sara is not a Black woman in search of a good man or trying to save a Black man, but one who is at odds with the man she loves because he threatens her very existence. As David Nicholson revealed in a write-up of Collins's work, not everyone appreciated this element of the film: "After the screening, a man asked Kathleen Collins-Prettyman if she had made the film. When she said yes, he replied, 'You're a traitor to the race,' and stalked away. And still later . . . talking to one of our better-known filmmakers . . . this director . . . told me he did not like *Losing Ground* because it was a negative portrait of a black marriage" (Nicholson 1988–89, 7). Such criticism demonstrates the burden placed on Black women filmmakers to do racial uplift work while ignoring other forms of oppression. It also exposes why comprehending the spiritual epistemology undergirding Collins's representations of love can help viewers comprehend just how much she was invested in decolonizing Western concepts of romantic love embraced by Black Americans.

Losing Ground opens with Sara lecturing on Camus, Sartre, and the existential movement to a class made up mostly of men. From the first frame of the film, Collins provides a jolting alternative to the historic representation of Black women on-screen. Sara stands before her class as a dominant master of knowledge, specifically knowledge usually associated with the white male body. The spectacle of this Black female body, then, arises from her intellectual expression. Further, Collins dismisses the idea that her film should engage conversations about acceptable Black women and representations of Black women, because Sara's lecture is about the rebuking of normalcy.

Sara convincingly explains in her lecture that, "'the natural order' . . . if there is such a thing . . . has been violated. Chaos exists. Not as a mental possibility—in the way that, say, Descartes might experience it, but as a physical and emotional fact." Sara, and by extension Collins, explores the schism produced in a Western metaphysics of duality as a forced and false division. There is no normal or natural. However, Collins also introduces a new order that will not negate the chaos. Later, Collins has Sara refuse Western enlightenment in favor of Louis Mars's concept of possession. In his criteria for a diagnosis of possession, the schism is not a negative event. Collins conveys this, first, with subtleties within Sara's characterization on-screen. She is conservatively dressed, her hair is pulled up in a bun, and eyeglasses mask the excitement that could be in her eyes. Sara's exterior does not reflect her interior, as displayed by her passion in the lecture, her choice of topic, and her rapport with her students.

The opening scene demonstrates that, in front of the classroom, Sara is not simply admired as an "intellectual authority," as critic Geetha Ramanathan has suggested (2006, 160). She is revered and her classroom remains a space where rituals to a god will unfold. "Most often the gods," Mars explains, "become incarnate during the religious gatherings, and . . . their appearance is activated in part by the psychology of the crowd" (1977, 13). In the film, Sara's students respectfully address her as "Professor" and "Dr. Rogers," but when a Black male student says to her, "You're terrific . . . always so alive and terrific . . . and your husband appreciates you," he isn't talking only about Sara's intellect. Later, the same student continues, "You're so full of life." Life, here, is not the pregnant biopolitical fantasy of pro-life advocates or the masochistic calls for submission and sacrifice by male-dominated religious institutions that come from being born again. Collins is producing a definition of life beyond Western humanist thought. In a later scene, Sara is speaking with a white woman student who visits her during office hours. The woman echoes the male student's sentiments: "You're so bright, and lively, a real inspiration." In the classroom, Sara's role is likened to that of the dancer in mysticism. Mars "call[s] mysticism emotive-kinetic if it requires the atmosphere of a dance, of a collective excitement in order to take hold" (1977, 14). Learning and teaching become a type of mysticism that is emotive-kinetic since it requires a collective excitement. Collins's film displaces notions of disembodied rationality in the process of education and learning and, in doing so, introduces a way to bridge the spiritual and intellectual in ways that benefit her character and her audience.

Collins's protagonist may begin the film espousing the ideals of Western metaphysics, but she does not stay wedded to them. She turns instead to what exists beyond the schism of body and mind. "Nothing I do leads to ecstasy," Sara tells Victor later in the film. So although Sara is creating the collective excitation for everyone else's ecstatic experience, for her students and Victor, she cannot generate the same for herself. Hence her exasperation at her student's focus on her husband: "A husband—what—What's this thing they've got about my having a husband?" In many ways, Sara's on-screen dialogue with her students takes us back to the question of possession that Collins's personal writings alluded to earlier as she tried to figure out how to maintain possession of herself as a woman in love.

Sara from *Losing Ground* is the opposite of the two woman protagonists in *Only the Sky Is Free*. Where Sara is in search of ecstasy, Coleman, as imagined by Collins, had found that ecstasy in flying. *Losing Ground* is deeply layered; one layer involves the search for ecstasy and another concerns why Sara does not comprehend that her mind can be a vital part of creating ecstatic experiences for herself and her students. Sara's students testify that they hope her husband appreciates her, but their comments also show that Sara is equally respected and desired by the Black male students and by the white male and female students. Their queries about her husband suggest that all the life displayed by Sara does not belong to her but to her husband, that its sole purpose is for his use and not hers. Sara's words, and her anger at her student's questions about her husband, are Collins's way of demonstrating the way in which men (not women) have been made into gods, or made to replace the gods (some of them female) who can and will possess subjects during the ecstatic process that women make possible. Acquiescing to this possession allows for capitalism's gendered dynamics of power and possession in civilized societies. Since Victor-as-demigod exceeds biopolitical life and can spiritually possess another being, Sara's lack of such a life will place her at risk of becoming a (material) possession. While the students may not understand such logic, Collins clearly showcases that this is Sara's understanding of the situation, because she creates a film that has Sara rejecting this order not simply with words but through action as well.

Collins begins a vital line of questioning about Black women's ecstasy and eroticism using Sara's final contestation of her students' interests in her husband. What does Black women's ecstasy look like? How is it used? Who is it for? Collins's answers insist that ecstasy and eroticism compose a definition of life not translatable by the biopolitical, and one necessary for toppling a heteropatriarchy that oppresses women. Thus, Collins sends Sara on a quest for ecstasy—specifically, the ecstatic process as defined by Mars: "mechanical or spiritual exercises, fasting, depriving one's self of sleep, orgiastic excitement, dancing, drunkenness, smoking—[which can] only take their full effect under conditions of mental direction, of an attitude of the spirit" (1977, 16). In short, Collins provides an adjustment to Sara's attitude of the spirit. Sara, not unlike the white Edna Malloy in *The Cruz Brothers*, will seek out and find her life. As in Collins's other scripts, many of the women characters pursue the ecstatic process. In *Losing Ground*, Sara receives assistance with her quest from her scholarly research on other spiritual traditions; from her mother, Leila, an actor who provides sage advice; and from George, a former student who asks Sara to act in his student film based on the Black folk ballad "Frankie and Johnny."

In one scene, Sara sits in the library researching and reading about her subject, ecstasy. As she reads from a book, we hear the words in her voice-over: "It does not come then exactly from without. Yet our consciousness, delving downwards, reveals to us, the deeper we go, an ever more original personality, capable of private ecstatic experience that is often undeniable in words. To call it ecstasy forces us to borrow from the theologians who have used the word in terms of man's immediate connectedness and/or apprehension of the Divine." Collins's use of voice-over invokes emotive-kinetic mysticism, and Collins reveals that Sara is able to work herself into a mental state that would produce ecstasy if only she could find the right text. As Collins continues to show us what a Black woman in search of ecstasy looks like, she also remains mindful of defining that ecstasy and exposing how and by whom it might be used or misused. Instead of shying away from any mention of eroticism, ecstasy, and sexuality for fear of being seen as not respectable, Collins shows Sara seeking out ecstasy in unconventional places.

In the library, Sara reads a book on Haitian Vodou, where she learns that possession and being mounted by a god can place one in a trance, yet "the ecstatic moment is, so to speak, after the fact"—that is, after coming out of the trance. Sara's thought process focuses on the interior experience of possession rather than on external commentary that might see possession as performance or spectacle. Collins's dialogue even considers how the gaze affects such interiority when Sara, seeking further evidence of or knowledge on how to experience ecstasy, visits a psychic and asks, "When you read someone—for instance, now looking at me. What happens inside you?" Sara needs to know not only what the woman sees but also what she experiences inside when she sees it. Collins refuses to allow the external gaze to dominate her representation of Black female experience, privileging the interior in everything Sara does throughout the film. Collins asks viewers to be like Sara with the psychic, to remain aware and ask what is happening inside. Is there a crisis of possession?

Various definitions of ecstasy identify it as a state of bliss often associated with sexual pleasure and the orgasm, but by situating ecstasy in a philosophical debate tied to stepping outside oneself to know that self, Collins challenges viewers to reimagine the realm of Black women's eros as a life force that does not require a split between body and mind. In the library scene, Collins and Seret Scott, who plays Sara, visually represent the connection between intellect, sensuality, and ecstasy by conveying physical and sensory intensity around these moments of intellectual engagement. Sara's voice-over is breathy, excitable, and without pause, while her body language exudes a level of tenseness shifting into excitability. Even as Sara seeks to feel and experience more, her career as a philosophy professor, one who thinks for a living, emphasizes that whatever she feels will not be divorced from consciousness. Throughout the film, Collins and Scott do a magnificent job of visually ensuring that the intensity and passion erupting from Sara are produced cerebrally but expressed corporeally.

Voice-over renders Sara's interiority and her search for ecstasy representable on the big screen without relying on the tired narrative tropes of searching for love, a good man, or sexual conquest. *Losing Ground* has no scenes of nudity. Victor is the primary active participant and instigator of anything sexual in the film. Nevertheless, the character of Sara deserves to be included in more conversations about representations of Black women as asexual or hypersexual primarily because she represents neither. Sara views herself as too orderly and logical, as having no connection to her feelings and emotions. She longs to connect to her body despite rhetoric that might make her feel less womanly or respectable for doing so. According to Collins, then, being more concerned with the interiority of individuals may yield an entirely new viewpoint and perspective so that we no longer think of love as a means to wholeness and unification, or of sexuality as something to be feared, or of filmmaking as the devil finding work. Collins uses considerations of ecstasy and eroticism to produce a depth of field that transforms and layers the flesh and blood of Black women's bodies and experiences on-screen, and produces cinematic language, in line with Sara's thoughts, that helps us uncover an original, shifting self invested in a private experience of connecting to the divine (ourselves) until we are joyously, rather than dreadfully, losing ground.

Collins forges new paths in demonstrating what Sara's quest for ecstasy looks like in the way she utilizes the camera to create visual representations of interior altars and visual spaces of worship that are not external institutions such as churches. On numerous occasions, Collins uses structures and shots of Sara in windows or doorways, deep in thought, to signify Sara's body as an altar for a greater force. Institutional spaces are then juxtaposed as external realities that incorrectly assume that Sara has to go outside herself to find what she seeks. Yet, as Sara continues to search for ecstasy, we see her enter buildings—a church, library, school, and telephone booth—to obtain information that will fulfill her quest, only to leave as empty-handed as when she arrived.

Collins further presents the need for such interior depth with striking film techniques and shot angles that position Sara as always looking first inside, then out, then back inside herself again. The camera in the opening classroom scene primarily zooms in on Sara so that we understand she is the dominating center of attention from any angle, a subject rather than an object. Collins then pans the camera out from Sara's position to the rows of Black male students and two white students listening intently and rapturously to Sara lecture. The camera privileges Sara's gaze and Sara's perception of her students before moving on to the students and their gaze at Sara. Collins forces viewers to confront that each gaze brings an individual context that shapes the depiction of the Black woman in the lecture hall and on-screen.

These moments are all mere preludes to Sara accepting the invitation of George, a former student, to act in his student film of "Frankie and Johnny," with a mysterious and dark actor named Duke. Once Sara begins acting in the student film, *Losing Ground* becomes a film within a film. This is done to visually demonstrate how Sara can simultaneously come to possess herself and experience ecstasy. Before Sara knows that Duke will be her co-lead in the film, she meets him in the library while researching ecstasy. Upon seeing Sara deeply engaged in her reading, he begins talking to her, eventually asking her, "What's the thesis of your paper?" Sara replies, "That the religious boundaries around ecstasy are too narrow." Sara and Duke continue to discuss the topic, highlighting the various ways ecstasy could be expressed outside Christianity, since, as Duke notes, "Christianity has had a devastating effect on man as an intuitive creature." Their entire debate provides a context for us to understand one of the reasons that Sara thinks her performance as a character in a blues ballad, a secular expression, might lead her toward the ecstatic experience she seeks.

"Frankie and Johnny" is a song about a passionate love affair, destroyed by the man's infidelity and the woman's violent and deadly response to the infidelity: "Frankie and Johnny were lovers. Lordy how they could love. . . . He was her man, but he done her wrong. . . . She shot her man, who was doing her wrong" (Gates and McKay 2004, 34). The ballad reflects the lack of passion in Sara and Victor's marriage. It is passion that draws Frankie and Johnny together, and such passion, when disappointed, turns to anger. In taking up the role of Frankie, Sara risks stepping outside her scholarly comfort zone and into the emotive-kinetic experience of another woman. Acting in the film could allow Sara to experience the possession she has discovered examples of through her academic research; it might also bring her closer to, as Sara claims of Victor's artistic identity, "all that private ecstasy . . . so detached and free." Collins, time and again, uses Victor's behavior to showcase the kind of freedom that comes with masculine privilege and identity and allows Sara to uncover ways in which she, or her ecstasy, does not have to be fashioned, as Victor proposes at one point, from the rib, body, and needs of a man.

Sara's mother, Leila, understands Sara's envy of and anger at Victor's ecstasy, but she also pushes Sara to move past her anger about such privilege. During conversations between Sara and Leila, we understand why Sara believes that her acceptance of the Frankie role will bring her closer to ecstasy. Like Victor, Leila is an artistic individual, an actor. Sara asks her, "How did someone like you produce a child who thinks so much?" Notably, Leila and Sara's conversations are matrilineal explorations of ecstasy that often turn to gender and sex, especially since Leila uses sexuality to outrage her daughter's repressed nature.

In one scene meant to convey the importance of female intimacy in Black women's search for ecstasy, Collins chooses low, soft lighting and close-ups of the two women sitting close together at a table, talking. They discuss the existence of woman and man in a manner that moves beyond an earlier scene in which Victor noted that woman, Eve, is fashioned from the body of man, Adam. Leila's perspective provides a vantage point on woman, as she psychologically deconstructs the sexual act of men penetrating women. She asks her daughter, "What does that do to you . . . that he lifts himself up, then puts himself down into someone else?" Leila turns to the act of sexual intercourse to embody the pursuit of ecstasy, self-creation, and subjectivity. Within this act, penetration allows men pleasure and power. It becomes, like the Haitian Vodou ceremony, an act of possession. Hence, men enjoy a godlike status in society. If gods are only male, and the only way to possess is via penetration with the phallus, then women cannot ever possess another body as men can; they can only be possessed.

Yet, as Ezili and other gender-fluid gods demonstrate, there are many ways to possess and be possessed. Leila has enjoyed moments of ecstasy when performing, as she tells Sara: "When I'm actually acting really well it's like that . . . I'm gone . . . I'm in complete control, yet gone . . . the gods have me, or Satan . . . somebody does . . . once after a show I couldn't seem to come back. I was perspiring and in a kind of trance." Leila's ecstatic experience is not one-sided; as Mars explained, "The gods show their contentment by increasing the crisis of possession" (1977, 20). Ironically, Leila reveals that her male partner's observance of such possession led him to stop coming backstage since the sight of her so enthralled in her own self proved to be too much for his male ego and sense of ownership of her body. Leila's ecstatic moment, similar to the ecstatic moment Sara reads about with regard to possession in Vodou, happens *after* the possession/performance. Leila challenges Sara to reflect first and foremost on herself in that moment so that she can understand that her ecstasy must be fashioned from her own body and not Victor's. Since she does not have a penis, Sara must find a way to reconsider ecstasy outside of penetration and monotheistic and capitalistic iterations of being possessed— that is, owned by another person—even if her attempts will contradict or upset the natural order.

The experience of being Leila's child provides Sara with one method to attempt this: acting. But ecstasy is a private and personal experience, and it is not universal for all Black women. Although Sara idealizes her mother's freedom in performance, Leila notes that her history of playing asexual mamas and mammies contradicts her own desire to portray a woman character with sexual agency. Her comments mirror Sara's desire to escape external expectations and find an even greater ecstatic experience. Hence, Sara inherits performance as a means of locating ecstasy and turns to it during her particular existential crisis.

Desire plays a key role in Sara's search for ecstasy. While shooting a scene, Sara becomes so lost in her performance as Frankie that when George, the director, asks her to kiss Duke/Johnny, she does not hesitate to kiss a man who is not her husband. Collins shows Sara experiencing another moment of kinetic-emotive mysticism: "In kinetic-emotive mysticism, a god reveals himself to man through a brutal breaking up of the self. A split takes place in the personality that brings about an overwhelming psychic disruption. Ideas, will, memory, and external actions are attributed to a second personality" (Mars 1977, 20). Duke, or some other god, is not the one possessing Sara in a moment created by the student director, George; rather, she possesses herself since she is performing who she thinks Frankie is at this moment. After filming is done for the day, Sara invites Duke back to her house to party with Victor, Carlos (Victor's friend), and Celia, a woman who has been sitting as a model for Victor. When Victor begins flirting with Celia in front of everyone, it is clear that inhabiting the role of Frankie has moved Sara into an emotional space instead of the logical plane that she usually inhabits. She angrily responds in frustration: "Don't fuck around then . . . don't take that dick of yours out and fling it willy-nilly here and there like it was artistic . . . pointing it at trees, and lakes, and women . . . like it was some artistic paintbrush . . . I got nothing to take out god-dammit, that's what's uneven, that I got nothing to take out."

Yet Collins's film-within-a-film approach presents a polyinteriority and consciousness that reveal Sara's ability to resolve the crisis. Sara's performance, rather than a corporeal appendage, provides one method for the ecstatic experience. However, as the film unfolds, it becomes clear that Sara does not understand that she already has other means to ecstasy, and this is a position endured by the Black female viewer as well. Sara's second path to ecstasy had always been her pursuit of knowledge, but society, via religion or commerce, does not value women's—especially Black women's—intellect. Black women have been taught to devalue the connection between their intellect and their bodies.

After Leila reveals how acting places her in a trance, Sara exclaims, "The only thing I've ever known like that is sometimes in the middle of writing a paper my mind suddenly takes this tremendous leap into a new interpretation of the material . . . I know I'm right." Sara's writing and teaching are just as powerful as Victor's paintbrush or Leila's performance, but they are always conceptualized as rational and not spiritual or mystical. Sara's interior gaze reveals the truth to viewers, even if Sara within the film does not yet see it. The opening scene of the students' gaze and Sara's lecture exemplifies this. She does indeed have something to take out, and she does so unconsciously in ways that others, her students, see very clearly.

Collins's suggestion—to search for ecstasy rather than love—is not a simple, one-size-fits-all approach to Black women's living. On the contrary, the film's exploration of ecstasy is rather complex. Sara, Victor, and Leila all position ecstasy as tied to creative endeavors and spiritual institutions and doctrines. Somehow all these models allow for an accessible connection between body and eros. However, because the film ends so ambivalently, we understand that Sara's journey is not finished and may lie in the hands of viewers. George's student film ends with Frankie shooting Johnny, but Collins's closing shot in *Losing Ground* is of Sara, however much in character, pointing the gun at Victor and pulling the trigger. Gloria H. Gibson-Hudson reads the symbolism of the final scene as a psychic transition: "As the bullet explodes[,] it is Sara's previous psychological state which is shattered to reveal a new person" (1991, 52). While I agree with this theory about Sara's new subjectivity, I suggest moving beyond traditional ideas of what Gibson-Hudson observes as the basis for the new subjectivity: "The blues structure provides the ideal cultural context for Sara's examination of self and transforming consciousness because the blues in many instances represents a cultural icon communicating sexual empowerment" (Gibson-Hudson 1991, 53). The blues, via Frankie the character, provides the director, George, with an ideal cultural context to explore Black women's sexual empowerment—something Victor the painter could not do on canvas. However, the conflation of Sara's love troubles with Frankie's love troubles in the blues ballad is erroneous. Sara's internal and external search for ecstasy, which moves beyond anger about Victor's cheating in their marriage, proves this. What transforms Sara is the experience of performance and possession that comes with acting out any character. The cultural icon at the center for Sara exists in a different realm of performance—Black actor and acting—and it provides Sara with the new subjectivity. At the end of George's film, Sara does not just shoot Victor; she shoots the two mediocre personifications of love, husband and Cupid. It now seems clear that filmmaking and directing were providing Collins with another way to examine the self and transform her own consciousness about love. She was becoming the cultural icon, a film director that could stand alongside the blues singer in communicating sexual empowerment, among many other experiences.

Though *Losing Ground* begins with a reflection on Western metaphysics, Collins refuses to keep her characters or the audience in that plane. The film also refuses to represent Black love as a unifying force—a love that can conquer any failings or oppressions—not because white racism makes such an ideal union impossible but because, in many cases, love based in Christian concepts of possession and capitalist notions of possession creates a crisis. However, if love is like the possession in Vodou mysticism, it need not require a negation of self. Such introspective aplomb seems grounded in an unacknowledged perspective that Black women have a right to pursue ecstasy in their lives, alone or with someone else. Collins's cinematic theorization of ecstasy is useful and powerful because it is both visual and rooted in a Pan-African vision of Vodou.

Black women as intellectuals—specifically Black women intellectuals in search of ecstasy—operate outside heteronormative spaces of normalcy, because institutional, domestic, and nationalist rhetoric insists that their roles and purposes are to fulfill the needs of a nation, family, or an institution before their own. Because Collins's Black female imagery and its meaning are determined by the self, there remains little room for conventions of Black respectability. Sara's quest for ecstasy challenges the romantic narrative of love presented in Hollywood films and Black independent cinema of Collins's era. Despite concerns that *Losing Ground* produced negative representations of Black families and Black people, Collins's exploration of the depths and precarity of Black love is justified because she situates her characters' conflict around the need to make sense of the vision, idealized in Western humanism, of a split self being unified or made whole through coupled or divine love. For Collins's film hero, this search means producing an expression of love, eroticism, and sexuality that evolves from an interior self whose value may conflict with social external logics of love and relationships. Collins began this meditation of dispossession with her second feature film, *Losing Ground*, and continued it in *Only the Sky Is Free*, but she ended it with another unproduced script about Black women expatriates: *But Then She Is Madame Flor.*

BUT THEN SHE IS MADAME FLOR: REMAINING
OUT OF TIME AND PLACE

The end of this chapter brings us back to William Greave's concept of symbiopsychotaxiplasm to discover whether Collins's critical and creative investigation into love provided her with any answers for her own life, or answers that she could share with her ideal audience. Is there a crisis of possession in love?

Is love a crisis of possession? Did her translation of Mars's ethnopsychiatry on Vodou influence her creative production, how she made love in cinema, and how she sought out new life and new worlds? The middle-aged woman protagonist in Collins's script *But Then She Is Madame Flor* suggests that knowledge about the crisis of possession is important for women who struggle with being out of time and out of place.

Love—especially tumultuous love—features as a huge concern both in Collins's creative endeavors and in her life. In 1961, while doing outreach work with Operation Crossroads Africa in the Republic of the Congo, she met Douglas Collins.[12] Both were aspiring creatives, and they traveled a lot in the early years of their marriage. Yet, as Collins notes in many letters, she never felt very secure in the life they were building. A failed marriage to Doug Collins and several affairs and relationships later, she would eventually marry editor and philosopher Alfred Lord Prettyman, who insists that *But Then She Is Madame Flor* is a metaphor for their relationship.[13] Between 1965 and 1966, Collins had encountered Prettyman and his then wife, Julie Poussaint, via Collins's friend Peggy Dammond. Their brief meeting and acquaintance was enough for Collins to visit Prettyman and Poussaint's home and have Prettyman cut her hair before she made her way to Europe to begin her studies. Collins and Prettyman did not see each other again until 1984 in Harlem, at a mutual friend's birthday party, where Collins reminded Prettyman that he had cut her hair nearly twenty years before. Both now single, they bonded over their common interests in philosophy, religion, and drama. In Prettyman's own words to me about their love, "We had an incandescent relationship. We were intellectual mates . . . combustible partners" (interview with author, 2012). Collins described her dynamic with Prettyman using a similar flair, writing in a cosmic-inflected journal entry, "It's something else—some feeling of a connection returned to us this time, this life time . . . we have drifted in and out of each other. . . . The hearing of your voice as I know you hear mine too specific for only one dimension, one present confession" (September 1, 1985). A haircut and a chance meeting become the universe's way of moving people through space and light to find a way to complete love with a new definition of life. But something more shaped Collins's creative representations of love and Black women: a concept of dimensionality that can only be felt, not seen.

Though Collins seldom laments it in her private writing, the double bind created from the intersectionality of race with gender was a primary concern in much of her unproduced work. She speaks about it on a personal level when she leaves her home country to study in Paris. She wrote to her friend back home about the experience: "You know Bluette, you have to really, radically, fundamentally understand that life in the United States—does not make sense—that you live inside the madness—that one lives madness—but we only manage to tell ourselves: Yes, that's true—and then pouf!!! You go to the corner to do the shopping, then you clean the house, wait for the children—So it goes."[14] Racism and sexism in the United States threaten Black life, and any impetus to leave or fix these problems is overwhelmed by the everyday process of trying to live. How and why do Black women do it? Is there a way to escape the madness and live? Going abroad right after participating in efforts to desegregate the South provided Collins with a wealth of new knowledge about race, gender, and being that she would draw upon in her later writings: "It is impossible to describe the feeling of freedom—not just of being away from my own culture, but also of being free from the people and the relationships that have confined me so much. I have the feeling that for the first time I can ask myself what kind of life I want to live."[15] Figuring out a way to move away from the irrationality of living in such a space is why *Madame Flor* sees Collins replacing the search for love with the search for new life.

Dispossession, disorientation, displacement, and love are the issues dominating *But Then She Is Madame Flor* (1986), an original screenplay written by Collins during the last few years of her life. Given how keen Collins was on the labor that language does to create worlds, it is useful to delve into what is initiated by the title's conjunctive "but then" in its intimation of an unspoken prior clause. The title exceeds grammatical function; "but then" is usually employed to emphasize an instance of two or more events or things occurring at the same point in time or space. *But Then She Is Madame Flor* answers in the affirmative the question that went unanswered in previous works: There is a crisis of possession and love is a crisis of possession. The simultaneity of the experience produces disorientation and displacement that Collins articulates in her homage to narratives about Black women expatriates. Collins's script uses the geographical and temporal vastness of transcontinental love to intervene on Black nationalists' narratives of heterosexual love. While she could have based a story on the lives of women such as Josephine Baker or Nina Simone, Collins provides a fictional character living a less-than-spectacular, phenomenally ordinary life.

Set in Aix-en-Provence in 1985, the script centers on Madame Flor, a Black expatriate in her early forties who owns and runs a country inn. The trajectory of Flor's life is interrupted when Ned, a Black American man vacationing in France, knocks on her door and reminds her that she is a Black American. The stage directions emphasize early on that shifts of time and place will occur based on where each character is located. However, in each case, the script directions emphasize

"*SAME TIME*" or "*FLASH BACK SEQUENCE BEGINS.*" The beginning of the film concludes one phase of Flor and Ned's relationship. In an early scene, while Flor is in France, crying in her room at the inn, Ned is in New York, recording a message to Flor:

> *NED still talking into his TAPE CASSETTE*
> What a silly novel we'd make, Flor . . .
> transcontinental romance, idyllic inn,
> middle-aged love. We fit into every cliché. (Collins 1986, 3)

Despite Ned's statement, there is nothing clichéd about the love story Collins creates. Flor is the opposite of Sara in *Losing Ground*. Flor came to France at age nineteen and stayed longer than she ever planned, because in leaving her home roots, she had made a space in which she could plant new seeds, could grow to be herself. However, as Flor explains in a letter to Ned, this is not a self that adequately translates into narratives of romantic love that she did not author:

> I know you hate that I keep notes on everything, you insist . . . that it explains why I live in "somebody else's country"—as you put it. . . . Let me say this right away . . . that you came as a complete surprise to me, I didn't expect you. I was just going about my life as I knew it when you walked in. (4)

From here, the script cuts to the first flashback: Flor is seen going over a menu with two chefs at the inn and then providing flowers for a guest suite. This is not a domestic scene depicting the labor of a wife and mother. As the script directions note, Flor runs a business: "*Montage. Flor wandering in and out of several guest rooms, exchanging brief words with different workers*" (5). The inn provides a unique architectural space for Collins to blur public and private boundaries that establish the limitations of women. In doing so, her character confronts capitalist notions of possession.

Flor tells Alfonse, her hotel manager, that she wants to convert an old barn to make the most of a view of an orchard. He chides her for saying it but never doing it. As she explains to him, "It's hard for me to believe that it's mine . . . all this . . . often I think it's going to disappear . . . to covert the barn . . . it's like saying . . . this is <u>mine</u>, I own it, I can do anything" (6). Throughout the screenplay, Flor talks with different characters about not wanting to feel rooted in one place or to be tied to something permanently. The rule of ownership, possessing or being property, has created a fear that embracing these ideas will result in a loss of her freedom.

The inn, then, becomes a metaphor for the crisis of possession in love and love as a crisis of possession. However, Flor's struggle is not simply about capitalist notions of ownership. Flor's conversation about architecture and space underlines how the inn has become a mode of her interior expression. She has created, built, and designed it in her own image. Not a room or a house, but an inn with multiple living spaces that may serve vastly different functions. We don't know the name of the inn, but then she is Madame Flor. In creating her own space/world, she has also created a space; a whole new world for other Black people throughout the Diaspora. As Allie, a Black thirty-three-year-old mother with two kids, tells Flor upon their arrival at the inn, "They [the kids] think you're enchanted and that the Inn is a palace" (7). Flor has this effect not only on children; as Allie later confesses, "I think of you as . . . complete . . . in ways I wish I could be" (8). Though it is easy for Allie to articulate what Flor represents to her kids, it is harder for her to name what Flor is to her, as Collins makes clear with her use of ellipses as beats, seconds, where thought and translation of a difficult concept are taking place. Allie's own interior struggle to locate completion of self outside of motherhood and marriage, in art and design, is juxtaposed against Flor's unease about owning property. They both experience psychic displacement. None of Allie's encouraging revelations stop Flor from obsessing over the foundation of her unease about fully possessing and owning the inn and herself. She tells Allie, "though I can't imagine living in the States. But to settle-in . . . finally feels like such a complete acceptance of being alone" (8). Yet, as much of the screenplay unveils, Flor is never alone. Moreover, she never expresses sentiments of being incomplete.

By the time Flor meets Ned (Flor's sister Lavinia had recommended the inn to Ned), she has owned the inn for fourteen of the twenty-something years she has been in France. At their first meeting, Ned compliments Flor on her command of the French language, but then sarcastically comments, "You probably find English tedious, perhaps a bit too real" (11). Essentially Ned calls Flor a snob, and he makes a memorable first impression. For Ned, Flor's choice to live in France is more than a rejection of her country; it also appears as a rejection of her race. He resides in a space and time where there is only one way to be Black. At the end of act 1, however, Ned speaks into the tape recorder, saying that he remembers thinking to himself, "She's not like any other woman," and thus provides the clause that precedes, "but then she is Madame Flor." Clarifying, he insists, "You're not like any other woman . . . you're too damn much yourself" (27). Moving beyond interior monologue, Collins uses journals and tape recorders to document how her characters work to integrate interior process with external social reality.

In another flashback, right before Flor agrees to a fishing trip with Ned, Flor dances alone in an empty room with lots of windows, enjoying the movement that her body's internal beats afford her. As in Collins's previous films, dance becomes the emotive-kinetics that prepares the characters for possession. The next act depicts the slow moments of Flor and Ned getting to know each other. On a weekend trip to Cannes, they shop, drink, talk, and dance late into the night, and eventually make love:

> **Close On:** *Flor and Ned in bed. Passionately lost in each other. HOLD*
> *FADE OUT* (53)

Predictably, when Ned must return to the United States, he asks Flor to come with him. Though Flor expresses unease at the thought, against her better judgment, she moves back to be with him. As they live together in the United States, Flor fails to reconnect with her sister Lavinia, struggles to get to know Ned's daughter, and deals with Ned's repeated remarks about her time in France as an act of "running away." The culmination of this disorder is revealed in the most ordinary and quiet way. After spending a day with Lavinia, Flor and Ned go to a restaurant for dinner. They are enjoying each other's company and making small talk when the waiter brings them their salad:

> **Flor** *(suddenly annoyed):*
> I don't eat salad at the beginning of a meal . . .
> The Waiter doesn't know what to do. (88)

According to the script, the awkwardness of the moment must convey "*Tight Silence.*" The scene ends with Ned telling Flor to eat her salad or "nibble on a roll," which she does. Everything is out of order, and Flor has trouble finding a place to fit in Ned's life. This scene is followed by more serious eruptions of Flor's discomfort at social events as well as in private settings between just the two of them. She tells Ned, "I feel the way I've always felt when I'm here . . . like I don't fit" (97), but he minimizes her feelings. She finally confesses to him, "I have to go home" (106). In the United States, she has to be Florence Coles and take on a life that has been crafted by others: "It was ugly, my life here, that's why I left. If I'd stayed, maybe I'd be like Lavinia is now, unable to forget, craving a mother none of us had . . . and I'm walking around these god-awful streets I feel so naked I can't breathe . . . I don't know who I am. I'm lost" (107). Trying to explain why she wants to go back to France, Flor insists on the need for a life made beautiful by her imagination and hands. She returns to France, and despite Flor having called it "home" in her speech to Ned, an irresolution remains for Flor about being there. In an atypical ending, Collins's script ends with Ned returning to France to live with Madame Flor.

In all three of the original cinematic visions of Black love discussed in this chapter, Collins clarifies that love is a crisis of possession and that there is a crisis of possession for Black women. Each script articulates love not as an emotional journey shared between two perfectly matched souls forming one union but as a spiritual conflict for Black women who have already found love in and of themselves. Collins was unable to solve the conflict between cosmology and ontology, expressed at both the individual and nationalistic levels, in which romantic love becomes a dispossession of women's own love of self. She proposed, instead, that Black women seek out and discover new forms of life not defined by the biopolitical or socioreligious—forms of life that could support an existence and acceptance of being out of time and out of place for Black women and men. Inevitably, her experimentations with genres of love in life and genres of love in art guided Collins toward using her natural empathetic talents and artistic skills to teach others how to move through multiple worlds without the crisis of possession.

LIFE OF THE MIND

Scene 3, *The Afterlives of Kathleen Collins*

TIME SHIFT:

Cut to long shot: Night sky, moon, stars . . . space

LOCATION:

Earth Satellite campus: a film school in space

CHARACTERS:

JOSEPHINA VASQUEZ. Mid-20s, Afro-Latina, androgynous, decorated veteran in the Moon Wars of 2216. Protégé of Kathleen Collins.

Eight to ten adolescent students of different races and genders.

V.O. NARRATOR. Digital voice / Collins as ghost

The instrumental opening of Stevie Wonder's "Visions" plays as students stretch into a two-minute mental warm-up for Josephina's class.

JOSEPHINA:

Listen to the music. Breathe. At the end of the song, clear the way for your vision. Remember, whatever they could not handle about their psyche, they have projected onto us.[1]

V.O. NARRATOR:

She prefers this to the meditation exercises I taught her long ago.

In a montage, viewers see a woman in a classroom, lecturing. THIS IS COL-LINS. She raises her hand and points to someone in the audience. THIS IS JOSEPHINA as a child. Her words repeated, at that moment, "You are freer than you think." Cut to adult Josephina echoing those words.

JOSEPHINA:

Therefore, you cannot defeat them by remaking yourself into their image. This war will not be won with violence, fresh bodies, or weaponized technology. You must create an empathetic technology of the mind. You, unlike them, must be fearless in seeking out and finding the languages that can accompany your new life-forms. Remember, these are the foundational rules established by the Cinematic Marronage Manifesto of the early twenty-first century.

V.O. NARRATOR, *over recorded images of the events described below*:

In the interplanetary wars, Josephina had learned that the system of hierarchies could be undone when new technologies of editing and translation took hold in their minds' vision. Reading about her teacher's past life as a freedom rider, translator, and film editor became an asset as she taught her students how to design neural interface technology that might save the lives of hundreds of their kind.

Neurobiologists and physicists had finally proved what the Baule people of Ivory Coast had theorized eons ago with masks and faith: that the third eye and its visual field were not simply a fantasy of occultism and mysticism. Based on her manipulations of space, light, and time, Collins founded the Near Space and Film Movement using jurisdictional zones established by the Law of Sea Convention, which allowed for peaceful use and innocent passage of near space zones. Josephina also created and designed the first brain-optical interface, linking computers with psychics to see what telescopes couldn't when quantum artificial intelligence was in its infancy. Her students, inspired by the history of Radio Free Dixie, also built the first free dark matter satellite and launched it from Ghana when black hole and dark matter satellites were unimaginable. In this time, they had figured out a way to circumvent the myopic cartographies of white empires on Earth.

CHAPTER THREE

FIFTH DIMENSION CINEMA

UNDERSTANDING WHAT A BLACK FILM studies professor makes possible is as important as understanding what a Black woman filmmaker makes possible. To do so means understanding that empathy, chance, affect, serendipity, intuition, and futurist thinking are as relevant as history, data collections, and archives. For Collins, it means understanding how she developed a philosophy of learning and teaching as a form of life and an expansion of a universe beyond what could be seen. As filmmaker, editor, and former Collins student Susan Korda explained, "She was highly perceptive. . . . Kathleen was all spirit."[2]

In the prefatory speculative imagining of a film school in space, unlike utopic renderings by Afro-futurists or space-age colonizers such as Elon Musk and Jeff Bezos, I am unable to imagine a future without another form of colonization in which settlers will assert sovereignty over time and space and, in the end, over dimensionality, which shapes reality as much as it does representation. I am only able to imagine a world where Black beings' future use of film and film technology becomes a fifth dimension cinema that addresses dangerous analytics of algorithms, artificial intelligence, and exploitation of space while thwarting the will to repeatedly adapt and manufacture comic books into savior cinema to be produced by Hollywood studio systems, cop mythology into law-and-order television procedurals steeped in carceral imaginations, and military culture into a panoptic weaponization of drones and surveillance technology.

In this book's introduction, I stress that attention to form and genre serves as intervention on the disembodied logics of biography and autobiography that fail Black figures. I theorize my uses of other creative forms in afterlife-writing as about interrupting the logic of film genres and film studies racialized as white settler cinema. Other critics have also noted that genre itself is a colonization of form and aesthetics that may have preceded national identity and culture (Nzegwu 2019).[3] Chapter 1 makes evident that, in working on her first script, Collins was able to locate a cosmology that would become the basis of her artistic identity and a method in which writing and filmmaking served as embodied erotic practice that would motivate her to keep writing even when she was not being recognized as a Black woman writer at work in Hollywood. Rather than attempt to fit into the very few predetermined definitions of Black film, she would have to teach herself and others to navigate around them until they could access another dimension. Contemporary Black film scholars outline the importance of pedagogy to the production and study of Black film. For example, film and Black feminist critics Beretta E. Smith-Shomade, Racquel Gates, and Miriam J. Petty, in their introductory assessment of Black media, explain that "the creation of a sustainable pedagogy not only displaces the model of one day of 'race and ethnicity in media' but also takes into account the power of Black film as an idea that productively complicates many of film and media studies' central methods and assumptions" (Smith-Shomade, Gates, and Petty, 2014, 53). Centering Black film, and film Blackness, in the teaching of film provides a means to decolonize the art and discipline while enabling a conversation on race and representation.

This chapter, then, builds on Gillespie's theory of film Blackness to argue that Collins used her unique position as a Black woman filmmaker and film studies professor to introduce and advance the anteriority of global Black visuality as a distinctive dimension for the future of Black filmmaking and film studies. Gillespie asks, *What if black film could be something other than embodied? What if black film was immaterial and bodiless? What if black film could be speculative or just ambivalent? What if black film is art and not the visual transcription of the black lifeworld?* (2016,157; italics in original). These questions seem similar to Collins's own queries, and she answered them with the creation of scripts and films. In addition, and most relevant here, through development of her film pedagogy, she provided students with tools that would allow them to propose different answers in their own time.

If, as Collins lectures her students, "You are freer than you think," then it is prudent for Black people to find or develop the technology to shift and accommodate our thinking. Teaching is a futurist and psychic technology of world-making. Filmmaking is a technology of moving images. Teaching filmmaking, then, is a technology of freedom movements than can enable Black people to counter physical and psychic racializing surveillance—"a technology of social control where surveillance practices, policies, and performances concern the production of norms pertaining to race and exercise a 'power to define what is in or out of place'" (Browne 2015, 16)—whenever and wherever it may occur.

Through my study of Collins, I am able to imagine her as a teacher in space, training students how to resolve the tensions and contradictions of placing Black living beings in any space being explored by white exploiters. My imagination, however, gives way to a film Blackness genealogy constructed from what VèVè A. Clark termed a "diasporic literacy," which "defines the reader's ability to comprehend the literatures of Africa, Afro-America, and the Caribbean from an informed indigenous perspective. The field is multicultural and multilingual, encompassing writing in European and ethnic languages" (11). Diasporic literacy applies to film and cinematic language, and it requires critical reciprocity. It is these elements that connect Collins to mentor and collaborator filmmaker William Greaves, and to her student and mentee filmmakers Ronald Gray, Susan Korda, Rebecca Williams, and Joseph Vasquez; they are linked by real and symbolic missions and visions for Black filmmaking. This thread is made apparent when perspective shifts from what might have been to the multiplicity of what is still possible, when attention to dimensionality forces us to think beyond a democratic public into a future where we can imagine humans having an anticolonial relationship to space. Film concerns of depth, direction, duration, and distance are four elements influenced by colonialism and empire, and in the new space age, Collins and Vasquez become teachers whose expertise in the multiple uses of light, space, and dimensionality informs their efforts to hinder the changing same of colonization and subsequent need for decolonization. Film pedagogy, I argue in conversation with the afterlife of Collins's teaching texts and philosophies, adds an ancient function and (psychic) dimension to filmmaking and its future developments.

In film studies, *first cinema* is designated as that of European and US capitalist-centric models in which film is an industrial art. *Second cinema,* or art house, is the alternative in which the auteur is granted more freedom of expression from the constraints of commodification and aesthetic formulation. *Third cinema* is conceived by filmmakers from the global South invested in a cinema of liberation that works "outside and against the System" established by first cinema (Solanas and Getino 2014, 238). *Fourth cinema* is "Indigenous cinema," which takes up indigeneity, colonial appropriation, and dispossession (Barclay 2003). First and second cinema incorporate Christian metaphysics and reproduce Christian humanist perspectives. Fortunately, in the process of decolonizing culture, third and fourth cinema function to develop Black and Indigenous national conscious and critique first and second cinema. These cinemas also understand and incorporate alternative metaphysics through aesthetics, content, and theme. Third and fourth cinemas attempt to outline what the political relationship to visual technology can and should be among Black, Indigenous, and people of color.

I argue in this chapter that the relationship between institution, power, education, and filmmaking in Collins's simultaneous evolution as a filmmaker and film studies professor demonstrates the necessity of a *fifth dimension cinema* in our current era, as opposed to a fifth cinema.[4] My theorization of a fifth dimension is derived not from physics but from esoteric spiritual traditions. Fifth dimension serves as a guiding metaphor for a cinema related to the expansion of consciousness about one's place in the universe as opposed to concerns about one's place in a nation and a subject representation that sustains Enlightenment ideals about reason and human being in twentieth-century filmmaking. Fifth dimension cinema's function is not only to highlight film as a tool for "consciousness" or delivering propaganda for resistance movements but also to highlight how the teaching of film is technology that intuits function and purpose beyond the representation of present realities.

Even if Collins had known that she wanted to be a filmmaker before she went to Paris to get her MA in French literature, what were her options? What conditions of the industry could facilitate dimensional Black representation on-screen, in the writing room, and behind the camera? Superficial strategies such as hiring Black actors for small roles or sparsely using color-blind casting in major roles never fully address the institutional, systemic, segregationist, and white supremacist path that any Black person wanting to make a film would encounter. Black-owned and -operated Lincoln Motion Picture Company, founded in 1916, and the Micheaux Book and Film Company, founded in 1918, began the era of race films, but none of these were spaces of imaginative freedom for women—as Zora Neale Hurston's limited forays into filmmaking can attest. Though these companies produced films that were commercial successes, they could not be classified as decolonizing films. The biographies of Oscar Micheaux, the earliest and most prolific Black filmmaker, capture the entrepreneurial and independent spirit of the filmmaker, who sold his films, with their talented-tenth plots, from the trunk of his car. Technological innovation was pushing film in new directions, but aesthetic innovation did nothing for the visual politics of difference. During the 1950s, when Eastman Kodak was shifting from Technicolor to modern Eastman color cinematography, *Brown v. Board of Education* was filed—and segregation continued long after Thurgood Marshall won his arguments to end segregation. Nevertheless, there were no intersectional revelations that would radicalize Hollywood films in regard to race and gender.

Like most other insitutions of learning, film schools were not fully integrated even though most of them were not in the South. The University of Southern California School of Cinematic Arts was founded in 1929. Dada artist Hans Richter founded the City College of New York's Masters Institute of Film, and it began offering the first bachelor of fine arts degree for film in the United States in 1941. The University of California, Los Angeles, established a theater, film, and television unit in 1947. New York University's Tisch School of the Arts originated in 1965. Walt Disney founded the California Insitute of the Arts in 1961. The University of Texas at Austin Department of Radio and Television began offering film studies in 1965, as did the Columbia University School of the Arts. The City College of New York's defunct Celia and David V. Picker Film Institute,[5] which Collins was a part of, was one of the few schools in the 1970s to conceive of a more balanced configuration of film study in considerations of race and gender. People who had access to film education in the United States were limited by race or gender. White logics played a role in the formative years of Collins's filmmaking career.

FOUNDATIONS OF A FIFTH DIMENSION CINEMA

Fifth dimension cinema is freedom from representation, freedom toward technology, and freedom from violent uses of visual technology. My definition of fifth dimension cinema relies on interviews with her students and two important video documents: a master class lecture that Collins delivered at Howard University (Collins 1984) and a video interview with Phyllis Klotman, in which Collins outlines and discusses her cinematic vision (Klotman 1984). It is evident, from the very beginning of the Howard lecture, that Collins's artistic and metaphysical philosophies are clear and intertwined: "When you think about film in the barest sense . . . it is nothing but space and light. It is the placement of people inside these two illusions. . . . Therefore, the first thing you should do when you think about freedom—about film—you have to think about the freedom to move people through space and light." Although this has been the basis of filmmaking since its origins, Collins's philosophies about space and light, when coupled with her attention to race and human being, are what provide the call for something radical. The lecture is a manifesto that Collins teaches, as opposes to writes, and in the lecture she details what she believes film should do.

At the beginning of her statement on film, she has a minor language-thought mix-up, using the word *freedom* before correcting herself and using the word *film*. Collins's subconscious understands film as freedom. It knows that film's two-dimensional surface exists in a curved dimension where freedom can be recursively broached and returned to, no matter where one begins in space and time. Before Collins could ever make a film, she had to dismiss the dehumanization of Black people, revise and reject Negro uplift, reject the metaphysics that helped construct the notion of racial segregation and its tools of visual colonization, and resist further entrenchment of race as an uncontested visible and biological category. In sum, she had to be free somewhere and sometime, not here. Then she had to figure out how to teach her students to do the same while also teaching them how to use and understand film technology and dislocate it from Western visual regimes.

Collins's words and teachings about light, space, and freedom are the foundation of fifth dimension cinema—which understands Black film both as a genre and field of Black studies that intuits the rise and evolution of anti-Blackness in visual technology and as a sacred practice of looking and seeking that refuses the material social pathology of representation and gaze in the methods of natural and social sciences. Collins's practice of understanding the ways in which Black bodies or Blackness interact with and use light to chart movement is based on an awareness not taught in film school. As a teacher of film, Collins developed a pedagogy that complemented some of the ideas from previous film movements. She was consistently developing a treatment for the colonizing impact of US film approaches and Hollywood industry protocols. She once explained, "The whole myth of Hollywood, the way film functions in this culture, has succeeded, artistically, in brainwashing all of us" (Franklin 2015, 35). Her vision far exceeded the reactionary race film era, originated and evolved alongside the beautifully militant Blaxploitation period, and grew and withered within the Black independent film movement in the lateness of the long twentieth century. It was a vision that evolved based on her experiences in the cutting room, in the classroom, and behind the camera.

She passionately argued, "How can we talk about picking up a camera when there is a sacred imaginary mythology around film, around Hollywood, around movies, and we would be breaking sacred ground!" (Franklin 2015, 36). Whatever white and Eurocentric ideologies exist about filmmaking and film, they do not compete with what Collins assigns as the function of filmmaking: sacred visual practices of secular humanism. Susan Vogel has written, "Looking and seeing are learned modes; visuality is not a uniform feature across human experience, but is a culturally constructed practice deeply affected by cultural categories or classifications that can usually be expressed through language and that embrace virtually everything in human experience, including the perception of natural phenomena" (1977, 66). For these reasons, Collins would turn to modes of visuality where the power of looking and seeking into another being could be reciprocal and, in turn, could subvert the dominance of the Western gaze toward marginalized subjects as possessions or objects.

In her film pedagogy, Collins claims an anterioriority of Black visuality rooted in intuitive and psychic elements that can transform material technologies into the practice of freedom and an ability to move people through space and light, even when institutional, societal, technological, and architectural structures are built to curtail movement and freedom. Collins's dedication to inner vision dictated everything she did in filmmaking, writing, and teaching, and it set her apart from many filmmakers during her productive years.

Fifth dimension cinema is a mode of visuality and optics based on what cannot yet be seen. When outer space and theories of colonialism, postcolonialism, and settler colonialism become the operating frames for modes of visuality, how does such a new worldview shift the frames for developing a cinematic and film theory about race, colonization, and technology? Fifth dimension cinema privileges alternative logics about light, space, and energy over the biopolitical. It asks Black film and cinema to revise its perspective of shadow and light from that of a veil to that of dark matter and melanin in an exploration of Black life and living.

Whereas most theories relying on space focus on scientific and technological disciplines such as physics, astronomy, or aerospace engineering, I am interested in non-Western approaches based in cosmology, consciousness, and perception as technology, such as meditation, astral projection, and remote viewing. As Babatunde Lawal explains of Yoruba visual philosophy, "The eyeball is thought to have two aspects, an outer layer (literally external eye) or naked eye, which has to do with normal, quotidian vision, and an inner one called *ojú inú* (literally, internal eye) or mind's eye. The latter is associated with memory, intention, intuition, insight, thinking, imagination, critical analysis, visual cognition, dreams, trances, prophecy, hypnotism, empathy, telepathy, divination, healing, benevolence, malevolence, extrasensory perception, and witchcraft, among others" (Lawal 2001, 516). Fifth dimension cinema asks Black film and cinema to locate alternative metaphysics and become a platform for exploration and experimentation, as opposed to representation or resistance alone. Fifth dimension cinema understands film and television as mediums capable of not only representing life experiences but also seeking out new life-forms that live and create outside the available optical/visual/scopic technology, such as microscopes or telescopes.

For this reason, fifth dimension cinema incorporates depth, thus moving away from the split caused by Cartesian logos, by understanding vision as a complex simultaneity of corporeality, kinesthetics, thought, and perception.

Maurice Merleau-Ponty reminds us that "depth is the means the things have to remain distinct, to remain things, while not being what I look at present. It is pre-eminently the dimension of the simultaneous. Without it, there would not be a world or Being" (1968, 219). Fifth dimension cinema promises a visual philosophy centered on a third eye (perception)—an entire system of visuality that does not begin and end with how the eye processes light, but rather pairs that processing of light with how the body processes darkness and force. It proposes to develop cinematic rendering, distribution, and marketing that does not solely invest in the public sphere; to deploy a higher consciousness, seeing with the eye's mind to deconstruct the myth of Hollywood and the US film industry; to resist technophobia; to bring an end to the overrepresentation of man; to provide examples of aesthetics that can serve as a technology of the living; and to exceed necropolitical representation and communication. Hence, fifth dimension cinema begins in a reorientation away from Christian metaphysics.

Stan Brakhage theorized in "Metaphors on Vision" that "there is a pursuit of knowledge foreign to language and founded upon visual communication, demanding a development of the optical mind, dependent upon perception in the optical and deepest sense of the word" (2014, 62). Fifth dimension cinema builds on this idea and establishes decolonial teaching as a form of knowledge production and development of the prescient optical mind; therefore, it challenges the curricula of film schools and film studies. As I explain, much of what Collins was doing in the editing room and the classroom would be hailed as revolutionary almost more than two decades later when Walter Murch's *In the Blink of an Eye: A Perspective on Film Editing* (1992) became a notable and popular book about film-editing, in part because of its thesis centered on feeling, emotion, and improvisation as opposed to technical elements aligned with rationality, synchronicity, and linearity.

The pedagogical inventiveness of Collins makes four important maneuvers that prepare the way for fifth dimension cinema. First, she tackles the unacknowledged Cartesian metaphysics that shapes the cinematic scopic field and designates film as being capable of only disembodied necropolitical art and communication. Second, she strategizes how to infuse cinema technology with psychic visuality in order to transcend the veil of race. Third, she asks what, if any, is Black people's relationship to visual technologies and then insists on a decolonial relationship to technology if it is not already there. Fourth, as I more fully explore in the next chapter, Collins's film pedagogy presciently addresses what Ruha Benjamin (2016) has defined as captivating technologies in technoscience and Simone Browne (2015) has called Black luminosity in Black feminist surveillance studies so as to issue a call for future Black filmmaking to adapt to the new modes of policing and surveillance that occur in evolving panopticons.

Theories of Black culture and representation have traditionally evolved out of concerns about the public sphere and Black social life, even when their metaphors originated in fields of knowledge where interiority or otherworldly questions are central. Such is the case with the most canonical visual metaphor in Black studies: the veil, as expounded by W.E.B. Du Bois in his theory of double-consciousness in *The Souls of Black Folk* ([1902] 1996). Du Bois's concept of double-consciousness originates in his occult use of the veil to provide insights on what had once been called the Negro problem. Its employment was meant to capture "those finer manifestations of social life which history can but mention and which statistics can not count" (Du Bois 1898, 20). Yet the veil, when translated into external social world schemas and combined with scopic technology, produces necropolitics and a culture of mourning.

Karla Holloway's *Passed On: African American Mourning Stories* details how African Americans "die a 'color-coded death' as a result of riots, executions, suicides, and targeted medical neglect" (Holloway 2002, 3). Holloway traces this culture of mourning back to Du Bois, as one of the forefathers of Black intellectual thought. "When Du Bois wrote of his son's passing as 'liberation' and that his child was 'Not dead, not dead, but escaped; not bond but free' . . . he revealed the cultural dimension of black America's experience with death and dying. . . . He cherished the thought that death had liberated him from living within the veil of race" (Holloway 2002, 6–7). Death cannot and should not be the only means of liberating oneself from the veil of race. Collins, unlike Du Bois, did something very different with the veil and second sight. Rather than embrace them as metaphor, she taught second sight as a corporeal technology for the production of art and culture.

The realities of segregation and an apartheid regime cemented in visual recognition of a hierarchy of differences require futuristic experimentation with form and medium so as to exceed systemic boundaries. Simone Browne's *Dark Matters* reminds us that legislation such as lantern laws dictated that, should enslaved Black people be out after dark unlit, or without a lantern, they could be punished or imprisoned. Understanding this as "an exercise of panoptic power," Browne terms the practice "Black luminosity"—"a form of boundary maintenance occurring at the site of the black body, whether by candlelight, flaming torch, or the camera flashbulb that documents the ritualized terror of a lynch mob" (Browne 2015, 67–68). Browne's concept of Black luminosity makes it out of the antebellum era of slave patrollers and converts it to a systemic practice in Jim Crow. Influenced by the aesthetic philosophies of a segregated world, Collins is confronted with several figurations of the visible and invisible associated with Black luminosity and race that go unaddressed in hegemonic aesthetics and theories of being. Black luminosity is also part of Hollywood filmmaking, such that making films means accepting such boundaries—Hollywood filmmaking is incompatible with recognizing that there are many ways to move people through space and light. We must now better comprehend the potential of what Collins imagined as the ability to move people through space and light.

WHEN THERE IS NO PUBLIC TELEVISION, NO PUBLIC TRUST: THERE IS ALWAYS SPACE

As is evident from figure 3.1—an image of Collins teaching a film workshop while wearing a T-shirt emblazoned with the cheeky slogan "A woman's place is in the House . . . and the Senate"—Collins perfectly understood the gendered spatial boundaries she was crossing as a Black woman filmmaker. She was ever aware of producing an alternative of space, something that Toni Cade Bambara theorized as world-making when she insisted, "I want to talk about language, form, and changing the world. The question that faces billions of people at this moment . . . is: Can the planet be saved from the psychopaths? What role can, should, or must the film practitioner, for example, play in producing a desirable vision of the future?" (Bambara 1996, 139). Bambara continues, "The filmmaker will then face a choice: either to devise a new film language in order to get that story told or to have the whole enterprise derailed by those conventions" (143). One of the mechanisms essential to radicalizing life-writing and devising a new film language remains the act of editing.

After completing her thesis on André Breton and surrealism as a cinematic notion, Collins acquired a job as a researcher at National Educational Television (NET), and later became an editor for the entity under its later iteration WNET. NET was founded and supported by a Ford Foundation grant for adult education. As a result of reduced funding due to concerns about radical topics being broadcast on more conservative stations, the network was later placed under the auspices of the Public Broadcasting Service (PBS) and the Corporation for Public Broadcasting affiliate stations in more liberal viewing areas. In film editing, Collins discovered another tool for crafting her language, one that did not rely on someone else's ideas of temporality and spatiality. With editing, there was no such thing as out of place. As an editor, she could construct many, many stories as opposed to one mythical universal truth. In addition to being a necessary part of the writing and filmmaking processes, editing, as Collins

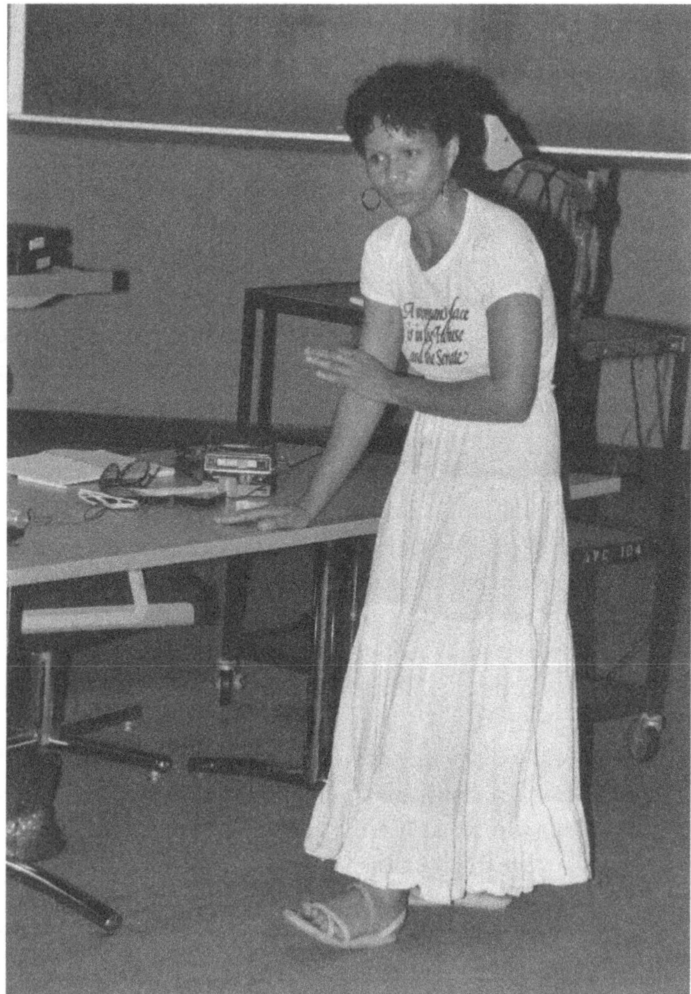

Fig. 3.1 Kathleen Collins speaking at BFC/Creative Use of
Black Film: Workshop/Festival of Films by Independent Black
Filmmakers, July 1983. © Black Film Center/Archive

learned at WNET, could also be a form of critical immersion in understanding
film technology and one's interior self.

For Collins, simultaneously completing editing jobs for public television
while teaching at CCNY provided a continuation of the process she had begun
in writing film scripts: thinking through and devising the new film language.
"I thought that [editing] was magical. And it's really the magic of being in that

cutting room that I remember now," she told Phyllis Klotman (1984), her face lighting up as she divulged how the unglamorous, technical process turned her on to film and its function in her life. Collins explained in the interview (1984) that editing provided her with both a methodology for unlearning harmful myths and a theory for reimagining approaches to representation.

Because Collins had the benefit of working with William Greaves in his capacity as a filmmaker for the United States Information Agency (USIA) and for his own production company, she learned firsthand what film could contribute toward countering myth. Greaves was open about his dominant philosophy in filmmaking and production as counter to racializing surveillance: "My interest in the documentary as an educational tool was further increased during a protracted period of study in Afro-American and Ancient African History.... I decided to get behind the camera and produce documentary and feature films which, in my small way, would help counter the one-hundred-year campaign of vilification in the media against the people of the African diaspora" (Greaves 1998, 61). In addition to Greaves's documentary filmmaking philosophy, his belief in experimentation and editing in the cinematic rendering of artistic life was expressed in his explanation of *Symbiopsychotaxiplasm* (Greaves [1968] 2006), now considered his most significant intervention and innovation. As Greaves put it, "These are the determinants, rather than the Aristotelian approach to drama—the traditional dramatic form of Sophocles or Ibsen or whomever. You're going for—let's call it divine action, another level of insight into the human condition, using cinema" (Knee and Musser 1992, 22). Clearly, Greaves's notion of "divine action" comprehends filmmaking as something other than the devil finding work.

Collins was credited as a member of the production crew on this important film as well as on a number of Greaves's other films. She learned her lessons well. Editing, as expressed in a letter Collins wrote to her friend Bluette Dammond, brought her closer to Greaves's theory of cinema as spiritual practice: "I have just finished a very beautiful film about Leger, the artists, and the workers. It was a very significant experience for me in editing—I had to open myself up to the images just as one opens up to music so that editing was no longer a means of manipulating images but of allowing them to play with almost unconscious transparency."[6] Simply put, Collins understood editing as a type of second sight. The letters that Collins wrote to friends and family, as well as the extent to which Greaves influenced her work, underscore why she must be contextualized as a trans-Atlantic and Diasporic filmmaker very much concerned with decolonial approaches to space and light. In Collins's case, the major symbols are not water or music, but space and light. Greaves provided Collins with opportunities that her education in France did not. In another letter to Bluette Dammond, written on her way to work on one of Greaves's films, Collins writes, "A letter en route to Jamaica. How life has moved on: I have been offered to write and be an assistant director on a feature film! I said yes, just like that. . . . School granted me a month off to do it."[7]

Greaves provided Collins with an opportunity to move beyond the role of editor and be part of an African Diasporic community of filmmakers. In a letter to her stepmother, Collins writes of her assistant director duties, "It never ceases to amaze me how much work goes into making a film. The Star, Calvin Lockhart, (whose [*sic*] very famous by the way)." Later in the same letter she notes that the film's producer "is a very wealthy Chinese man (there are a lot of Chinese here, along with English, Dutch, and Germans), and he's an avid bridge player."[8] Though the letter does not reference the film's title, the details revealed make it clear it was Greaves's film *The Marijuana Affair* (1975). The plot of this failed reggae film, a would-be Jamaican cult classic because of its Bahamian star Calvin Lockhart's portrayal of a detective, centers on a corrupt police force in Jamaica shutting down the marijuana trade in order to allow cocaine to enter the United States. The Chinese producer of the film was none other than Lucien Chin, a well-known Jamaican boxing promoter and businessman. Collins expressed how important the editing experience, as well as travel to the Caribbean, was to her vision. She wrote of the islands, "I've visited (Trinidad, Nassau, Haiti), I'd say Jamaica is the best and warmest."[9]

As New York filmmakers trained in Canada and France, respectively, Greaves's and Collins's attention to their craft was shaped by their experience of race in the United States as well as by the freedom they found to explore their craft outside an industry's Black luminosity—that is, the institutional racism endemic in Hollywood and in US film schools. The experiences of shooting and making films outside the United States provided a comparison for what they experienced in the United States. They would not be the same. One experience would provide a glimpse at numerous possibilities; the other would delimit any future considerations of becoming a filmmaker. Notably, for Collins, the magic of editing also occurs in a cultural space struggling to define its purpose, identity, and audience and one quite distinct from commercial or auteur cinema—public television.

From 1961 through the 1970s, film manifestos on third cinema were being written, but few of them addressed public educational television, which became a haven for early US Black filmmakers. In the 1970s, while Gil Scott-Heron and James Baldwin were critiquing television and films and Michel Foucault was examining the state's panopticon and its citizens, Collins was developing her form as a practitioner and teacher of films. Her work as a film editor on Black public affairs television programs such as *Black Journal* as well as *The Great American Dream Machine* and the *51st State* (Klotman and Cutler 1999, 123) provided a solid foundation for what would become her cinematic vision. This work also was a continuation of the progressive politics she had promoted as a freedom rider. *Black Journal* originated from the timely parallel of political unrest (particularly the Newark riots, which were examined by an NET-commissioned documentary) and the radical artistic mission articulated in the Carnegie Commission on Educational Television report, "Public Television: A Program for Action" (1967), also known as Carnegie I. The report has been noted as the basis of the Public Broadcasting Act of 1967.[10] Twelve years later, the authors of Carnegie II, "The Public Trust," succinctly acknowledged, "In retrospect, what public broadcasting tried to invent was a truly radical idea: an instrument of mass communication that simultaneously respects the artistry of the individuals who create programs, the needs of the public that form the audience, and the forces of political power that supply the resources" (Carnegie Commission on Public Broadcasting 1979, 10). Sadly, the same report stressed that the Carnegie program for action had failed for very specific reasons: "We find public broadcasting's financial, organizational and creative structure fundamentally flawed" (11). As Ralph Engelman's *Public Radio and Television in America: A Political History* explains, the report called for different funding structures and the abolition of corporate public broadcasting as a result of cable channel growth, satellites, and other technology (Engelman 1996, 185). Government spending on public television, which had been robust in the 1960s, was attacked by the Nixon administration as well as by leftist Democrats who felt public television needed to be a more democratized form of communication. Public television's early attempts at independence from both state and market ended with the election of Ronald Reagan, who stressed marketplace solutions.

While most assessments of Black public television have rightly focused on *Black Journal* and *Souls* as radical political platforms of Black Power and the Black Arts Movement, the series *The Great American Dream Machine* is especially relevant to the type of writer/filmmaker that Collins was becoming in the 1970s. According to Greaves, Collins was a film editor on the controversial satirical variety show that aired on PBS from 1971 to 1972. In providing commentary on American life, culture, and politics, *The Great American Dream Machine* presented a combination of short comedy films, musical performances, street interviews, documentaries, and animated shorts. Behind the scenes, its production team included important media stalwarts such as Jack Willis, Sheila Nevins, and A. H. Perlmutter; in front of the camera were stars such as Penny

Marshall, Chevy Chase, Albert Brooks, and Andy Rooney.[11] Unlike her editing jobs for the USIA, which centered on subtle peddling of nationalistic propaganda, the series allowed Collins to hone her magical editing skills. *Dream Machine* had no narrative, host, or restrictions on genre or form, and by editing it, Collins learned that editing could be a useful tool for narration.

June Givanni's "A Curator's Conundrum: Programing 'Black Film' in 1980s–1990s Britain" highlights how, outside the United States, institutional support and infrastructures ensured a time when "television, the industry unions, and local government" worked together to develop independent cinema via Black filmmakers workshops and showcased the output on Channel 4, a UK public-service television station (Givanni 2004, 61). Givanni goes so far as to assert that the vision was so expansive that it "embraced notions of 'Third Cinema,' cinemas of resistance, cinemas that existed in spite of social and economic or political pressure. They all seemed to have a common and shared position: not only to tell stories of experiences excluded from the agendas of Hollywood/Bollywood and European cinema, but also to find ways of subverting the conventions of filmmaking to serve their own specific project in storytelling" (62).

Notably, Givanni observes that this did not eliminate challenges and tensions regarding audience expectations around race and ethnicity. Still, in the United Kingdom, third cinema was doing extraordinary work challenging the ideological and economic interests of the Western film industry; such a vision for television was consistently being undermined in the United States by those who feared that the mission of public television and film was politically too left leaning and not fiscally worth the risk. As Greaves bluntly stated of his purpose in working for public television and against the grain of commercial, "As an Afro-American film and TV producer, I, for one, haven't time to be either entertained or entertaining. . . . [Black producers] must develop programming which prepares the minority community for assuming the responsibilities of leadership a sick society is forcing upon them" (Greaves 81, 1970). A desire to align with third cinema was missing from Black filmmaking and public television before Greaves, but his approach to filmmaking as enlightenment was being taken up elsewhere, too. It was an issue that one filmmaker and professor tried to address with the founding of the Black Filmmaker Foundation and its publication of significant research reports on Black filmmaking and public television.

As Warrington Hudlin and George P. Cunningham (1978), codirectors of the Black Filmmaker Foundation, wrote in "Black Filmmakers, Black Audiences, and Public Television: An Examination of Issues and Options for the Future," public television, with its proposed mission to serve the public good, had failed not only Black independent filmmakers but also American art and culture more generally. The entire document was a scathing critique of public television and Carnegie II. Hudlin was an up-and-coming independent filmmaker who had produced and directed the critically acclaimed documentaries *Black at Yale* and *Street Stories*, which were aired on WNET via its Independent Focus series. Cunningham was chair of Africana studies at Brooklyn College (CUNY). Recognizing the ways in which commercial television and film of the 1970s had produced Black sitcoms and movies, Hudlin and Cunningham noted, "Public television has not paid enough attention to developing, caring for, and exposing the artist as an American, much less the artist as a Black or as a Hispanic. The problem here is very complicated and centered around the ideas of defining American culture" (Hudlin and Cunningham 1978, 3). They also took issue with public television's support of white filmmakers and their visions of Black life and culture: "Many Black independents describe the Black subject-white filmmaker phenomenon as media colonization" (5). The report and the Black Filmmaker Foundation showcased a necessary relationship between film education and filmmaking for Black independent cinema going into the 1980s. This relationship was one that Collins consistently utilized to her advantage as a Black woman filmmaker whose vision for Black film and filmmaking was in stark contrast to that of previous Black filmmakers, because it did not court commercial tastes or covet the Black audiences who consumed commercial films.

Years later, Collins would tell Phyllis Klotman that not even the offer of a coveted producer job for a major television network could persuade her from her path as an independent filmmaker whose mission was shaped by space, not the public sphere:

> I don't really feel that whatever creative work that is going to come out of me will come out successfully if I have to work off other people's formulas.... I might presumably be producing ... television drama.... I don't think I would have ever gotten the chance to direct at all; I would have never gotten the chance to write my own scripts. I don't think that other avenues would have been open to do any of the films I've done at all.... And so to that degree I consider it a necessity that I do it independently. And I can't imagine ever veering from that. (Klotman 1984, video)

With this refusal, Collins outlines what constitutes independent filmmaking for her. She also, through a practice of not refusing teaching jobs in the same way, underlines how teaching filmmaking can structure the nature of independent filmmaking.

TEACHING THE VISION OF OUR MINDS

When her first original screenplay could not be made into a film, Collins was discouraged. She placed her filmmaking dream aside and began writing plays. Several years later, when film study was becoming an academic subject of interest, City College would pay her to be one of the few Black women to teach screenwriting and film theory courses. Her academic credentials in French cinema as well as her production experiences as an editor for public television allowed her to make a living. As she would note in the late 1970s, while also making her own films she came to teach "with an incredible direct efficiency. Tolerate no lateness, no unnecessary absenteeism, refuse any extra-curricular involvement."[12] It also allowed her to continue developing her philosophy about what film should do.

In the public sphere, teaching is often framed as an occupation in which knowledge is both transferred and produced. In *The Oxford Handbook of Film and Media Studies*, Warren Buckland's chapter "Film and Media Studies Pedagogy" delves into the teaching of film and media studies in higher education. Seeking to address pedagogy debates in Britain and the United States, Buckland notes a schism between traditional views of teaching (the professor-as-expert trains students to be active critics and to see film as a force of social change) and progressive ones (the teacher centers student experiences of film and media as expertise and emphasizes the positive and pleasurable aspects of film). He also introduces a distinction between surface and deep learning, and analyzes both print and digital film textbooks (Buckland 2008, 528). Yet film studies education as centered in a state apparatus of higher education cannot be disconnected from debates about the function of film and the public sphere.

As practitioners who are also artists know, teaching an art and practicing an art are two very different things. The processes rely on different cognitive, embodied, and psychic elements; simply put, they require the flexing of different mental muscles. Teaching requires an engagement with present and future audiences who may or may not be open to a transfer of knowledge. Yes, teaching can manifest radical visions for self and the world, but it has been understood solely as an endeavor in which a subject or disciplinary object is passed along. Collins intuitively understood the liberatory value of teaching, even if she could not articulate it during interviews. She admitted to Klotman, "Commitment to teaching, for some reason, has remained with me in spite of my heart being very much committed to making films. But the teaching is still very much a part of it" (1984, video). However, what should be gleaned from Collins's understanding of teaching, film, and pedagogy is that the act and experience of teaching are themselves a form of knowledge about light, space, and dimensionality; that is, teaching is about enlightenment. The familiar refrain and image associated with cinematic representations of death and the afterlife often show a character going into the light, after being told to "go into the light."

Collins's explorations of what constitutes life, the representation of life, and the afterlife were not about the life and death of the corporeal body; rather, they pose a question about enlightenment, the birth of ideas, and the translation of creative energy. Could she generate enough light with filmmaking alone for the cultivation of new ideas and idioms in multiple spaces? Merleau-Ponty linked the beginnings of human life to his era's philosophies of visual aesthetics and painting: "We say that a human being is born the moment when something that was only virtually visible within the mother's body becomes at once visible for us and for itself. The painter's vision is an ongoing birth" (1968, 129). He was building on Max Ernst's surrealist notion of the inner life/world/imagination of the artist, specifically Ernst's insistence that, "just as the role of the poet . . . consists in writing under the dictation of what is being thought, of what articulates itself in him, the painter's role is to circumscribe and project what is making itself seen within himself" (Ernst 1960, 34). Teaching is a performative and visual art, and Collins's discussion of teaching film makes this obvious. She provides a synchronous model of vision and knowledge production based outside Western sciences or the discourses of job trades.

To understand cinema literacy and film pedagogy outside of an institution, film manifestos must be produced and placed on par with both film theory and film production. Although the manifesto is not the only form in which questions about film's relationships to the public sphere and to pedagogy can be engaged, the medium's function of dismantling the very codes and systems being manufactured by seeking out or creating new forms is necessary practice for avoiding the replication of colonizing regimes. In their articulation of revolutionary cinema, Fernando Solanas and Octavio Getino wrote: *"I make the revolution; therefore I exist.* This is the starting point for the disappearance of fantasy and phantom to make way for living human beings" (Solanas and Getino 2014, 240; italics in the original). Collins learned that through teaching, she could use film to revolutionize genres of the human and recover ancient modes of knowledge, making use of light and space.

Of Collins, former student Rebecca Williams noted, "We didn't know a whole lot about Kathy. . . . We knew she had studied in Paris. . . . She was unlike any Black woman I had ever met in my life."[13] Williams, now an English professor at Essex Community College and a politician, met Collins in 1979 when she enrolled in her "Introduction to Filmmaking" course. She would go onto to take production courses and work on *Losing Ground* with Collins in 1981. Williams described Collins as a teacher who ensured that students experienced both rigorous classes in the day and film production at night, so as to cultivate a film community that "was very much like family."

Ironically, as Collins told Klotman, "When I first started teaching film, I don't think I knew anything about teaching film. I knew a great deal about editing." She continued, "When I first came to City University it was a young department, we were all trying to figure out what film was in terms of teaching it, and of course the history and the aesthetic courses were the easiest to teach because you could go back to the history of cinema and build them on that—but the production courses were generally very sloppy. And the students would take a course, in let's say 8 mm cinema, then they'd take a production course in 16, but there was no thread going through all these classes" (Klotman, 1984). Nevertheless, by the time Collins made her first two films, she had already been developing an approach and methodology for film based on storytelling and language.

In the video recording of the Howard University lecture, we see Collins as Howard film students may have seen her—and as her own film students saw her. She wears a white blouse, with silver earrings dangling, fluorescent lights and sunlight reflecting off her jewelry; her hands are constantly moving as she explains herself and her work. She was all light in motion: wavelengths of enlightenment and particles of creative energy beckoning the students to "come into the light." Film editor and teacher Susan Korda, Collins's former student, aptly captures Collins's pedagogical presence: "She was this kind of icon. She was lovely, delicately built. She had this wonderful smile and laugh, but she was a hard-ass."[14] Williams agreed with Korda that Collins was "tough" both theoretically and practically (in both film theory and film production), but noted that Collins refused students' elevation of her as an authority and higher power. Williams recalls her repeatedly saying to them, "I'm not a mentor." She seems to have wanted to refuse a mantle and pedestal that could have impeded students' growth or her own evolution as a filmmaker.

In the lecture video, after Collins is introduced to the Howard film students, she notes that her talk was advertised as bringing in the "lowest-budget independent filmmaker around," someone who could tell students the "secrets of how to make film stock out of fishes and loaves. . . . It is not a miracle I can hope to pull off" (Collins 1984). She continues, "In order to get at how I think about making movies at a low budget, I have to be able to give you the theory . . . the narrative theory behind which or that supports my reasons for making movies." These words are crucial to understanding the personal manifesto that directed Collins's filmmaking away from the publics of film and filmmaking and toward filmmaking as a private and personal configuration of space, toward an inner space absent in the commodification and industry of the art. It is a vision manifested to address technological innovation, the impact of integration on film viewing and filmmaking, and the accessibility of various materials to be adapted to screen. For example, when Collins discusses technology and African Americans, she speaks of a community intimidated by technology: "It is not that difficult to pick up a pen and write, to stay within a tradition and pick up an instrument, or to deal with painting. It is very hard to face the gigantic technological achievement—which can be painted white—of this society which is film, video, the computerized technologies that come out of the handling of image and sound. We as Black people have a reluctance to come to terms with true technology—technophobia. To do good movies you have to solve the technological problems. It is a tough industry" (Franklin 35, 2015).

Her earlier statement perfectly accounted for white racist structures' impact on Black representation. Yet, when speaking of technology, Collins notes Black communities' vexed relationship to technology. Such words seem harsh, but they are instructional and critical feedback in an era when they are not altogether untrue. It took decades for filmmaking to be elevated to the upper echelons of Black cultural politics in the way that theater, poetry, and art had been. Some of this resistance was about the costs of equipment and production. In addition to her comments to the Howard students about financing films, the many grant applications Collins submitted throughout her career demonstrated that technology related to film was far more expensive than picking up a pen, pencil, or paintbrush. Collins's comments arise from her experiences as a student, teacher, and editor of film during the 1970s and 1980s. Other than Howard University, few Black institutions were fully dedicated to producing literacy about film and film technology during this era. Collins's comment is certainly an audacious signal of the need for film education and literacy in Black communities. Nevertheless, teaching film made it possible for Collins to address what she perceived as Black technophobia. As Williams and Korda both noted, Collins often used her position at CCNY to ensure that students had access to technology for making their own films.

Teaching film also seems to have clarified how different Collins was as an independent filmmaker. For example, in talking with Klotman, Collins recalls her early days as a film professor at CCNY, developing film production classes:

> What I did with another teacher, a woman named Jo Tavner who was
> there at the same time. . . . And we actually sat down for several months
> and thought out how you should introduce film in such a way that
> students could gain a systematic sense of it as a language and then experi-
> ment in their films with the language. So you would never say to a student:
> go out and shoot and then we'll look at your footage. You would say to
> a student: we're going to examine the frame. Now you're going to shoot
> thinking about the frame or thinking about one concept pertaining to the
> frame. (Klotman 1984)

Whether she was teaching a lower-level introductory course or an upper-level
capstone course, or spearheading the Senior Festival at City College—a year-
long course that met four times a week—Collins believed in helping students
to become fluent in one cinematic language and then allowing them to autono-
mously discover their own cinematic language. According to former students
Williams and Korda, Collins required senior festival students to complete
a one-on-one script analysis session for two months, workshop scenes with
the class, participate in an acting and improvisation workshop, study camera
and lighting works, and analyze shots of final locations—all before beginning
shooting.

An analysis of Collins's teaching situates her work as still necessary and
relevant to our current understandings of visual media, visual technology, human being, and world-making. She attests,

> What we ended up doing was duplicating the process by which one actu-
> ally experiences film when you're watching it, but on an unconscious
> level. . . . So now, actually what I do when I teach . . . is, I try and work the
> students into a grasp of a language. . . . And the more sophisticated they
> can become about apprehending that language, the more critical they can
> become when it's used sloppily, when it's used incorrectly. . . . And there-
> fore, they become their own best critic. (Klotman 1984)

In our interview, Williams reflected that her exchanges with Collins were far
from coddling or nurturing, especially when it came to the social reality of being an aspiring Black woman filmmaker in the 1980s. After applying to Picker
as a sophomore and not being accepted, Williams was upset and attributed the
loss to racial politics. She noted that Collins was critical of her position and her
film project at the time, saying:

> She [Collins] said, "Look you're either going to make a good film or you
> don't make a film. You think that I don't understand your struggle. You

think it's been easy. . . . You know nobody's going to listen to you if you
ascribe your struggles, which are partly social but also aesthetic struggles,
just to race. Nobody's going to listen to you. . . ." She said the work just
wasn't good enough and that if you really want to do this you just can't
give up.[15]

As Williams learned when she faced adversity in film school and film competi-
tions, the problem is not that there is no space for Black film; the problem is
that there is little training in seeing all the space that exists for the creation
and development in Black film. Collins's words to Williams are telling given
Collins's early experience with trying to get *Women, Sisters, and Friends* made,
and her fortitude in making *The Cruz Brothers* and *Losing Ground* years later.
Would such words from a mentor have made a difference in her own trajectory?
Did she regret giving up too soon? Collins's words seems to have made a difference, as Korda noted of their senior year in Picker Institute's student festival
competition: Vasquez took first prize, Williams second prize, and Korda third
prize their senior year. Collins was consistently teaching her students to place
the camera up to a different set of eyes—or, as Ousmane Sembène wrote, "At
the moment the eyes of the body closed, the eyes of the mind were opened"
([1960] 1995, 12).

Korda explained that she "learned a lot from [Collins] about teaching," and
recalled that most of Collins's classes included meditation and breathing exercises: "She would have people meditate in class, and I think that the exercise . . .
breathing meditation . . . and then [they would] go into the first scene of your
film. It was a technique about bringing life into the piece . . . a way of exploration." Classroom exercises also featured one-on-one time with Collins, scene
immersion, and acting workshops with actors such as Duane Jones. Collins
understood filmmaking as having a metaphysical function far beyond what
Western humanist thought could conceive. Williams related that Collins had
no qualms about assigning students to visit psychics or about doing her own
readings for them, seeing these readings as personal and professional experiences that could shape modes of vision and perception. All these exercises were
meant to establish a different sensory relationship with the world and to utilize
filmmaking to support a new metaphysics.

Collins's film pedagogy opposes Louis Lumière's claim that "cinema is an invention without a future"[16] and asserts that we need not accept the metaphysics
that produces such a statement. As I have speculated, cinema is most certainly
an invention with many futures. Though Lumière may have been observing
that the invention of cinema does not have to be predetermined or have one

particular future, the statement already includes a specific point of view, a system designating visual technology to certain proscriptions or opposition to proscriptions. Unequivocally, the teaching of film, cinema, and media inside and outside institutional state apparatuses influences those futures.

STUDENTS: CINEMATIC INVENTION WITH A FUTURE

There exists no better example of how reciprocity in learning benefits teacher and student than the collaboration between Collins and her former student Ronald K. Gray. Gray was cinematographer and coproducer on *The Cruz Brothers and Miss Malloy* and *Losing Ground*, and Collins said of him, "Ronald is probably more responsible for my becoming a filmmaker than anybody. He was a student of mine at City College and he would get angry at me for all the work I did on other people's films, saying that if we just got a little bit of money we could make a movie" (Nicholson 1988–89, 10). In DVD extras of *Losing Ground*, Gray notes the serendipitous learning experience. Gray would go on to become a noted filmmaker, cinematographer, editor, and teacher. Like Gray, writer David Nicholson would highlight Collins's impact on him after an interview, stating: "the hours I spent with Kathleen Collins Prettyman affected me profoundly," and "I knew she would always be one of my mentors" (Nicholson 1988–89, 7). However, this chapter's closing interest in symbiopsychotaxiplasm directs me from these more publicly acknowledged student-teacher-mentor collaborations to a less-acknowledged relationship of reciprocity and futurity—that between Joseph B. Vasquez and Kathleen Collins. Vasquez serves as the inspiration for my speculative afterlife-writing at the beginning of this chapter. Though both Williams and Korda mention Vasquez as a film classmate and identify the possible mutual influence between Vasquez and Collins,[17] the materiality of such a connection is made vague and ephemeral due to their early deaths and the lack of attention their work has received in film studies.

A young Puerto Rican filmmaker, Vasquez played the student cinematographer/ cameraman, as opposed to the filmmaker, in *Losing Ground*. Twenty years after Collins completed her first script and failed to make it into a film, her former student saw the release and critical and commercial success of his film *Hangin' with the Homeboys* from New Line Cinema in 1991. Though Vasquez had been shooting 8 mm movies since age twelve, his time at City College had been enriching. He graduated from CCNY in 1983. According to Williams and Korda, Collins had some influence on the young filmmaker. His first film, *Street Story*, was made for $30,000, and his second film, *Bronx Story*, was made for $360,000. After *Bronx Story* and *Hangin' with the Homeboys*, New Line signed him to do two more pictures (M. Harris 1991). The opening scene of

Hangin' with the Homeboys features Mario Joyner (Tom), Doug E. Doug (Willie), Nestor Serrano (Vinnie), and John Leguizamo (Johnny) in one of their earliest features. On a subway train, Tom, Johnny, and Vinnie malevolently approach Willie in front of a group of white onlookers who become afraid of the men. After threats are exchanged, the young men throw Willie on the ground as if to beat him up, before erupting in laughter at the fearful reactions of the white riders. Tom enunciates in a faux British accent, "Ladies and Gentleman, thank you for attending another performance of ghetto theater." In the midst of what was the renaissance of Black independent filmmaking, the so-called New Black Wave era—in which films such as *Do the Right Thing, House Party, Hollywood Shuffle, Boyz n the Hood,* and *Straight Out of Brooklyn* courted Black audiences—Vasquez's film told a complicated and humorous story about internalized racism in Puerto Rican culture as well as divisions between Dominicans, Puerto Ricans, and African Americans. However, as he once intimated to *Fresh Air*'s Terry Gross, he refused to model himself in the mold of Spike Lee (Vasquez 1991).

On further reflection, *Hangin' with the Homeboys* showcases the influence of Collins, whose filmmaking career centered on not mythologizing individuals. In the opening scene, Vasquez makes clear his intent to refuse the rhetoric of Black urban life that was being constructed and instead to deal with anti-Blackness and intraracial conflicts, as Collins had done years before him.

More recently, the production and release of *The House That Jack Built* (2013), a film whose screenplay was written by Vasquez, demonstrates why a brief conversational mention of Black film genealogy in this regard becomes important. The plot of the film is aligned with the themes of identity, domesticity, and interiority of masculinity that Collins takes up in her film *The Cruz Brothers and Miss Malloy* and in her noteworthy play *The Brothers*. As Jack, the film's protagonist, tells viewers via voice-over at the beginning, "All I ever wanted was my family to be happy. . . . There are few things that a man loves. . . . That's his home. That's his family." An independent domestic drama about a Puerto Rican family in the Bronx featuring a drug dealer's romantic notions of family, alongside critiques of machismo, toxic masculinity, and homophobia against Afro-Latina lesbians, would have been a hard sell for critics of the 1990s, who were prone to pigeonholing films into the genres of New Queer Cinema, LA Rebellion, or New Jack Cinema. Vasquez, too, was out of place and out of time. Unfortunately, like his mentor, Vasquez died young, at the age of thirty-three.[18] What he left behind also has its own afterlife, and it deserves to be taught and shown.

The fictional Collins—her school, her cinema, and her manifesto—imagined at the beginning of this chapter is very much based on the real Collins, whose teaching and pedagogy overcame the tensions in representation and filmmaking by introducing her ideas of freedom and second sight to discussions of the public and commercial impulses in Black independent filmmaking. With a vision of film centered on alternative modes of seeing and distribution—that is, on disseminating cinematic knowledge via a unique classroom space as well as through movie theaters, television, network, or cable—Collins understood and practiced education and pedagogy as an untapped form of distribution as well as an expansion of cinematic space that could resolve the dilemma of representation politics and access to technology in Black filmmaking. Further, the expanse that she offers insists that filmmaking is not only a skill, trade, or art for representation; it is a space in which the unification and interconnectedness of what goes unseen in the universe can be actualized in the simultaneity of production and observation of light as it encounters Blackness to produce another world with many futures.

In examining the relationships between three major factors that Collins approaches in her films and writings—reciprocity in pedagogy to provide depth and futurity; inner vision to counter the veil; and use of space and light as enlightenment—I assert that she escapes and overcomes several limitations of US film and film studies. Collins's beginnings as a filmmaker were shaped by multiple experiences, and examining her teaching career alongside her time as an editor in educational television reveals how she came to have a philosophy about film editing and directing that centered on decolonization, despite her deliberate veering away from the Afrocentric politics usually ascribed to decolonial aesthetics and art. The late arrival of an audience for Collins's scripts and films is a failure of publics and counterpublics regarding race, gender, and aesthetic openess. The afterlife of her creative and productive moments in the classroom provides a blueprint for fifth dimension cinema. As I explain in the next chapter, with the making of her first film—*The Cruz Brothers and Miss Malloy*, in the interim of a fifth dimension cinema called for in this chapter, Collins practiced a type of cinematic marronage so relevant for current movements centered on anti-Blackness, visual technology, and freedom.

MOCAMBO LIFE

Scene 4, *The Afterlives of Kathleen Collins*

Long Take: Manifesto—Dawn

V.O.

Vous êtes plus libre que vous le pensiez!
You are freer than you think!

Nous ne mourrons pas d'une matière noire.
We will not die a black matter.

    l'adapter
    Adapt it

éboniser la vie
ebonize life

Vivons dans la matière noire!
    Let us live in black matter!

vivons comme de la matière noire!
Let us live as black matter!

Manifeste cinématographique de marronage
Cinematic Marronage Manifesto

CHAPTER FOUR

CINEMATIC MARRONAGE

COLLINS, IN ANOTHER OF HER afterlives, leaves to worlds of Black people an infinite treatment for the unforeseen psychological ills that occur in the present and afterlife of racializing surveillance that refuses to let Black people picnic, play, watch birds, vote, sleep, drive, sit, learn, or any other . . . living . . . while Black verbiage. Adaptation. Though the excerpts from the fictional manifesto are not the words of Kathleen Collins, they are adapted from ideas presented in Collins's lectures and interviews as well as adaptation decisions she made in creating her first film, *The Cruz Brothers and Miss Malloy* (1980). They are written in two of the languages that she spoke, in addition to the other, nontextual language that she sought and achieved fluency in, with its own grammar and dimensionality. The imagined manifesto about adaptation is also inspired by the militancy of Aimé Césaire's "Le Verb Marronner," Fernando Solanas and Octavio Getino's "Toward a Third Cinema," and Jorge Sanjinés's "Problems of Form and Content in Revolutionary Cinema." These three texts provide a contextualization for uncovering the quiet militancy and artistic resistance shaping Collins's first film, an adaptation of Henry Roth's novel *The Cruz Chronicle*. When Collins made *The Cruz Brothers and Miss Malloy* for $5,000, it was not in the context of Black independent cinema, which from the 1970s to the 1990s was often classified as an oppositional space to commercial Hollywood. Collins's film, rather, was part of a less-discussed movement of public television that is proving to be as significant to the history of Black filmmaking in the United States as independent film movements. The film's one screening was on PBS.

Adaptation was a central component of Collins's career. In her Black Film Center/Archive interview with Phyllis Klotman (1984), Collins reveals that, like

James Baldwin, she was raised in a religious household and that cinema as an idea had not occurred to her until she took an elective course about the adaptation of literature into film during her studies in Paris. It was in this course that she began to see how to keep cinema from being the violent form Baldwin articulates, to envision adapting literature to film as "a process of translation," and to realize that she had a good eye for watching film. When placed in conversation with her decision to adapt a novel for her first film, Collins's instructional statements about film can be transformed into a manifesto about adaptation as an abolitionist genre and a practice of cinematic marronage. Adaptation provides a way to address the tensions and limitations of representational politics in regards to race and gender, while also presenting universal themes of an artistic piece and expanding the possible ways to translate the inner world of a character in relation to those themes without necessarily having to privilege external social reality.

Because Collins, like so many other artists of her time, believed that "Black people in America are classic outsiders" (Collins 1984), she used the camera and film to illuminate Black experience beyond mythological othering—something that is important to our current era's need to adapt film and visual technologies away from the dehumanization that occurs in the surveillance and policing modalities. Sylvia Wynter's examination of the police acronym N.H.I. (no humans involved) considers the impact of such dehumanization and its originating source as tied to a metaphor of vision and hierarchies of difference. She asks: "Where does this 'inner eye,' which leads the society to choose mass incarceration in dealing with the post-industrial new poor ... come from? Why is this eye so intricately bound up with that code, so determinant of our collective behaviors, to which we have given the name race?" (Wynter 1994, 47). Linking Wynter's discussion of police brutality with Collins's strategies of film adaptation can reveal to students of Black film and Black studies a starting point for thinking about film's use in cinematically imagining alternatives to the gratuitous reproduction of carcerality and surveillance on screen. Can the manipulation of space and light, or the movement of humans through space and light, help us transcend the logic of N.H.I.—a logic produced by an inner eye that fears darkness—so that we can adapt technology in more vital ways?

Collins's films might not ever be viewed as connected to Black Power or the Black Arts Movement, but their underlying focus on depicting outsider experience continues to be relevant to the social justice efforts of contemporary Black communities. She explicitly announced, "No one is going to refuse me the right to explore my experiences of life ... and the humanism of that experience ... is the last hurdle we have to transcend" (Collins 1984). As I argue later, *The Cruz Brothers and Miss Malloy* implemented the concepts of communal creativity and freedom as marronage, thereby eliminating the impact of carceral imagination and a cinema of policing on her non-white characters.

Though Collins's move to France after her involvement in the Civil Rights movement was in pursuit of a postgraduate degree in literature, she learned there how to edit, adapt, and make original films outside the Hollywood and US film school systems. Not unlike William Greaves's training in Canada, this training outside the United States would impact her filmmaking. The experience was important in shaping the vision and philosophy she would develop for her films. Césaire's oft-cited poem "Le verbe marronner" (The verb to maroon), written in response to Haitian poet René Despestre, details the links between poetry and revolution and provides an entrée to how Collins's filmmaking was shaped by the Black Arts Movement and Black thought outside the US film system as well as in it:

> *C'est un problème assurément très grave*
> *des rapports de la poésie et de la Révolution*
> *le fond conditionne la forme*
> *et si l'on s'avisait aussi du détour dialectique*
> *par quoi la forme prenant sa revanche*
> *comme un figuier maudit étouffe le poème*
>
> It's assuredly a very serious problem
> the relations between poetry and Revolution
> content conditions form
> and if one took thought also for the dialectical detour
> by which form exacting its revenge
> smothers the poem like a cursed fig tree.[1]

Césaire provides an anticolonial approach to revolution and literary art forms that we can adapt to Hollywood filmmaking and its segregationist approaches to film and cinema. As Gregson Davis's translation and engagement with Césaire's work explains, "In inventing a verb, 'to maroon' (*marronner*), based on the noun denoting slaves who escaped from the New World plantation to live in autonomous communities, the speaker hoists aloft the banner of artistic freedom and resistance to cultural totalitarianism" (Césaire 1997, 17). Césaire's engagement with both surrealism and Négritude, as Davis notes, was about resistance and form, politically and artistically. He understands that prior to the very physical acts attributed to maroons (both *petit* and *grand*) of flight and survival, a mental and spiritual process of flight and survival happens.

Years later, Neil Roberts, in his book *Freedom as Marronage*, expands Césaire's focus on form, genre, and poetics to dissect the sociopolitical attributes of this move and provide a definition: "Marronage is a total refusal of the enslaved condition. Interpreting maroons' systematic opposition means developing alternative imagined models of freedom through the process of intellectual marronage (*le marronage intellectual*), an epistemological blueprint functioning as a corollary to the enactment of actual flight" (Roberts 2015, 13). For Collins, the imagination and practice of freedom as marronage occur in her escape from the structures of Hollywood filmmaking, centered on whiteness and white supremacy, as well as from those of early twentieth-century Black filmmaking, centered on uplift and aesthetics that rely on documentary, realism, respectability, normativity, and Black authenticity. Collins was insistent on changing the grammar of the cinematic language available to Black filmmakers as well as the forms and genres, the tropes of freedom.

I choose the term *cinematic marronage* for Collins's practice of film adaptation because the category of Black independent filmmaking does not adequately capture her refusal to accept the psychological and mental colonization produced by the US film system, sustained by Jim Crow techniques of segregation and characterized by physical apartheid and psychic apartheid (in genres, forms, spectacle, etc.), as well as the economic disenfranchisement caused by the Hollywood industry. It does not sufficiently connote the grueling spiritual flight from a tradition of filmmaking and film technologies manufactured to enact epistemic violence on Black bodies so as to sustain settler colonialism and its white supremacist institutions. It does not adequately attest, as described in the previous chapter, to how teaching film studies and working in public television became places for maroons to practice intellectual and artistic freedom. Collins, however, acknowledges this. Though she does not use the exact language of cultural imperialism, aesthetic empire, or institutional structure, she does acknowledge the very detrimental foundations of US filmmaking: "Film is the largest, most powerful, most potent myth. And we have not thought about how that myth applies to us [Black people]. We don't believe it applies to us. So, we can't believe ourselves as filmmakers when we talk about John Ford, Huston, Bette Davis, John Wayne, and so forth. Hollywood is the one mythical world that America created! The Gods and Goddesses of America are film stars! They're the Greek mythology of America, and we don't know who we are in that mythology" (Franklin 2015, 35). Collins's critique begins where all good decolonial projects begin: with assessing the role of myth in particular societies. Collins broke sacred ground with *The Cruz Brothers*, making what some critics classified as a non-Black film, seeing it only as a film about a white woman and three Puerto Rican brothers, as opposed to an African Diasporic concept of Black people dealing with white flight. Collins takes flight from myths of Blackness in Hollywood film and from the burden of monolithic cultural representation in Black communities.

Her cinematic marronage also incorporates a concerted effort to think of the craft and technology of film (and specific elements and processes therein) not simply as tools to express or visually represent freedom but as a technology that could itself be a form of marronage: "Marronage is a multidimensional, constant act of flight that involves . . . four interrelated pillars: distance, movement, property, and purpose" (Roberts 2015, 9). In sum, where white institutions and state apparatuses make film a tool to eroticize violence, Collins understands it as a tool of eroticism that challenges state and individual acts of violence. Editing and adaptation might be described as artistic and aesthetic practices about distance, movement, property, and purpose. Though many people might not write it this way, it is clear that this is how Collins broadly thought about adaptation and editing.

When interviewer Oliver Franklin notes that Collins is a writer and queries her about her choice not to use her own scripts for her first film, she offers a reply that showcases how adaptation becomes the cinematic practice of "to maroon": "I would like to do my own work, but I thought it was dangerous, before understanding the distance one needs from one's works, to translate literature into film. So, I started with another work I admired with similar themes and problems, and yet by instinct I would have some distance because it wasn't my work" (Franklin 2015, 33). Her first film provides the distance and movement with characters whose experiences of gender, race, class, and nation differ from her own life experience and cinema practices, but it also takes on purpose in modes especially significant for Black life and living, as discussed later. Camera angles, light, filters, and location selections provide individual moments of flight and escape for the greater journey that Collins's pictures entail. Moreover, her belief in distance in the work needs to be juxtaposed with white male filmmaking, which centers itself in every film, even when the historical and social experience being filmed is not white or masculine.

I choose to position Collins's cinematic marronage (fleeing Hollywood cinema) as flight into black/dark matter, linked with the positive connotation of the term *blacken*. While to blacken, or ebonize, according to Western and European dictionaries, has numerous negative connotations, they all agree that the terms connote "to deepen." Bringing metaphysical depth to scopic visuality, as described in accounts from her students, was a major element of Collins's film pedagogy. Adaptation became a primary way that Collins could seek out and find new life, deepening or ebonizing other folks' work to produce an entirely new world or galaxy. She may not have invented a verb, as Césaire did, but she did work to ebonize—that is, blacken—her subject matter appositively and to deepen what the film industry could do for minoritized subjects.

As I further argue in this chapter, a cinematic marronage manifesto is necessary in the current context of the political movement Black Lives Matter as well as more fascist cultural movements such as the cinema of policing underwritten by the long-existing carceral imagination. A cinematic marronage manifesto speaks to the necessity that Black film studies consider the decolonization of cinematic film technologies in issues of surveillance, police states, and Black bodies. This manifesto is about genre innovation and technological innovation. Both the cinema of policing and the carceral imagination have exacerbated the dehumanization of Black people and the increased killing of Black people by state agents. This chapter does not intend to rehearse or provide a broad overview of carceral studies; rather, it seeks to direct Black film studies, via Collins's example, away from the cultural moorings of the carceral state and imagination.

GENRE AND PREGENERIC MYTHS: CINEMA OF POLICING AND CARCERAL IMAGINATION

When Carlos Alvarez wrote his film manifesto arguing for a radical cinema in Colombia—one that could be carried out by filmmakers, farmers, and other laborers—he did so not only to challenge class structures but also to assert film as a militant tool of resistance to challenge the state violence arising from a carceral imagination. He stated, "Nor will it be easy if the police and the forces of repression discover that this cinema is not agreeable to them. It is not practical to have to run weighted down with a heavy projector. This will be an everyday part of film making, and it must be taken into account starting now. And solutions must be found" (Alvarez 2014, 390).

The end of the twentieth century brought a technological solution to issues of mobility and film equipment; it is not necessary for rebels to physically be on the run with a heavy projector or 8 mm and 16 mm film reels. But the police and forces of repression remain a threat when cinema or filming is not agreeable to them. The dangers of police harassment and brutality have not been curbed by technology. The role of systemic and institutional state violence in this is apparent, but less obvious is the role of cultural representations of law and justice that bolster the "necessity" of institutional forces. Representation of police and law enforcement in cinema is a problem whose roots stem from a larger assumption that law enforcement and surveillance are natural, an absolute truth, that must be imagined when one constructs human cities, builds humane societies, and protects human rights. For Black filmmakers on the run, it is not practical to have this weight to carry. Applying the words of Alvarez to Black filmmakers, radical cinema must take into account the everyday fugitivity that goes into the making of film as well as the everyday role of freedom as marronage in Black life.

In the twenty-first century, we, the descendants of free and enslaved Africans and Jim Crow survivors, record our murders and deaths and the murders and deaths of others on moving image technology, cameras and mobile devices, engineered for entertainment and communication among human beings across the globe. We, the descendants of free and enslaved Africans and Jim Crow survivors, represent our suffering, trauma, and pain to counter monstrous, dehumanizing, and stereotypical misrepresentation by others. These distorted images are distributed to movie theaters, streamed and broadcast online and on the news, and bootlegged on a global scale. Body cameras, dash cams, and street cameras meant to surveille and protect, a pseudo-form of automated law and order, instead record acts of violence, murder, and death. This panoptic can be turned on and off, edited, distorted, or lost. What those in power do with the images depends on a twentieth-century holdover strategy about awareness, consciousness, and evidence suited toward a public sphere meant for a specific genre of the human, a relic of the industrial and information age, that has no intention of evolving into a nonhierarchical form of life.

Black filmmaking and film studies can no longer create in and through this tradition; they must shift to a sense of space not arranged by the public sphere, with its deceased vision of public service and public good. Police brutality videos are a late twentieth-century genre invention attributed to George Holliday's Rodney King video and amateur filmmaking aesthetics. However, this genre has had previous iterations in form, producers, and audience. One might ask how, given Melvin Van Peebles's formidable contestation of police brutality, *Sweet Sweetback's Baadasssss Song* (1971), we have been reduced to recording our murders and deaths at the hands of law enforcers, or making spectacles of them as evidence that will not be used or ignored, without creating a cinema in which transformative justice for those deaths are streamed or storylines representing abolition and the dismantling of inadequate institutions are screened or streamed weekly.

In the era of mass criminalization and the prison abolition movement, we need only start with the problems and failures of life-writing to narrate this particular aspect (state violence) of Black life in print and video. Any presentation of police brutality must consider the political and legislative changes spawned by video as well as explore aesthetic possibilities not seen in twentieth-century films. In detailing the role of individuals in African American communities as both witnesses and participants, Elizabeth Alexander asks, "What do the scenes of communally witnessed violence in slave narratives tell us about the way that text is inscribed in African American flesh" (Alexander 1994, 85). We might ask a similar question about violence witnessed in the carceral state.

Since the Rodney King video, moments of collective spectatorship in Black America have been stuck on a repetitive refrain left over from slavery. As one fictional character, Great Gram, has explained of justice in the Americas, "Because they didn't want to leave no evidence of what they done? so it couldn't be held against them. And I'm leaving evidence. And you got to leave evidence too. And your children got to leave evidence" (G. Jones 1986, 14). In this era, however, the purpose of making evidence is not to simply bear witness to the exploitative nature of carceral society or to demand justice or reparations for those crimes against humanity—or so says Ursa Corregidora, a descendant of Great Gram. We have already held up the evidence on these crimes. As Alexander noted of the King video, "Videotape imprints constructed bodily histories on a jury's consciousness, and, in a national arena amplifies or denies the story an African American body appears to be telling" (Alexander 1994, 96). With this new realist genre of film, then, we must become like the fictional Ursa Corregidora, who refuses Great Gram's request to make evidence with her body, and we must let go of Bayard Rustin's call to be angelic troublemakers, a pivotal civil rights strategy and situated in the white logics of things.[2]

The remainder of this chapter incorporates lessons from Collins's film adaptation of magical realism and pedagogy to explore the ways in which a film without police, prisons, or judicial systems might enunciate resistance to a cinema of policing and the further evolution of the carceral imagination. By contextualizing Collins's *The Cruz Brothers and Miss Malloy* as linked to a divestment from carceral states and societies, I demonstrate how her work proposes that we imagine freedom and care as opposed to safety and protection. By asking her characters—and by extension, her viewers—to reimagine their relationships with one another and their ghosts, Collins insists that a world can be created where freedom and care for others can be exercised without police.

Collins begins *The Cruz Brothers and Miss Malloy* with Victor Cruz and his friends stealing a car in a suburban neighborhood, as the spirit of his dead father warns him to be extra careful since their family is cursed, or they simply have bad luck. The film thus opens with an act of grand larceny, but it ends with a reimagining of a major pregeneric myth of Hollywood cinema, inherited from the common law of the early US empire: the protection of communal property at any cost. Communal property and common law make up the pregeneric myths of many genre narratives in Hollywood film in general, but in crime and action genres in particular. *The Cruz Brothers* is not a film about the carceral state, but the film imagines what it would mean for people throughout the African Diaspora to live beyond the carceral state and the imagination that spawns it. Though her film contains some generic elements from drama, action, and comedy, Collins crafted a maroon genre for her ideal viewer—herself or like-minded folks. Fleeing or not engaging the theme of carcerality while addressing the ills of capitalism and property rights challenges both the carceral imagination and the state.

Given all the work being done in carceral studies, the twentieth century's long proliferation of film genres based on these pregeneric myths can no longer be seen as having neutral or apolitical plots and themes. In Ruth Wilson Gilmore's *Golden Gulag: Prisons, Surplus, Crisis, and Opposition in Globalizing California*, a brilliant appraisal of the prison-industrial complex, Gilmore begins her heartfelt argument for the abolition of prisons with a poetic narrative about light. She opens with a description of a busload of prison abolitionists on their way to a rally to confront state lawmakers about California's prison-industrial complex: "A small group of riders . . . started to count sightings of intensely golden glows that eerily poked depth into the flat blackness. These concentrations of light in farmland are many of California's new prisons" (Gilmore 2007, 4). Gilmore's recognition of how light illuminates the erected structures across the landscape, and therefore reveals a system of labor and death being maintained by a state, insists that prison abolition must also be about moving people through space and light. She describes this as a concern of both perspective and critical imagination. Gilmore examines how the United States advanced beyond obvious codes of racial discrimination, stating that "racism is the state-sanctioned and/or extralegal production and exploitation of group-differentiated vulnerability to premature death. Prison expansion is a new iteration of this theme" (2007, 247).[3] As for this policy's intersection with culture, Caleb Smith's *The Prison and the American Imagination* notes that "state discipline . . . was not only an exercise of power against a condemned body but also a public spectacle with a carefully managed system of meanings and values. Surrounding the act of violence, even shaping it, were symbols of power and subjection, an elaborate poetics of punishment" (Smith 2009, 8).

Others have also dissected the cultural ramifications of carceral imagination. *Carceral Fantasies: Cinema and Prison in Early Twentieth-Century America*, by Alison Griffiths, examines how cultural inventiveness feeds into the carceral fantasies of a necrophilic spectator, asking why we are "fascinated by images of punishment, more extremely, the extinction of life, and how has the popular visual culture throughout the ages catered to this lurid curiosity" (Griffiths

2016, 13). Ruha Benjamin likewise takes up the subject of carceral imagination in her discussion of critical race and science and technology studies, stating that "this conceptual lens is not only applicable to those processes that are directly tied to prisons and police; rather, I propose an expansive understanding of containment that trains scholarly attention to the underside of technoscientific development—who and what are fixed in place—classified, corralled, and/or coerced, to enable innovation?" (Benjamin 2016, 150). Benjamin's questions are important to this chapter's discussion of technology and carceral practices, especially in comprehending how the creative arts can be utilized to produce and support narratives that embolden the underside of technoscientific development.

Filmmaking is a technoscientific development. Upon emancipation and with the advent of new technologies, the slave narrative gave way to newswriting and life-writing for African Americans, while for white Americans, as D. W. Griffith's *The Birth of a Nation* (1915) would show, the modern technology of film became a new tool of propaganda for a US police state based in white supremacy. If Hollywood filmmaking and independent filmmaking descend from Westerns vested in imagining freedom and democracy as the fruits of a Western expansion that depends on Native American genocide, and from domestic dramas that require Black submission and enslavement, then other innovations within the film genre are needed. Though Melvin Van Peebles's *Sweet Sweetback's Baadasssss Song* spawned the new film genre of Blaxploitation, based on political themes and cultural innovation, it was not enough to dismantle and unseat the carceral imagination and a cinema of policing.[4] Though the US film industry may be reluctant to produce films centered on the Ku Klux Klan, Hollywood industries have continued to take the genre inventions in *The Birth of a Nation* and produce a genre of television and film media we might denote as judicial decree or a universe of *Law and Order* shows, spin-offs, and imitators.

Much of the writing on criminality and prisons regarding race, film, and television addresses stereotypes and representations without addressing the genre's underlying purpose. We must instead ask what the Western, crime, and horror genres do—or do not do—with society's notion of moral authority, regardless of how their specific plots or themes deal with race, class, or gender. Debates about race and representation typically call for limited reforms of the film and media industries. In a *Huffington Post* article titled "Hollywood, the Police, and Ourselves: A Shared Responsibility for a Better Future," criminal justice theorists Franklin T. Wilson and Howard Henderson draw links between marginalized individuals' lived experience in police states and representations of Black people in law enforcement or criminal roles in film and television. Much of the article focuses on how casting choices and shows influence how cops and citizens internalize the racialization of particular roles, but it also makes a broader call for change based in the metaphor of casting choices: "Hollywood portrays what we choose to watch on TV and for what we are willing to pay the price of a movie ticket. The police are public servants and they answer to what we demand. Whether you are a Hollywood executive, a corporate sponsor, a progressive Police Chief, or a common Jane or Joe that wants to see a less divided society, we will all play a role in creating a new and better future. If we choose to cast ourselves in that role" (Franklin and Henderson 2016). After setting up a utopic and universal rendering of the public goodness of police, the authors pose several questions, such as: "Would changing the typical formula for police officer and detective roles help change the racial characteristics of who watches such programs and possibly begin to influence who chooses to be a police officer?" The authors unintentionally state what is understood: that Hollywood films and television media serve as propaganda outlets for a sustained police state. They ask, "Do Hollywood depictions, or lack of depictions, enhance or cause misguided expectations of what a career in law enforcement will involve?" and "Do Hollywood depictions, or lack of depictions, play a role in who applies to city, county, state, and federal level law enforcement agencies?" The article's simplistic focus on representation cannot escape the mythical absolute truth of police as a necessary "public good," and such thinking sets the stage for more subtle forms of state repression.

As Jared Sexton argues in "The Ruse of Engagement: Black Masculinity and the Cinema of Policing," answering these questions with more diverse casting choices can be more problematic than empowering: "These various guises of black empowerment, particularly images of black masculinity as state authority, should not be simply contrasted with the associations of illegitimacy, dispossession, and violence that seem to otherwise monopolize the signification of racial blackness. Rather, the former should be understood as an extension of the latter" (Sexton 2009, 39–40). Sexton notes that the casting of actors such as Sidney Poitier, Denzel Washington, and Jamie Foxx as cops becomes a form of anti-Blackness (even in vehicles directed by Black filmmakers such as Antoine Fuqua), especially when we consider not only systemic racism in Hollywood but carceral practices within US society. This "subtext of ongoing black captivity that Fuqua's work can neither transcend nor do without" (Sexton 2009, 60) has been taken up in other Black films that operate outside the cinema of policing, specifically in Black independent filmmaking.

Black filmmakers have made strides in addressing, if not transcending, the subtext of Black captivity. Yet it cannot be enough to locate and applaud these films. We must also ask other questions. What does resistance to police state and police brutality look like in US films, and what are such films allowed to convey about being? Do such films break free from masculinist and patriarchal visions of spectacle, violence, and force? Do they depict the everyday, ordinary, and minor actions of living that mentally clear space to imagine existence beyond the carceral state? Do they rely on the same moral authority that is embedded within the carceral state and carceral imagination? Some of the most powerful Black films about police brutality and violence, while critiquing the police state, maintain this posture. After Sidney Poitier portrayed Mr. Tibbs (*They Call Me Mister Tibbs!*, 1967), his less acclaimed role was as Jason Higgs in the drama *The Lost Man* (1969). The film depicts what happens when, after robbing a bank to help imprisoned Black men, an ex-army lieutenant turned Black militant shoots a cop and goes on the run. Later, Melvin Van Peebles's *Sweet Sweetback's Baadasssss Song* would offer a possible solution to the everyday presence of police brutality in the form of a radical Black Panther Party politics and Blaxploitation aesthetics. Almost twenty years later, in 1989, two films provided divergent approaches to police states: Spike Lee's *Do the Right Thing* and Euzhan Palcy's *A Dry White Season*.

Films about police brutality have become a genre in which a narrative about the morals of individuals (rogue, corrupt, racist, etc.) is imposed onto a narrative about a police state that refuses to acknowledge systemic issues or answer the question of its own organizational necessity. The makers of such films want to return viewers to a trust in the moral authority of objective public institutions, in a world in which moral authority is defined as "trustworthiness to make decisions that are right and good" (Hunter 1991, 119). The problem with such a narrative is that moral authority is a flawed concept, because it never specifies for whom such decisions are good. Arguably, if such fundamental assumptions actually existed in the public spheres of law and justice, a police state would be unnecessary, as would enforced or voluntary segregation. Black and white Hollywood filmmakers, and some independents, have attempted to make Black lives matter on-screen without addressing a question asked by Paula X. Rojas in the title of her essay "Are the Cops in Our Heads and Hearts?" Rojas looks to other world movements, particularly Latin American freedom movements such as Augusto Boal's *Theatre of The Oppressed* (1985) workshop exercise "Cop in the Head" developed in the 1970s. Taking her cue from Boal, Rojas outlines ways to "identify the cops in our heads and hearts, [and] release us from the US-centric tunnel vision, and expand our dreams of possibility"

(Rojas 2007, 213). Films that do not relieve themselves of this incessant narrative may exude the precarity and unsustainable energy of the first militant posturing, but they are unable to address the central question, Are the police in our heads and hearts?

Certainly, this is the case in Lee's and Palcy's films, both of which feature political controversies rooted in police states. *Do the Right Thing* takes up the issue of police brutality against African Americans—specifically, the riots that ensue when the character Radio Raheem is killed by the New York Police Department. Its moral narrative is delivered via Da Mayor's (Ossie Davis) line to Mookie: "Always do the right thing." The film's ambivalence about what that might be—whether it's the blaring soundtrack of "Fight the Power" or the outright riot that ensues—highlights how moral authority, when contextualized within the realities of different film audiences, can be controversial. Some reviews accused Lee of wanting to incite violence among Black audiences, which put Black viewers and critics, along with Lee himself, face-to-face with the film industry's limited carceral imagination.

Even when a film is critically praised for taking up police brutality, Black filmmakers still have to deal with the ramifications of Black representation and the cinema of policing. Set in apartheid South Africa, Euzhan Palcy's *A Dry White Season* explores police brutality against Black people as a global phenomenon and presents the same moral questions as *Do the Right Thing*, but through the eyes of white protagonists struggling with witnessing and opposing white supremacy. Cast with A-list white Hollywood actors, the film cannot center a Black subject or protagonist in its query about what it means to do the right thing. Palcy's white characters believe that the police state, clearly formed to violently maintain apartheid, must be reformed as opposed to decommissioned to enable postapartheid unity. Privileging the narrative of moral authority and moral dilemma, these two powerful films cannot transcend calls for Black fugitivity if abolishment is unimaginable or untenable.

LA Rebellion filmmaker Charles Burnett has been the most successful in answering Rojas's question with an emphatic yes. Burnett, however, purposely makes it difficult to see whether there is a way out of, over, or under the influence of carceral imagination. Though Burnett's *The Glass Shield* (1994) was seen as his most commercially viable film, due to its wider distribution via a collaboration with Miramax, it sets out to break the fragile myth of "serve and protect" that rules in policing narratives supported by a gold shield. The film is especially significant for this book because it plays with life-writing and the biopic to challenge the realism and logic of such a narrative. Burnett combines several real-life incidents of police brutality involving the Los Angeles Police

Department. *The Glass Shield* reimagines John Eddie Johnson's experiences as the first Black officer to integrate the Signal Hill Police Department as well as the Ron Settles police brutality case handled by attorney Johnnie Cochran in the 1980s. Burnett examines the evolution of the relationship between Black biopic and carcerality, and in doing so, he emphasizes the Black biography's dependence on moral dilemma and moral authority.

Burnett intends for viewers to understand that they come to the film with an internalized narrative of what it means to police and be policed in US society. The beginning of the film fades in on a vivid blue screen before a jump cut to an enlarged comic strip panel showing a white man holding a gun to the chin of a white woman as sirens are heard in the background. The scene cuts to another comic strip panel, of criminals being chased by sheriffs and police, culminating in a shoot-out in which one gunman tells the cops, in the text bubble: "Don't Try to Be a Hero." Gunfire erupts and the one Black officer in a sea of white cops is shot. The last comic strip panel depicts the Black cop bleeding with his white brethren surrounding him and a dialogue bubble that reads, "You Proved Yourself, Your Shield Is Made of Gold." The camera pans out from the comic strip panel to the comic book hanging in the locker of the Black protagonist, J.J., in his sheriff's uniform about to begin his day. The dream sequence ends and the reality of the film begins. It is hardly a typical opening for a crime or police film in the United States.

Burnett spoke about Miramax's initial opinion of his first cut: "When they [Miramax] picked up the film, they wanted to change it to be more of an action-packed kind of thing, guns and language . . . more four-letter words and . . . what happened was they did a test screening in New Jersey and this was not the audience for the film" (Burnett 2017). In addition to the test screening, Miramax released a trailer that was a questionable preview of the actual film contents, other than featuring a brief appearance by Ice Cube to make use of his hip-hop reputation. Burnett, who was introduced to third world cinema by Elyseo Taylor at UCLA, knew how to critique the myth of the police state using the very forms of culture that house the myth.

Burnett's film does more than simply declare the fiction in the idea that the police are a public good; it demonstrates how that fiction is conveyed—that is, how it is visually, graphically, and colorfully drawn in the cultural archives from childhood into adulthood. The aesthetics deployed throughout the film (filters in blue, red, orange, etc.) ignore the black-and-white of television procedurals, conventions of truth and realism. Positioned as a naive and good-hearted young man, J.J. ends up lying for one of his white brothers in blue after the white colleague threatens the life of another Black man. Burnett says the point of J.J's story was to ask, "How could you have good intentions and end up being corrupt and be a part of the conspiracy . . . the criminal element in the police department. . . . All it takes is one little mistake, one little lie that you think you're doing the right thing. . . . And that's the thing that initiates all of these problems" (Burnett 2017). Though Burnett is talking about his character, or even alluding to the real-life inspiration for J.J., the statement also applies to US society and its rhetoric and creative fictions about the police state. The lie that policing works, and that society needs it, becomes the mistake that Burnett ends up critiquing, as opposed to the actions of individual officers. Moreover, rather than participate in the cinema of policing, as some contemporary filmmakers do, Burnett shows the price his protagonist pays for colluding with the state when he loses his job for perjury, while the white officer gets immunity after acknowledging that J.J. lied.

When J.J's commander, Captain Massey, says, "Now if criminals don't fear God; they will this badge and division," the intrusion of moral authority is made clear. Yet the gravity of the critique is undercut by a line of dialogue from J.J's Black girlfriend after she learns of his actions: "I can see through that badge. It doesn't hide the evilness." Her statement returns to a concern about individual failings. Though made years after the Rodney King video of police brutality, which eventually led to the LA Riots in 1992, Burnett's attention to film and media is represented only via the news conferences and celebrity attorneys shown in the film. Political circumstances and technological inventions stress the necessity of doing away with the carceral imagination and a cinema of policing just as silent films and Blaxploitation have faded and given way to other genres.

I'M LOOKING FOR MY LIFE (FORM): BEYOND A CINEMA OF POLICING AND CARCERAL FANTASIES

The questions Collins was interested in answering about Black life with her first film also occur in current narratives in the era of Black Lives Matter, but the expression of her answers and art might fit more aptly within surrealist and post-Négritude frameworks. Such is the case with *The Cruz Brothers and Miss Malloy*, a loose adaptation of Henry Roth's problematic novel *The Cruz Chronicle* (1989), about three Puerto Rican brothers (Victor, Felipe, and José) and their ghost father (Raymondo). A film about three Puerto Rican brothers connecting with an elderly white woman, Edna Malloy, may not appear to be about carcerality and race, but if we intend to make our way out of carceral imagination, then we must begin with an intentional vision of safety, freedom, and human being sans carcerality.

In the hands of Collins, the character of Edna Malloy is a necessary foil for and engagement with the history of white women who utilize police/state agents to enact violence against Black bodies.[5] They do so because they are racists, but also because modern white life and living are rooted in white supremacy's necropower aka manifest destiny. Collins's dialogue for Malloy demonstrates this time and again: "Would you mind if we talked about death.... Death is terrible, when you can't ever remember having lived," says Malloy to Victor after they have spent some time getting to know each other. Malloy's words should be contrasted with the words and experience of the Cruz brothers' dead father, Raymondo, so that we understand that Collins is actually interrogating whose life gets to matter. Is death terrible for Raymondo? Has he been able to live? Edna's dialogue reveals how Collins understood that a film that boldly approaches and questions life and death, as opposed to fearfully runs from them using metaphors of crime and punishment, can shift debates about freedom, security, and prison.

As Caleb Smith has explained, "In criminal law the living dead are produced through 'civil death,' a legal fiction indicating the status of a person who has been deprived of all civil rights.... Historically, U.S. civil death statutes have dictated that the felon may not vote or make contracts. He loses his property" (Smith 2008, 245). According to Smith, the state can and does mandate what life is like after prison, a type of death. Smith's theory, however, does not take into account the necropolitics impacting Black social life. What is Black life in the United States like before prison? If one is poor, don't the legalities and emphasis on property, or lack thereof, produce social death? Collins's adaptation of Roth's novel was a successful attempt to produce a new genre of film as well as a method of filmmaking that considers Black life on the run. Collins's film showcases that adaptation is the practice of marronage as freedom.

For Collins, editing and adaptation became a film method in which she could go against the grain of realism and documentary aesthetics in detailing the impact of a carceral society on families of color. She proposes that telling a story is not simply an act of witnessing, but a way to make and enact fugitivity in our daily lives. Collins's *The Cruz Brothers and Miss Malloy* is not a film that would be read as being about policing, state violence, militarization of the police, surveillance, or police brutality the way Melvin Van Peebles's *Sweet Sweetback's Baadasssss Song*, Spike Lee's *Do the Right Thing*, Charles Burnett's *The Glass Shield*, or Ryan Coogler's *Fruitvale Station* are. It is more in line with Haile Gerima's surrealist feat *Child of Resistance* in the ways that it attempts to move beyond the carceral imagination and carceral fantasies as well as the cinema of policing.

It was possible for Collins to envision and develop a narrative film that addresses state violence as carried out by the judicial system without relying on foundational elements situated in a cinema of policing or a carceral imagination in part because, consciously or not, she began with a concept of film as the practice of freedom as marronage, as outlined by Aimé Césaire and others. Collins takes flight from myths of Blackness and Hollywood film to invent a practice that would be difficult to tie to any of the Black movements in existence during the years she made films. Collins needed to challenge and undo the carceral imagination of white Hollywood and Jim Crow America. Though Collins's experiences with the carceral state were much different from those of someone like Assata Shakur, how Collins came to think about freedom and prison might be linked to her two arrests for protesting in Albany, Georgia, in 1962. Newspaper accounts record Collins's experience as well as her description of how white protestors received different treatment from the US judicial system (see Worrell 1962; "Jersey City" 1962).

A Black woman with an almost-doctorate in French literature, Collins would not allow US cultural mores to be the only elements shaping her depictions of Blackness. Using the world and Black experiences throughout the world— more specifically, her own experiences throughout the world—she would adapt and edit other artists' work before writing her own films, plays, short stories, and novels. When Oliver Franklin asked Collins about race and her decision to make *The Cruz Brothers*, she redirected the question to a focus on problems of narrative filmmaking:

> **OF:** There has been a lot of discussion about definitions, especially the definition of a "Black film." You have made a film without any Afro-Americans in it, yet it is a Black film perhaps because you directed it.
> **KC:** That's your answer. There can't be a monopoly on form or content. I'm interested in solving certain questions such as: How do you do an interesting narrative film? So, I simply wanted a story that would be sufficiently difficult for me to want to solve some problems in narrative filmmaking. (Franklin 2015, 33)

Although Collins does not challenge Franklin's approach to race and art at this moment in the interview, her lecture at Howard University delineates the intersection of problems in narrative with philosophies about race (Collins 1984).[6] In addition, *The Cruz Brothers and Miss Malloy* absolutely challenges the notion that her films are not Black films, because she directs it and because she uses a global approach to Blackness and narrative that exceeds the era's biological or nationalist construct of race. One of the ways that Collins sought to solve problems in narrative filmmaking was to resist the turn to reality—or to one reality—as touted by US films depicting Black life.

Collins's confrontation with the aesthetic and political dilemmas dominating what it means to be a Black filmmaker demonstrates that she was also a filmmaker very much in tune with post-Négritude ideals. As defined by film scholar Mark Reid, "The 'postNegritude' project interprets essentialist and dualistic myths about whiteness and blackness, masculinity and femininity, heterosexuality and homosexuality, civilized and primitive as forms of dying colonialism" (Reid 1997, 3). Collins's decisions to adapt a white author's novel and to focus on subjects whom Franklin doesn't read as Black, while providing them with dialogue that ebonizes them in ways that belie Franklin's assumptions about their fair skin and positionality, refuses the forms of dying colonialism.

Collins described Roth's novel as "the closest thing to a full American version of *One Hundred Years of Solitude* by the Latin American writer [Gabriel García] Márquez. What Roth had done was to translate into American language, style and content the kind of mythical figures that populate *One Hundred Years of Solitude*" (Franklin 2015, 33). Yet, perhaps because Collins had a personal relationship with the author, her assessment of early versions of its chapters offers a far more generous read than what is warranted by the final novel. Shaped by a US carceral imagination and its fantasies of Black and Latino families and communities, Roth's novel traffics in horrible stereotypes and displays a necropolitical approach to the magical realist genre of fiction, which was meant to deepen narrative depictions about communities of color. The novel begins: "Raymondo Cruz's life did not begin until he died. Many years ago Raymondo, unable to provide even minimally for his family, tried to rob a bank with an empty water gun and was up-ended by a sharpshooting bank guard's stream of fat juicy bullets. Bleeding to death on a filthy West Side street, Raymondo heard a raucous hooting mob cheering his failure; the little man lay on his back mourning for his young sons—Victor, Felipe and José—now alone and helpless with the evil and mad Maria Cruz. What a momma!" (Roth 1989, 1). That none of this narrative makes it into Collins's film adaptation is telling.

To be clear, Roth's use of a ghost is not what produces the necropolitics in the novel. Rather, Roth's inability to execute techniques of magical realism in ways that comprehend why the genre comes to be useful for many minoritized communities who invent and innovate the genre leads to necropolitical encroachments. Portions of the novel were published as short stories in the 1970s, and the entire novel was published in 1989. In both eras, police brutality, structural inequalities in race and class, and issues of ethnic belonging were being widely discussed in the United States. Yet Roth's fiction seems disconnected from the culture it purports to be interested in. He references Cruz in multiple ways as a sorry father with no real work ethic. The Cruzes are a petty-crime family mired in bad luck. Roth's descriptions of the mother, delivered via Raymondo, are just as superficial: "That woman is evil, oh she is the devil" (Roth 1989, 53). In short, the novel cannot escape carceral fantasies about brown bodies, and, deservedly, it has received little attention over the years. Were it not for Collins's film, it could be easily forgotten.

However, Collins's adaptation mines and expands particular moments in some of the novel's chapters to create a world for the characters that enriches her portrayal of their journey, and she does so in a manner that exemplifies an understanding of how the genre of magical realism must function for the marginalized characters. From the beginning of her short film, Collins frees Raymondo and Victor, the eldest son, from the clutches of a white carceral imagination. The film opens with twenty seconds of voice-over dialogue and a black screen, before viewers see a Chevy and then Victor exiting it. Thereafter, a dialogue between father and son ensues:

> **Raymondo:** Beware, have nothing to do with Cortez. He's a third rater, never destined for success.
> **Victor:** Dag! Relax papa. We're not stealing the car, just stripping it.
> **Raymondo:** Beware my son! Americans care more about their cars than they do family. They will kill you for sitting on the hood.

Though this dialogue occurs toward the middle of Roth's novel (on page 102), Collins's decision to open her film with it demonstrates her interest in making a film that would critique US capitalism and its emphasis on material possessions. Further, the conversation between the living and the dead provides an ordinary order to the psychic dimension of the characters' lives. The film refuses much of the novel's one-dimensional characterization of the Puerto Rican characters. Collins's film also refuses moral judgments about the Cruzes' life of crime. Her film accepts Raymondo's career choice as connected to his commitment to being a devoted father who can provide for his family, even in death.

After the opening larceny scene, the screen goes black and we hear the father's voice narrate the details of his death during a robbery: "I would not greet death like the usual bullet-riddled loser. . . . I would not stay put and rot in some pauper's grave. . . . I cut out and found my sons to watch over." The scene jumps from a black screen to a shot of the sky and then trees, until a dilapidated house in an abandoned neighborhood comes into the frame. From there, Collins moves the narrative into answering questions about where life ends and begins for communities of color impacted by imperialism, colonization, and capitalism through Victor's meditation of the material and immaterial.

Collins's adaptation of the novel far exceeds the vision provided by Roth's novel and takes as its source a brief encounter detailed in a ten-page chapter titled "The Brothers and Miss Malloy." In another chapter, titled "The Word," Roth suggests there is a greater purpose to the boys' coming of age, when Raymondo charges his sons, especially Victor, to record the Cruz family history from his and their memories. As the eldest, and the only brother who can see their father's ghost, the character of Victor becomes a bridge between the living and the dead. He talks daily into a recording device and with his father about the world around him. In one scene, Victor asks, "How do you like our little town, poppa? The whole place is falling flat on its mush face. Urban renewal could begin here tonight. But don't worry the whites that live around here don't care shit about progress. Damn I forgot to turn my machine on." Initially, it seems as if Victor unquestionably takes on the duties of writer and historian. Collins's film, however, moves away from privileging this patrilineal mythmaking and focuses on the brothers' loving relationship with one another and with their father's ghost, as well as their interactions with the elderly white Irish woman, Edna Malloy, to create a narrative about living in black matter and about the vapidness of life and living in white supremacist capitalist structures.

As Victor speaks into the tape recorder on-screen, his monologue describes the provincial town they have come to inhabit, away from their Bronx beginnings: "They don't mind Main Street creaking and cracking. Or all the old buildings leaning down like they're hunched backed. 'Cause, man, if that means that no new coloreds come around to live and make trouble, then let it all fall down. So what if the place is sinking and the houses is dying faster than the owners. One thing nobody worries about is being mugged. This is still a dumb, gentle place. Only we got robbed here and that don't count." Victor's monologue covers a range of topics, including racial progress, urban renewal, gentrification, indigeneity, and dispersal and displacement. It provides the kind of social commentary not found in Roth's novel but maintains the novel's commitment to magical realism.

Victor's commentary also addresses the manufactured moral panic about crime that then leads to prison expansion. As Gilmore has noted, "To sum up: there is a moral panic over 'crime'—civil disorder, idle youth on the streets, people of colour out of control, women and children without husbands and fathers, students who believe it is their job to change the world (not merely to understand it) and political alliances among organizations trying to merge into full-scale movements. In other words, there is a social crisis. And there is also an economic panic—capital disorder, or the profits crisis. These crises collide and combine into the crisis that prison 'fixes'" (Gilmore 1998–99, 177). But prison itself is an institutional space designed for the mental entity that precedes it: the space of unfreedom. Which begs the question why anyone would imagine a thing, a space, and a world in which not everyone can be free and therefore they are not free. Is it because unfreedom is the equivalent of poverty in the United States? Ruth Wilson Gilmore theorized about this relationship decades before Michelle Alexander and Caleb Smith. Countering theories of prison growth in the United States that attributed it solely to moral panic about a contemporary crime problem, Gilmore stated, "In my view, the expansion of prison constitutes a geographical solution to socio-economic problems, politically organized by the state which is itself in the process of radical restructuring" (1998–99, 174). Collins's first film unequivocally understands this premise, which is why the Cruz brothers and their father are maroons.

Collins's attention to class and carcerality is subtle; she presents the conditions that might lead to a life of crime but also the conditions that feed into panics that justify the prison-industrial complex. For example, Raymondo consistently talks to Victor about making sure that they find work and maintain a suitable home, expressing an ingrained belief in the Protestant work ethic and patriarchy. He advises at one point, "A man must work, even if he is on his knees." Yet the middle brother, José, counters these ideas. Evicted from their residence in the city, José talks about the dilapidated shack that they occupy, living as marooned subjects might. He says, "We ain't got no phone, but we got a house," to which the youngest brother, Felipe, counters, "A shack with no walls and a leaky roof." Later José continues, "We eating tonight with our own fingers in our own joint. That's still amazing. Living in this sweet little town . . . not the Bronx or the home. Man we could be in a movie." The irony, of course, is that they are in a movie, one that looks like no other movie in Hollywood. José's exterior world, previously filled with living in group homes and separation from his brothers, finally matches the interior world he has created for himself as a child of the Bronx.

The freedom the brothers find outside the city comes across in the imagery provided by Collins's cinematography. There are beautiful shots of the brothers' interactions among trees, greenery, water, and natural light. As the brothers walk and run across a dangerously high wooden bridge, making their way to a basketball court where they play, a mid-twentieth-century Rolls-Royce appears behind them. The film reveals later that car is Edna's, and that she had been watching the brothers for some time. When Miss Malloy catches the brothers trespassing, she does not call the police. She inquires about hiring them to restore her house so that she can throw one last party before dying. They accept the month's work of clearing overgrown vegetation in the yard and gardens, painting rooms, polishing floors, and washing windows.

Collins refuses to make Miss Malloy the white savior, but she also does not make the brothers magical charms for Malloy. The Cruz brothers' scenes with Miss Malloy provide a contemplation of life, death, and freedom. Collins's dialogue about death, as well as Miss Malloy's insistence about her purpose—"I'm looking for my life. Have you seen my life? Somewhere in this house. Will you help me find it"—indicate that the well-off Edna is dead. Though the law upheld by biopolitics suggests, as a result of her being a property owner and a citizen, that she is alive and free, the film and Edna herself are clear: she has not been living. The house becomes a metaphor for Miss Malloy's life as well as for the Cruzes' aspirational living. The father warns that "this is not a happy home," and indeed Edna exhibits some eccentricities as well as bouts of mental instability and dementia. She also talks to ghosts. Once Victor, José, and Felipe become immersed in their work at Miss Malloy's house, Raymondo no longer visits them.

As the film progresses, the interactions between the brothers and Miss Malloy become less about their work and more about each character's interior life, or more specifically the theatrical performance of those lives. For example, José, who expresses interest in acting, "begins disappearing like he's a damn ghost," according to Victor. Viewers soon learn that José has been seeking out Edna and discovering a shared love of theater and performance. In many ways, Collins's representation of these scenes acknowledges ideas from Augusto Boal's *Theatre of the Oppressed*, in which he theorized that "[t]heatre is a form of knowledge; it should and can also be a means of transforming society. Theatre can help us build our future, rather than just waiting for it (xxxi). José begins performing with Edna, and with his earnings, he buys a camera to capture what he experiences. "I'd like to take your picture, Miss Malloy," he says to her, but José is drawn more to the house than he is to Miss Malloy. As Victor observes, each room in Miss Malloy's house represents a different life. José, and soon thereafter Victor, discovers new parts of himself and life while working on it. In many ways, the theatrical play between the characters allow each character to get beyond the cop in the head earlier referenced by Rojas. Moreover, Victor and José, the two brothers actively engaged in using technology to express their inner worlds, also end up engaging Edna differently than does Felipe, who avoids her. Victor and José converse, dance, and do acting performances with Miss Malloy. Felipe becomes and remains dismayed by his brothers' interactions with Edna, and by the fact that Victor has not heard from their father. However, he continues to work alongside his brothers. Acting, filmmaking, photography, and restoring of the houses are all creative expressions, or uses of the erotic, that displace they ways in which carceral imagination would represent dominant relationality between these characters.

When they have finished restoring the house, Edna takes out a phone book and asks them to help her with invitations for the party. They are stunned to learn that she has no friends or family, and that all of the work they've done will be so she can host a party for strangers. At the end of the film, the brothers go to collect their final week's earnings. Arriving at Edna's house, they find a sign posted on the gate that reads "No Trespassing by Order of the Police." Miss Malloy, they learn, has died and left them her Rolls-Royce. The sign and the will return viewers to the dominance of capitalism, law, and order. On the surface, the brothers' lives seemed to have improved as a result of their willingness to work and their encounter with white benevolence. Yet Collins resists this usual trope in a scene in which Raymondo comes to Victor after a month of silence, proclaiming, "The spell has been broken. She's dead. You three are alive with fat wallets from a job well done." When Victor declares that he does not want to talk about it, Raymondo insists, "Speaking into the magic tape makes a sour tale sweet. . . . On the tape your unpleasant voice makes the tale a legend heroic." Raymondo embraces the use of technology to alter the harsh realities of his sons' lives and ignores the reality in which they must still navigate US socioeconomics.

Unlike his father, Victor has moved beyond the myth of exceptionalism and the dualities produced by external matters. He says, "To be a legend, you got to make waves . . . or lose real bad or be real lucky. We only had to have you shot up and us abandoned to finally make it here. End of story." Victor understands that the conditions under which such heroism are exhibited derive from deliberately ignoring a broken system that enforces inequality. This is something that their father never learned in his life, but perhaps in his afterlife he has the opportunity to learn from his sons. The brothers' moments of performance with Miss Malloy, in addition to their craft in restoring the house, reveal a secular humanity less governed by carceral imagination and the state. With *The Cruz Brothers and Miss Malloy*, Collins was able to avoid forms and thought that could have dulled her vision of Black life. Reid reminds us that "a postNegritude analysis interprets the overlapping relationship between destructive residue [racism, sexism, homophobia, classism, and ethnocentrism] and certain forms of black conservatism, liberalism, and nationalism. 'PostNegrtiude' acts to subvert racism, sexism, and homophobia through womanist subversion of white and black patriarchal modes of production. It resists classism and ethnocentrism by affirming that black cultural identity is constantly unfolding to reveal its relationship to secular humanity" (Reid 1997, 3). In addition to the way that Collins ebonizes her characters in *The Cruz Brothers*, she promotes a use of recording technology that reckons with the cinema of policing and surveillance.

CINEMATIC MARRONAGE NOW (?)

Collins's interview with Oliver Franklin reveals what some might see as problematic ideas about Black people, film, and technology. She tells him, "It is hard for us to become artists in it because the high degree of technical competence intimidates us. That is probably why we have tended to do documentary films. It is much easier to pick up a camera and shoot than to understand everything about lighting, color, film stock, editing, sound, narrative convention, narrative structure, actors, and so forth" (Franklin 2015, 35). Rather than conceding this as arrogance, I see this as Collins again acknowledging that film technology has origins inside Western tradition. Moreover, it draws attention not only to technophobia but to the lack of a Black politics that could envision filmmaking as important to Black political resistance and external social movements. Her concerns about technophobia and race politics are why she introduces a focus on technology in her film adaptation—a theme that was not central in the novel.

"Victor is the family historian. He talk and talk into his machine," claims Raymondo in the film. Despite Raymondo's statement about his son's relationship to technology as archival, Victor's relationship to technologies of communication is speculative: "Did you get that machine? That's my poppa. Sure would be something if you got a ghost loud and clear. Poppa," he says extending the microphone into the air to his father's ghost. For Victor, the recording of his words is meant not only to archive the reality of his life or his father's life but also to explore his interiority in ways he cannot with his father or his brothers. While such exploration is understood as implicit in journal writing, too often conveyed as a feminized form of expression, technologies such as tape recording are more often associated with the rational realms of medicine and law and, if artistic, with music.

Collins's dialogue and technological depictions are specifically African Diasporic, as Roth's novel does little to develop meaning and symbolics around the tape recorder in his rendering of the ghost and son. Collins, like Erna Brodber in her novel *Louisiana*, sees the potential of technology in a magical realist tale. Years before our current age of surveillance, digital self-automation, and cinema of policing, Collins and Brodber theorized tape recording devices as tools that could enable communication between the living and the dead or afterliving.

These are two very separate forms of necro-communication based on differing definitions of life: one based in the material, biological, and rational erected out of a mind/body split; the other based on the material, psychic, and imaginative, born from aesthetics and the form of things unknown. Collins fled from the US film industry's necro-telecommunications and uses of film technology. Technology, her work argues, can be a bridge to magical realism as much as to realism, and it can help produce an alternative necro-telecommunications.

Collins, with her disregard for moral authority and guidance about technology, is an apt guide in the post–Rodney King era of carceral imagination, in which the irresolution of moral authority has become more complicated. More recent scholarship has shown how scopic technology and legal discourse have become updated tools of white supremacy that brutally dehumanize the Black subject while maintaining the moral authority of whiteness. In "What I Learned about Police Brutality Videos from Studying Lynching Photos," Koritha Mitchell documents that photos and videos of racist violence can often reinforce white supremacy. Mitchell explains that while lynching photos may have been celebratory mementos, police brutality videos are often filmed with the good intention of witnessing for justice. Nevertheless, she notes, "Being able to provide evidence often fails to yield the desired response—not only from the criminal justice system but also from fellow Americans in the form of basic human empathy" (Mitchell 2016).

Likewise, Benedict Stork's powerful piece "Aesthetics, Politics, and the Police Hermeneutic: Online Videos of Police Violence beyond the Evidentiary Function" argues that George Holliday's Rodney King video provided a lesson to police departments on how to use video footage as evidence in the defense of a police officer: "Both the tape and the procedural documents constitute, within the legal evidentiary setting, paired texts: one determining the meaning and value of the other, which in turn acts as a material supplement for this determination. The videotape was, just as any other piece of video evidence, greeted in court by an official police hermeneutic that adjudicates the specific questions relevant to this particular case of police force, and establishing the grounds of adjudication itself, and laying out the conditions of possibility for whatever verdict the jury might reach" (Stork 2016, 4). Videos can no longer be discussed solely as evidence, since their presentation to jurors in court changes nothing. Instead they have become the basis for a form of entertainment that provides tropes to neo-slave narratives shaped by post-Négritude motives. "'PostNegritude' wants to bring the videotaped beating of Rodney King into the churches of white middle class America," writes Reid about the means of distribution and the role of film technology in resistance (Reid 1997, 15).

Such is the case when we look at film and television works about police brutality that have been made since the Rodney King incident in 1991. The representation of such stories, however, is not a sign of change as much as it is a neoliberal response to generate capital off timely issues. While filmmakers and producers may have good intentions, the formulas for presenting the issues remain unchanged and underline concerns about audience and accessibility. Spike Lee's *Rodney King* (a recording of Roger Guinevere's one-man show about the incident) has recently been available for streaming on Netflix. In 2017, Fox aired a ten-part episodic series, *Shots Fired*, about tensions surrounding the event of a Black cop shooting a white teenager. When show creators were asked about the narrative of *Shots Fired*—which begins with the shooting of an unarmed white teenager by a Black cop instead of the shooting of an unarmed Black teenager by a white cop—the executive producer of the show, Gina Prince-Blythewood, replied, "We felt inverting it was a good way to allow people to identify with the character and understand what we feel" (Docterman 2017). This is not freedom or freedom as marronage. This is a literary device akin to the use of white authorial voice and sentiment honed during the writing and publishing of slave narratives to gain freedom. The purported inversion of the law-and-order narrative cannot overcome anti-Blackness. As Collins's work insists, adaptation can be a more radical decolonial process since its impact and success must consider the everyday part of fugitivity that goes into the making of Black cinema and film, the everyday part of freedom as marronage in Black life, and the deployment of technology as a means to multidimensionally decimate and undo the original myth.

Twenty years after the Rodney King video, Ryan Coogler's *Fruitvale Station* (2013) is one of the few contemporary biopics of a victim of police brutality, providing a day-in-the-life approach as opposed to a birth-to-death narrative. Coogler, in choosing to adapt new stories, police testimonies, and private cell phone footage of spectators, uses the new technology to tell a story that humanizes the victim, Oscar Grant, and comments on the inability of visual technology, without new narratives, to do anything other than undo such humanizing. *Fruitvale Station* exists somewhere between a battle cry and the ambivalence of moral authority displayed in earlier Black films. Its innovation, however, remains in its positioning of the everyday and ordinary, which Rojas identifies as pivotal in becoming less reliant on institutions and the spectacle of violence. Cell phone technology also plays a role in this. *Fruitvale* opens with a black screen, and we hear a conversation about New Year's resolutions between Oscar and his girlfriend, Sophia: "I'm going to cut carbs," declares Sophia; Oscar says,

"I want to quit selling trees." With this entry into Grant's life, Coogler returns to the slave narrative strategy of conversion from immoral life to moral life. He is already making evidence to argue for Grant's humanity. The film then cuts to cell phone footage, first blurry and then focused. A title card provides place, time, date: Fruitvale BART Station, New Year's Day 2009, and Oakland, CA, 2:15 a.m. The cell phone video is grainy, moving and rotating with the user's body. Notably, however, Coogler does not rely on the video footage as evidence in the same way the court cases or users intended, or even as Grant himself might have intended.[7] He instead uses cell phone technology as an aesthetic that showcases human communication and the human empathy it is meant to serve rather than replace.

Throughout the film, viewers see spoken and text conversations between Grant and his loved ones. Coogler imposes text messages on the screen before a pit bull is killed by a hit-and-run driver; when Grant texts his mother a happy birthday message; when Grant texts a buddy after heeding his mother's message to not drink and drive; and, during the arrest in the BART station, a text from Sophia comes across. These are the communications that go unseen in cell phone footage of the video of his murder, and they are a stream-of-consciousness narrative. After Oscar is shot, viewers see him left lying on the ground bleeding, and we hear his phone ring after he has said, "I have a daughter." The camera zooms in on the vibrating and ringing phone; on the other end is Sophia, desperate to communicate. In the film, technology is not simply a way to make evidence for a system that does not recognize the humanity of Black people; it is a line of communication visibly representing that this person is connected to others who love and care for him. They, too, are connected to him. This show of humanity, never able to be entered into the official record, should take precedence over spectacle, according to the ending of the film, which shows footage of a 2013 vigil for Grant at the BART station.

Fruitvale Station demonstrates that if Black filmmakers cannot make films dangerous, they can attempt to use them as tools of de-escalation and de-weaponization. While attentive to technology practices in the twenty-first century, the ending of *Fruitvale Station* does not intend to serve as a tool of propaganda for abolitionist movements in this century. Black people may have overcome the era of technophobia Collins addressed, but we have now entered a new era of technophobia tied to the speculative and the experimental and that highlights an entanglement with realist genres whose only purpose is to witness for a kangaroo court. We do not have to choose between using technology as a mode of archiving the real, as Raymondo asks, or as a practice of freedom as marronage, as Victor does. We must do both.

What it means to film and not intervene upon seeing incidents of police brutality is a question that Black film studies needs to take up with complexity, though it has been broached before in regard to Black public spheres and counterpublics. The act of filming and streaming fails to solve the dilemma that precedes it: How are everyday people intervening on acts of violence carried out by the state? Is there art that can teach us different modes of intervening, modes less reliant on judicial outcomes in which witnessing and testimony matter only if you are not Black? Black film studies needs to better engage the question of the carceral imagination not simply in terms of representation, entertainment, and artistry but because of what Shana Redmond writes about in her intimate and personal essay, "A Family Like Mine." Redmond recounts how much in-person visitations with her father in prison meant to both of them as they struggled to survive his captivity for years. She offers her personal history in response to news "that hundreds of US jails and prisons have terminated in-person visits and replaced them with virtual sessions by phone or computer. . . . Incarcerated women and men continue to be treated as carrion for vulturous telecommunications companies (via prison brokers and administrators) who justify their actions by trotting out the familiar ruse of security" (Redmond 2017). Years earlier, Collins's film adaptation of Roth's novel showed how the dead require communication that exceeds technoscientific developments. She not only predicted the necro-telecommunications of our current era but also suggested how to resist it by focusing on life and living outside of the material—that is, by centering our embodied and haptic interactions with one another.

Finally, the psychological and political ramifications of technophobia, filmmaking, and challenging the carceral imagination are highly gendered in ways that Collins and her descendants failed to recognize. For example, Ava DuVernay's Netflix documentary *13th* was critically acclaimed and received several awards and nominations. However, the film's attention to the carceral state did little to acknowledge gender. As writer Samantha Master wrote in her review, "The film's power is tempered by a glaring omission: black women's stories" (Master 2016). Here, the documentary genre, politics, and technology are competing elements erasing the intersection of gender with the New Jim Crow. This particular technophobia cannot continue to be ignored.

While the streaming and shared images of teenage girls at schools or pool parties being brutalized by state agents force us to add more names to more #SayHerName hashtags, they cannot take the place of propaganda shaped by aesthetics and genres that work outside the confines of the law. Black beings can no longer bear the burden of being martyrs or serving as video evidence of injustice. The filming of police brutality should no longer be seen as a tactic that will ensure justice. When we place the advent of cell phone, dash cam, and body cam recordings of police brutality alongside the well-established genre of police procedurals and prison dramas produced by the Hollywood film and US television industries, we have to ask more of Black filmmaking and film studies to combat this representation of life, of Black life. How do we accept and move forward to the new life that Collins alludes to in her Howard University master class lecture, when she insists, "You are freer than you think"? The answer will provide the possibility of a new worldview that could launch a sustained abolitionist campaign filled with both information and propaganda.

MAKING THE CASE FOR ASSATA

Despite these inroads, Hollywood cinema and US film schools continue to produce students and methods that engage in carceral imaginative practices. With the production of Lena Waithe's lazy, sloppy screenwriting of Black fugitivity in *Queen and Slim*, Katheryn Bigelow's questionable reimagining of police in *Detroit*, and news that Taylor Hackford is set to direct the biopic of prominent Black attorney Johnnie Cochran, focusing on his experience with defending victims of police brutality, it is important to insist on renewed consciousness about a cinema of policing and carceral imagination in representing Black life as it intersects with the US police state. In simply referring to this as misrepresentation or stereotypes in art and film, we ignore the carceral as well as artistic institutions being maintained. In any case, this genre, most often called the police procedural, is a form of propaganda for a police state and the prison-industrial complex. One difference between the abolition of slavery and the abolition of the US police state is that while there may have been laws and cultural literature advocating for slavery, other laws and cultural works were simultaneously advocating for its abolition; the same cannot be said for the carceral state today. As critics and policy makers advocate for the abolition of police and prisons, the culture industry continues to serve as a propaganda machine for the state. Hence, we might ask, What does the cultural arm of prison and police abolition look like—or if it does not yet exist, what might it look like?

Collins must be placed in traditions and genealogies that she has not been associated with, as her film and lectures provide a crucial mapping of where to go from here. Television and film are still technoscientific developments, and the use of them by novices, artists, and industry professionals needs to be part of a larger conversation about carceral fantasy and carceral imagination as it impacts Black communities and other communities of color in the twenty-first century. Haile Gerima's *Child of Resistance* (1973) alerted viewers to this more than forty years ago, but his film's declaration is just as relevant in the era of Black Lives Matter. Fundamentally we need films that release us from the prison that slavery and colonization has created in our minds. As we wait for those films, we need cinematic marronage to showcase how multiple freedoms are not only won but maintained. We need films that delve deeply into the meanings of life and living, because such questioning shifts imagination away from necropolitical models and prepares individuals to be open to the abolition of the US police state and prison-industrial complex.

Years before the Rodney King video, Black people had imagined a mode of escape from the carceral state and its everyday violence without the help of film or video. A literal break from prison, the escape and marronage of Assata Shakur, became a beacon of hope against US empire for radicals across the African Diaspora and a spectacle of failure and disorder for US empire and its carceral imagination. Yet Shakur's story remains unfilmable in the US cinema industry, even at a time when its representation on-screen is most needed. A cinematic adaptation of Assata Shakur's life story would require further evolution of cinematic marronage.

"I want to live in a country where freedom means something," says Shakur, speaking about her afterlife, or the early days of her marronage in Cuba, in Gloria Rolando's documentary *Eyes of the Rainbow* (1997). Shakur remains in Cuba because of police brutality and a US police state that manufactures a narrative of her as a terrorist. Rather than allow her film to be shaped by the moral authority narrative structure typical of biographies and biopics, Rolando forgoes the US myth of Black citizenship that depends on the benevolence of an authorial white citizenry. She instead relies on Afro-Cuban articulations of freedom that merge the mythology of Oya (a warrior goddess) and Cuban music with Shakur's biography to create something akin to a cinematic biomythography as opposed to a documentary. Ten years earlier, Shakur had documented the details of her life in *Assata: An Autobiography* (1987). Shakur's life-writing articulated Black women's experiences of "freedom" during Jane Crow as well as their experiences in the prison-industrial complex. Yet it is Rolando's biomythocumentary that presents a challenge to nationalist ideas of freedom as democracy and a carceral imagination that consistently refuses to depict Shakur and other activists as political prisoners of US empire as opposed to criminal fugitives of the US state. Collins's attention to adaptation as a type of cinematic marronage, accepting her words "You are freer than you think," becomes a first step toward comprehending Assata Shakur's story as a coherent past, present, and future narrative of Black women victimized by police and carceral institutions. Her narrative exposes Black women as fugitives who must not only #SayHerName but also practice freedom as marronage. Such a practice might mean fleeing to another country, or it could entail the use of art, culture, and technology to create a space to which to flee.

Having seen one of the few early screenings of *Losing Ground* in Atlanta, the illustrious Toni Cade Bambara wrote, "The late pioneer black woman filmmaker Kathy Collins Prettyman was a liberating sign" (Bambara 1996, 128). Knowing all too well that the masculinist and militant renderings of the term *revolutionary* would never capture Collins, Bambara carefully selected *pioneer,* the fourteenth-century etymology of which is "foot soldier who prepares the way for the army." Collins was preparing the way for an army of rebel, maybe guerilla, filmmakers.

Collins left this world long before she could see, and perhaps benefit from, the consistent calls for diversity behind the cameras in Hollywood with hopes that someone might shift the stereotypical dehumanizing images of people of color on-screen. She did not see the technological innovations of digital cameras, phone cameras, YouTube videos, body cameras, dashboard cameras, and viral videos become virtual witnesses to track movements or archive experiences such as concerts, plays, and sporting events that might become of material, more so than affective, value. She would not live to see the use of recording equipment and drones to surveille, categorize, and document the humanity and nonhumanity of individuals and communities that she strove to represent as human. Yet her philosophy about film has much to say to these newfangled uses of cameras, visual technology, and films.

Black America has moved from on from the beating of Rodney King, recorded on video by George Holliday, a white immigrant, to the intimate livestream of the murder of George Floyd and Philando Castile, and to Korryn Gaines filming the invasion of her home. The words of Kathleen Collins, spoken more than thirty years ago, provide one reason that Darnella Frazier, Gaines, or Reynolds could remain poised behind the camera in ways that they could not once they were a part of the frame. In returning to the previous chapter's theory of fifth dimension cinema, Collins continues to offer ideals that support the theory: "You are freer than you think, because the screen that is around you is so thick. That behind it, you can do an awful lot of thinking, awful lot of figuring out. It'll take a long time for the world around you to even catch up with where your ideas are. Because you are not even being perceived as a thinking being" (Collins 1984). Her statement exceeds the passivity of witnessing and archiving murder and insists that there is something more to be done with this technology.

In returning to Shakur's words about living in a country where freedom means something, Black filmmaking and film studies must, as Collins suggested earlier, reckon with the myths of Hollywood and refuse one genre of filmmaking, inventing alternative genres in its stead. Only when cinematic marronage is the foundational premise of representing the lives of victims taken as a result of state violence—that is, police brutality—can afterlife-writing as biography or biopic become a useful form for US film. This is what *The Cruz Brothers and Miss Malloy* offered: an innovation of genre and a radical ideology about technology. Black film and television in the twenty-first century must do more than represent; they must teach us that we are freer than we think. They must become a practice in freedom as marronage.

KARKINOS LIFE

The Hallmarks of Cancer: An Afterlife
Like the Midwestern Hallmark tradition
founded in 1910 in Kansas City, Missouri
The hallmarks of cancer are cellular greeting cards
that surprise varied and numerous recipients
. . . expressing in dire creative fashion and form
As a microscope becomes a camera depicting
the numerous occasions

      Wherever she may be, whatever time she may be

      birth, survival, evolution, and afterliving

      As they are wont to do

            in a cycle of birth, founding, remission, anniversary of
                remission, death, afterlife

            Narrating to a diagnostician slow to refuse

            hesitant to imagine a nonbiological sentiment

            An unpatentable and impossible copyright

The Hallmarks of Cancer

      Genuine, efficient, and predictive

      Have no well wishes for the ones who

      Choose to make possible

      the simultaneous growth of two lives

            With womb, heart, and mind

            as they care and lie and lie and care

            their way through illness

            secrecy, hope, silence, fear

                death

The Hallmarks of Cancer

> Express their deepest sympathies and condolences
>
> To breast, large or small, filled with mammary glands that once made milk
>
> To nourish and feed noncarcinogenic growth

The Hallmarks of Cancer

> care enough to send the grimmest best
>
> so that incorporation of pink ribbon advocacy profits off survivor sentiments
>
> As everyone hopes for a cure and capitalizes off treatment

The Hallmarks of Cancer

> see with pristine clarity
>
> a North Star that microscopes can never magnify enough
>
> presciently charting their freedom route and tactical evasion
>
> from repeated attempts to enslave, diminish, catch, or kill
>
> the things that were supposed to be free but could not stay free

The Hallmarks of Cancer

> will not acknowledge their anteriority
>
> > precolonial
>
> before contracts of empire initiate
>
> tumor taxonomy . . . Oncology
>
> > present and postcolonial
>
> extending into movement, media, and stages

The Hallmarks of Cancer

> cannot explain
>
> > tarot card readings
> >
> > foretelling of a Black feminist poet(h)ics
>
> that intuits its own rise
>
> in ancient corpses
>
> mummified in hieroglyphed coffins that insist
>
> in the confessional words of an impossible Black woman filmmaker
>
> > searching for new life
> >
> > "Death marks the end of living in the future(?)"[1]

CHAPTER FIVE

BLACK FEMINIST POETHICS
AND CANCER

BLACK WOMEN WRITERS STUDY CANCER, not in search of a cure but in search of cancer's definition of life—a newfangled genesis of living arising from cellular confrontation with death. Kathleen Collins once asked, "What is cancer in my body? They say it's attacking the bones and the spine. That it's already eroded one vertebrae. But what's the exact nature of the erosion— viral, lymphatic—in other words how does it manifest itself?"[2] According to the American Cancer Society, "Collectively, blacks have the highest death rate and shortest survival of any racial/ethnic group in the U.S. for most cancers." It also notes that "breast cancer is the most commonly diagnosed cancer among black women" and that "breast cancer incidence rates among black women increased rapidly during much of the 1980s" (American Cancer Society 2019). Though there has been much biological research and technological innovation since then, as well as more focus on racial disparities, the mortality statistics for Black women with breast cancer continue to increase disproportionately to other women in the United States. Collins's question, then, "What is cancer in my body?" remains an unanswered one relevant to many Black women today. As Audre Lorde chronicled in two nonfiction works, *The Cancer Journals* (1980) and *A Burst of Light: Essays* (1988), many Black women become well-informed patients who are critical of the medical profession when it comes to caring for and healing non-white bodies: "The struggle with cancer now informs all my days, but it is only another face of that continuing battle for self-determination and survival that Black women fight daily, often in triumph" (Lorde 1988, 41).

Throughout an almost daily series of spiritual reflections about her ex- perience of stage-4 breast cancer, in a volume entitled "BOTA Diary III,"

Collins interrogates everything she knows about herself alongside what she does and does not know about the disease. BOTA, for Builders of the Adytum is an esoteric or occult spiritual practice centered on meditation and the tarot (*adytum* means "inner shrine" in Latin). The practice was founded in the early 1900s by Paul Foster Case. Though there are no statements about when Collins gravitated toward it, she did receive a certificate and exam for her study of the organization's teachings on mysticism and occult. Her openness to esoteric and non-Western spiritual traditions coupled with a stage-4 cancer diagnosis directed her toward this particular path.

While Collins privately posed these questions in "BOTA Diary III," scientific and medical research on the cause and treatment of cancer has sought answers at the microscopic level. Self-sufficiency in growth signals, insensitivity to antigrowth signals, limitless replicative potential, tissue invasion and metastasis, the evasion of cell suicide, and sustained development of new blood vessels are the six factors that form the hallmarks of cancer in scientific terms. These six modifications in cell physiology are the focus of a pivotal review of existing research, "The Hallmarks of Cancer," published in the journal *Cell*. Authored by Douglas Hanahan and Robert A. Weinberg, the study has become a canonical piece of scholarship in cancer research, shifting biological and epidemiological approaches to cancer. The authors theorized that no matter the type of cancer or its location, "the vast catalog of cancer cell genotypes is a manifestation of six essential alterations in cell physiology that collectively dictate malignant growth" (Hanahan and Weinberg 2000, 57). Upon completing their assessment of the six alterations of a healthy cell to a cancerous cell—what they describe as "acquired capability"—Hanahan and Weinberg emphasize that "those researching the cancer problem will be practicing a dramatically different type of science than we have experienced over the past 25 years. Surely much of this change will be apparent at the technical level. But ultimately, the more fundamental change will be conceptual" (57). They later insist that new metaphors, processes of interpretation, and systems of rationalization (67) will emerge. The review was pivotal in moving the study of cancerous tissue and cells away from a reductionist approach to an antireductionist approach, resulting in new treatments as well as the recognition of new cancers.

Ironically, Hanahan and Weinberg's research and understanding of malignant growth continues to narrativize an empirical definition of life, specifically cellular life, whereas Black women writers who study cancer have consistently narrated cancer as a form of being that exists beyond the biomedical definition of life. However, when fully considering Hanahan and Weinberg's thesis, we should be able to grasp how the hallmarks of cancer reveal a form of afterlife whose very existence is meant to reject the biological imperative and finality of death. Cancer, it would seem, lives *only* in the future.

In the fall of 1988, the same year that Audre Lorde published *A Burst of Light*, Collins succumbed to stage-4 breast cancer at the age of forty-six. With the exception of her husband, Alfred Prettyman, few people knew about her terminal illness during the last year of her life. Collins's decision to closely guard her diagnosis was a decision that impacted her family, as Nina Collins has written about elsewhere (N. Collins 2016). Despite her secrecy about her terminal diagnosis, Collins spent her cancer years engaged in what Lorde described as a "continuing battle for self-determination and survival" (Collins 1988, 41). Collins would meet cancer's acquired capability with her belief in adaptation and generate a tremendous amount of writing about alternative forms of life before passing.

This chapter examines interviews, plays, and diary entries that Collins completed during the last five years of her life to highlight how she discreetly and discursively addressed the biopolitics in Western health and medicine and the circuits of dispossession in alternative healing communities. In "'Transversing' the Circuit of Dispossession," an essay about labor and land dispossession, Denise Ferreira da Silva asks that we "speculate about the kind of shift in thinking that would allow a radicalization of the historical materialist framework. . . . For a radical reconsideration of these boundaries—a reinterpretation of the circuit of dispossession and its points of entry—that privileges the aesthetic is key if we are to trace the dis/continuities between today's and earlier practices of resistance. Both tasks, we must not forget, are necessary if we are to design practices that better disrupt the deployment of State-Capital power in the global present" (da Silva 2014b, 284). Encouraged by da Silva's words, I apply her question to the historical materialist framework of Western medicine, particularly in breast cancer narratives. This chapter's conversation about the human and resistance from that which is considered inhuman, cancer cells, seeks to understand both the role of cancer in shaping Collins's search for new forms of being and, more broadly, Black women's intuitive refusal of today's cancer culture, which is held in place by biopolitical forms of life. Black women attend to the aesthetics narrating our understanding of cancer as a disease, and its subsequent treatments, because biomedical discourses have yet to adequately account for the immaterial forces that may account for cancer's refusal to self-terminate or expire.

I begin with these questions: What is the shift in thinking that would allow a radicalization of the historical materialist framework of breast cancer? What and where are the circuits of dispossession and points of entry that have Black women resisting and refusing a biopolitical narrative of their illness? In broaching what are often understood as axiologically opposed strategies to treatment and healing, Collins outlined how racism and colonization shaped Black women's experiences within each realm, ambivalently representing how and why they may or may not rely on treatment or healing protocols to deal with their diagnosis. By exploring her quartet of one-act plays *Begin the Beguine* (1984) as well as her "BOTA Diary III" (1987), this chapter highlights how Collins's quest to live in the future, philosophically different from the race or search for a biological cure, leads to a recognition of alternative ways of being and becoming influenced by an anteriority that precedes the end of her exterior social life as a Black woman dying from cancer and whose futurist interiority exceed human mortality.

Collins's writings reveal her philosophical ideas about Western medicine, alternative medicine, and her critiques of early survival rhetoric related to breast cancer diagnosis and treatment in the 1980s. I place her various forms of writing within the context of medical and cultural narratives about what was happening in cancer research and awareness during the 1980s. I then discuss why her decision to explore these issues through the medium of playwriting, as opposed to the nonfiction personal essay, assisted her in continuing a self-determination process less dictated by the demands of Black middle-class heteronormative social life and the rationalization of the biomedical realm. While her words and methods of studying cancer did not result in a cure, they did produce an ontology that she had worked to develop throughout her artistic career: to live outside the logic of life and become whatever she was to be.

Collins was a philosopher always interested in the metaphysics of being. If death marked the end of living in the future for her, then being and becoming were processes of moving forward, inevitability, and possibility. The collective ideas in her work during the last years of her life suggest that she believed a public pronouncement of her fatal illness would cease both her present and future existence. Collins's approach to writing about dying from cancer and living in the future asks that those who share a lack of faith in the biomedical acquire or use their gifts of the speculative in order to exceed the power and control of biomedicalization—not because there is no use or value in treatment, therapies, et cetera, but because access to those elements may be limited or are not possible for all forms of life. Before delving specifically into Collins's works, a brief examination of cancer culture provides a context for how we should read them.

A LIFETIME OF CANCER CULTURE

In the last decade, several medical and public health articles as well as significant cultural studies have provided a broad history of cancer. When Ken Burns's production company and director Barak Goodman decided to adapt

Siddhartha Mukherjee's *Emperor of All Maladies* into a PBS documentary, *Cancer: The Emperor of All Maladies*, the film's medical humanities approach ushered in a new medium for the continued advocacy for and awareness of cancer treatment (Goodman 2015). Mukherjee's history and biography of cancer was thorough, going as far back as ancient Egypt's well-known surgeon Imhotep, who outlined how to diagnose a case of breast cancer: "This is a case of bulging masses. . . . Bulging tumors of the breast mean the existence of swellings on the breast, large, spreading, and hard" (Mukherjee 2010, 40).

Though the book and the film positioned themselves as invested in matters of cancer that epidemiology and oncology are not, including ancient narratives outside the biomedical realm, they still undervalued how Imhotep came to know cancer despite lacking modern technology: "Herodotus and Imhotep are storytellers, and like all stories, theirs have gaps and inconsistencies. The 'cancers' described by them may have been true neoplasms, or perhaps they were hazily describing abscesses, ulcers, warts, or moles. The only incontrovertible cases of cancer in history are those in which the malignant tissue has somehow been preserved" (Mukherjee 2010, 42). Soon after the publication of Mukherjee's book, archaeologists unearthed Egyptian female skeletal remains in Qubbet el-Hawa from 2000 BC, and CT scans revealed breast cancer. Here, we see medical advancement as superior because it verifies what could not be verified in a nonbiopolitical society. Notably, cancer exists before and after Western medicine's microscopic gaze.

Recently, feminist-influenced monographs have initiated comprehensive and layered critiques of both medical institutions doing cancer research and cancer nonprofits and philanthropic organizations in ways that demonstrate that ethics and good intentions have done little to help women navigate cancer. Anne S. Kasper and Susan J. Ferguson's edited collection *Breast Cancer: Society Shapes an Epidemic* (2000) provides several perspectives about the policy making around cancer research, capitalism, and the health industry, and history of the breast cancer activist and awareness movement. Maren Klawiter's *The Biopolitics of Breast Cancer: Changing Cultures of Disease and Activism* (2008) offers a mixed-methods study of the US breast cancer movement that details the influence of the feminist health movement, AIDS activism, and support groups on the lives of women with breast cancer. More recently, Emilia Nielsen's *Disrupting Breast Cancer Narratives: Stories of Rage and Repair* (2018) asks readers to rethink everything they know about survivor narratives. Each of these studies is important for contextualizing Collins's closely guarded secret of her diagnosis as well as understanding the artistic work that she produced to make sense of the diagnosis.

Klawiter provides a poststructuralist approach to the study of breast cancer health and movements, outlining its earliest iteration as "the regime of medicalization," which meant that "cancer treatment moved from the home to the hospital; surgeons were installed as the sovereign rulers of the kingdom; breast cancer was discursively constructed as a curable disease, and women exhibiting the 'danger signals' of breast cancer were reconstituted as the new subjects of the regime" (Klawiter 2008, xxvii). During this early regime, intersectional approaches to the study of the disease, in which considerations of class and race would factor, were less discussed than was gender. The narratives around breast cancer at this time centered on eliminating the disease at a cellular and anatomical level, as opposed to a wholistic patient outlook. Moreover, women could simultaneously be confronting a diagnosis and dealing with sexist, paternalistic, and patriarchal control over their body within medical institutions, which feminist health movements sought to combat (Klawiter 2008, 8–9). The 1970s and 1980s saw a transition into a regime of biomedicalization in which cancer clinics—or the "cancer cartel," as Audre Lorde called it—trafficked in "what Michel Foucault terms the 'anatomo-politics of bodies' . . . the emergence of informed consent, the proliferation of surgical procedures, the growing use of adjuvant therapies, the rise of new discourses of risk, the redefinition of patient and physician roles and responsibilities, and the development of rehabilitation programs that diminished the isolation of breast cancer patients" (Klawiter 2008, xxvii). Studies such as Klawiter's expose how US ideologies of individualism and personal responsibility in health and medical culture create patient identities that undermine revolutionary institutional reform regarding treatment and cure for marginalized people. Certainly, during this particular era, in which mammograms and patient education began constructing a subject who could become more of an active agent in preventing and containing her own illness, conversations of class and race should have been more pertinent.

Lisa Cartwright's *Screening the Body* delves into how new technologies around the gaze, imaging, scopes, and cameras came to serve as diagnostic tools, with the American Cancer Society generating rhetoric about making screening by X-rays or mammograms a priority. Yet, she notes, "Without question, knowledge and authority are exerted through the surveillant techniques of disease management; however, certain bodies are systematically excluded from this gaze. . . . Though medicine may control bodies and communities it images, it also offers imaging as a class and cultural privilege" (Cartwright 1995, 146).

Cartwright's statement is pertinent for our study of Collins, a filmmaker whose very calling was to challenge the exclusionary gaze of Western men, be it via film, scan, or scope. During her second experience with breast cancer,

Collins was consistently raising questions that suggest that medical answers could neither satisfy nor unsettle her own cinematic gaze. As she wrote in her BOTA diary: "Could it resemble cancer and yet not be cancer? The pattern of the erosion, or rather the nature <u>and</u> the pattern should dictate the <u>healing</u> procedure. I must clearly be able to envision the pattern if I'm to envision the cure" (January 4, 1988). Moreover, Collins's previous and less invasive experience may have also influenced her relationship to medical treatment based on the oncological gaze.

Though she died on September 18, 1988, in a letter to Peggy Dammond, eight years prior, it is clear that she had endured and won an earlier battle with cancer, when she revealed, "Just about three weeks ago exactly I underwent four hours of massive surgery for what they thought was lymph cancer. two small nodes were cancerous in the original biopsy. Bluette knows but I asked her not to tell your family."[3] Collins had also mentioned years earlier having to deal with an illness, during a 1986 interview with film critic David Nicholson. When she offered no specifics, Nicholson returned to her mention of having been sick, "When were you ill?" (Nicholson 1988–89, 9). Collins did not answer directly, and she chose instead to discuss the making of *The Cruz Brothers*, emphasizing her tremendous sense of self-determination, vision, and power. It is only after she has spoken at length about her art and production that Nicholson revisits the question: "But just to tie it back, after this it was that you became ill." She tells him "Yes. It was in 1980. We had just finished *The Cruz Brothers* and it had just started getting a lot of attention. And that's when I got ill. The timing was uncanny" (10). Based on this exchange, for almost eight years she dealt with an initial breast cancer diagnosis, treatment, and remission and then with a stage-4 metastasis diagnosis and treatment, all during a pre–pink ribbon era of advocacy and awareness. Collins's revelation, her hesitancy in discussing what she had revealed, and her eventual fuller discussion indicate what must have been her ongoing process of trying to understand how and why she had cancer.

Whatever middle-class beginnings Collins had come from, her adult life was a weird configuration of racialized, classed, and gendered subjectivity that most narratives of health activism, feminist organizing, and racial uplift could not narrate into a coherent patient identity: a struggling Black woman artist working in a medium few of her race and gender did; film professor working at a white public university; and a divorced, then remarried, working mother. What practical issues of health insurance did she deal with while trying to continue to make films and to make financial ends meet? What was the emotional toll of fighting cancer, fighting a white film industry, and fearing that she would involuntarily abandon her family via illness or death? What possible modes of expression could process and make sense of cancer's acquired ability to live only in the future?

Undoubtedly, the search for answers to similar questions is why Emilia Nielsen's ethnographic and textual study of affect in breast cancer narratives stands as such a significant scholarly treatment of breast cancer narratives. It joins Barbara Ehrenreich's personal essay "Welcome to Cancerland" (2000) as a counternarrative intent on intervening on the cancer movement's dominant and public "inspirational," "uplifting," or "positive" narratives about breast cancer, and it stands as one of the few book-length studies to do so with a succinct focus on narratives created by people with stage-4 breast cancer. Because stage-4 breast cancer is consistently the most terminal form of cancer, and those writing the narratives are rarely survivors, the anger and rage often present in these narratives have been disparaged by a broader cancer-free public; they do not make for compelling PR campaigns for cancer research and awareness.

Nielsen relies on Hilde Lindemann Nelson's theories about narrative repair—which insist that, "because identities are narratively constructed and narratively damaged, they can be narratively repaired" (Nielsen 2018, xii)—as important to understanding the significance of counternarratives. Nielsen asserts, of Audre Lorde's *A Burst of Light*, that "Lorde . . . writes to repair, not to cure, other Black women with metastatic cancer facing the end of life" (143). This could also be said of Lorde's *Cancer Journals*, written six years before *A Burst of Light*. In each work, Lorde appears to argue for repair of a broken system of health and medicine, repair of an environmentally dangerous society, and repair of her identity after a mastectomy. However, while Nielsen finds repair as potentially more valuable than narratives of cure in women's breast cancer narratives, I propose that Collins's writings alternate between narrative repair and something else. As she would write in "BOTA Diary III," "MY VERY FLESH IS THE SEED-BED FOR A NEW LIFE, FREE FROM BONDAGE TO TIME AND SPACE" (August 8, 1987). Her diary entry reveals that she can no longer accept that death marks the end of living in the future. Collins's search for new forms of life, as discussed in previous chapters, provides insight into the recursive infinity of cancer culture as long as the biopolitical and biological remain the only available conceptions of life and death.

Biomedical factors are not the only elements impacting the narratives of breast cancer survivors and patients. Based on contemporary research and scholarship on the culture of cancer and cancer narratives, specifically with regard to personal responsibility and politicization of the patient, it would be easy to read many entries of Collins's BOTA diary as impacted by a rhetoric of self that emerges in self-health movements or by a rhetoric of holistic sickness seen in complementary and alternative healing communities, in which "discursive construction of breast cancer transforms it from a discrete physical disease of the breast to a much larger problem potentially involving all areas of a woman's life (and possibly past life). This reframing is what we call holistic sickening . . . a process through which discrete corporeal diagnosis is widened into a broad assessment of trauma, misfortune . . . stunted spirituality, bad food choices" (Sered and Agigian 2008, 627). Without a doubt, the diary entry that Collins composed in January 1988 could be read as an example of a stage-4 breast cancer patient blaming the self and utilizing the language of holistic sickness:

> To my subconscious:
>
> Out of despair and loneliness my self-conscious reasoning has sent a message of destruction to the cells of my spine, back and pelvis. From now on you must reverse that message to one of love and union by flooding the area with healing golden light to revitalize and renew those cells immediately.

However, as I detail later, because Collins's BOTA diary is not the only prose that she produced about illness and healing, I find it more useful to think through how different forms of writing and the aesthetics they incorporate can offer nuanced thinking about the complicated cancer narratives that Black women writers create. While much of the research on such rhetoric attends to neoliberalism and its undermining of more radical, less capitalistic concepts of medical and health care not centered on individuation, most do not engage concerns about how colonialism and settler colonialism affect spiritual practices and healing traditions. Understanding the historical context of health movements, body politics, and biosociality provides some possible insight into why Collins might have kept her illness a secret, but aligning that context with Collins's artistic goal of decolonizing the gaze allows us to gain a comprehensive understanding of the writing she produced during this time, which concerned illness, alternative ideologies of healing, and original theories of life and living. What considerations of race and health care shaped her knowledge about cancer diagnosis and treatment? Were there many Black women artist survivors who thought about the world and searched for new forms of life as she did?

OUT OF TIME: "BOTA DIARY"

As highlighted in previous chapters, Collins was interested in various spiritual practices. She was a theology and philosophy major, and much of her later work centered on questions relevant to these fields of study. Long before she turned away from oncology as the only solution to cancer and turned instead to the BOTA tarot, she wrote in an earlier daily journal, "I know I lead my life psychically . . . I don't know why this is so . . . why I try to stay in touch with what can take me further, make me stronger, give me greater self-containment" (2019, 54). The BOTA tarot served as a suitable form to narrate her journey since it was a psychic tradition based in storytelling tools for holistic healing. As Collins indicated, "The Tarot Keys are exact pictures of the TRUE <u>SELF</u> . . . not the personality . . . they are not attitude of emulation, but <u>facts</u> of <u>being!</u>" (July 25, 1987). Collins's BOTA diary stands as an entirely novel form of diary writing: She records tarot readings, talks to a god, talks to her higher consciousness, outlines her medical treatment plan, and unfolds her creative vision. She believed the cards were more than a sufficient diagnostic tool for any one body dealing with haints, or things that don't seem like they can be shook loose. In this fifth life, it seemed that the thing that would not shake loose was cancer.

As a philosopher, Collins saw cancer as another metaphysical puzzle to be solved. It was not that she didn't believe Western science and medicine could treat the cancer; it was that she was sure Western medicine could not heal what caused the cancer to occur in the first place:

> My basic premise is that all illness is psychic disconnection of some kind. . . . The nature of illness and female success and the capacity of the female to acknowledge its own intelligence is a subject that interests me a lot. Because I think that women—if there's any way that I am a feminist, because I don't really think of myself as a feminist—but if there is any way in which women tend to be self-destructive it is in that area of creativity where they actually feel their own power and can't either acknowledge it or go into it as much. . . . They can't go to the end of it. They get scared and they retreat into illness or into having too many babies or destructive love affairs with men who run them ragged. Somewhere or other, they detour out of respect for their own creativity. (Nicholson 1988–89, 9)

Such ideals were not Collins's alone; other Black women writers voiced similar theories. Toni Cade Bambara wrote, "And my mama—not one to traffic in metaphors usually, being a very scientific woman—would add, 'Yeah, speak your speak' 'cause every silence you maintain is liable to become *first* a lump in your throat, then a lump in your lymphatic system" (Bambara 1996, 225). Bambara, a filmmaker and writer of the healing novel *The Salt Eaters*, died from breast cancer seven years after Collins, whom she greatly admired. In between their living and dying of breast cancer, Collins and Bambara theorized illness and healing throughout various cultural mediums. The two women demonstrated interest in concepts of reciprocity deemed important in Indigenous spiritual practices, as opposed to Western medical traditions.

In *Science, Colonialism, and Indigenous Peoples: The Cultural Politics of Law and Knowledge*, Laurelyn Whitt explains that "indigenous knowledge systems typically place considerable significance and value on alternative ways of knowing the world, particularly on gaining access to the perspective of the other-than-human. . . . This commitment to a non-anthropocentric epistemological pluralism, to coming to know the world through perspectives that are diverse and not restricted to that of humans, runs directly counter to the commitment to anti-pluralism typical of the dominant knowledge system" (Whitt 2009, 34). Though tarot cards are not specific to Indigenous populations, they rely on reciprocity and alternative ways of knowing.

With her BOTA diary, Collins establishes a subgenre in breast cancer narratives that is less interested in the pink ribbon survivor narrative, angry politicized narrative, or Christian salvation narrative. She provides instead a narrative of self-determination. In one entry, Collins writes, of the BOTA tarot, "Whenever I return to the hierophant, love and powerful individuation occur in me" (June 16, 1987). A basic summary of the hierophant's meaning, in most tarot card decks, easily aligns with Collins's living. When turned upright, the card symbolizes education, learning, and spirituality; when the card is reversed, it symbolizes rebellion, unconventionality, and nonconformity. Further, tarot card readings and practices are very distinct to the individuals and communities that practice them, because the cards—in their images, colors, and symbols—come with a world order that may or may not be culturally relevant for any one person or community. Of BOTA tarot, Collins wrote, "Why do I love their Key above all the others, why does it wake from me such potent and overwhelming feelings?" (June 16, 1987).

In "BOTA Diary III," Collins insists that "it is through subconsciousness that one enters the FOURTH DIMENSION" (July 3, 1987). The diary records the many exercises she dedicated to her subconscious during her illness. She performs almost daily tarot readings for herself. Her diary entries mix details about the cards she draws and her interpretations of them. Sometimes she provides a clue to the type of reading by spacing the key numbers on the page as though recording their places in a table reading. From there, she submits a question, meditates, and answers. For example, one entry reads: "Begin Key 21—The World . . . Space preoccupies me. That I move within ALL THAT IS. Have my being with ALL THAT IS. That there is no self, enclosed body, but extended matter existing above and below, to the east as to the west, to the north as to the south that the decomposition of form (mentally) is the recognition of

SELF, the mirror" (July 6, 1987). The cards she draws for herself and the keys aligned with each card are part of a conversation with the natural world.

These exercises are about transformation and transition into what Collins understands as the fourth dimension. "The transformation drama is clearly the hallmark of Afro-American literature, of our culture. . . . It is an imperative for our survival," Toni Cade Bambara explained some time ago when discussing film (1996, 205). Her words resonate with the theme and function of Collins's private diary writings. Transformation as the hallmark of Black culture instigates a challenge to the biopolitical narrative of dying from the hallmarks of cancer. A rhetoric of transformation was necessary for Collins to survive in her next life. In a letter to her daughter, Nina, days before Collins's forty-sixth birthday, Collins would confess, "The other day . . . I was driving somewhere and I saw the old form that was me leave my body. It's gone. I know it. And I am alert only to what the new form is saying, speaking. I feel tremendously aware, to an extremely sharp degree, of what is occurring around me" (July 2, 1985). The BOTA diary's rhetoric of transformation is part of a larger Black women's writers' tradition that scholarship on breast cancer narratives ignores, even as it may attend to racial and ethnic differences. Collins could not and would not ignore this tradition.

BLACK FEMINIST POETHICS OF CANCER

The cluster of barely middle-aged Black women writers who lived with or died of breast cancer throughout the 1980s and 1990s (Toni Bambara, Kathleen Collins, Pat Parker, Audre Lorde, and June Jordan, to name a few) were not genetically related, but they could be read as psychically linked in the natural world through their artistic practices. Some would even turn to the word and non-western healing philosophies to theorize illness. In "Toward a Black Feminist Poethics," Denise Ferreira da Silva offers an essay that links the writing of all these women, asserting that her thesis is "primarily a speculation on a Feminist Poethics of Blackness, which includes the outline of a description of existence without the tools of universal reason, and the narratives of science and history that sustain the transparent trajectory of the subject of universal reason and its grip on our political imagination" (da Silva 2014a, 82).

Encouraged by da Silva's speculation, I ask and answer: Why did these Black women who wrote of being and toward becoming . . . why did they, when so inspired, write of healing as a laying-on of hands? Why did they continue to imagine their own well-being and that of their communities, to imagine an affective and effective interiority of a touch, to imagine a release of all the many external things that attempted harm or harmed them? To imagine being without logic and empiricism? Why did they continue to imagine that they could ever be healed in this way? To imagine all the being and becoming, when there is no cure for white supremacy male patriarchy in sight, and where there seems to be only life even as they die from the logos of bio? A Feminist Poethics of Blackness leads to a Black Feminist Poethics of Cancer.

Collins pondered such connections, alluding to them as a future conversation: "I have this feeling of being very connected with Lorraine Hansberry. . . . And I have this strong feeling that there is this conversation that I have to have with Lorraine Hansberry at some point in time" (Nicholson 1988–89, 8). After reading Collins's diary and plays, I submit that she was having this conversation with Hansberry, and others, across time and space, throughout her writing.

Collins seems to have already constructed a belief system that fit the practices of the principles of BOTA, as evidenced in the 1986 interview with David Nicholson about illness, art, and success. Although the interview, published after her death in *Black Film Review*, is between Nicholson and Collins, I read it as a conversation that Collins was also having with Lorraine Hansberry. At one point during the interview, Collins tells Nicholson, "The thing that interests me about [Hansberry], probably more than anyone else, is her illness. She died very young, and she died basically eaten up. My theory is that she was not only way ahead of her time, but that success came at a time when she was not able to absorb it without its destructive elements eating her body up" (1988–89, 8). Reading the Nicholson interview and the BOTA diary together, it becomes clear that the rhetoric of transformation shapes both. Collins is interested not only in her own transformation but also in that of other like-minded Black women. Just as Lorraine Hansberry, Audre Lorde, Pat Parker, June Jordan, Gloria Naylor, Gayl Jones, Toni Morrison, and Toni Cade Bambara worked in multiple forms and aesthetics to take up concerns of race, gender, sexuality, class, and illness, so, too, did Collins.

Later in the interview, Collins continues to speculate about reciprocity and to draw connections between sickness and abuse or misuse of women's creative imagination—a thesis that fails to translate into Western medical language of treatment or cure. The reality, however, is that Collins seems to have come to this conclusion both before and after trying medical approaches to her diagnosis. Her choice of alternative medicine and a homeopathic approach to dealing with her disease was not the result of a rush to judgment or impaired judgment. Since it appears that some years earlier, she had been diagnosed with breast cancer and taken Western medical advice to overcome and survive it, her final resolution to forgo that approach on her second diagnosis is informed by a different way of knowing—a Black feminist poethics.

Collins's BOTA diary demonstrates what Edouard Glissant would term the right to opacity "that is not enclosure within an impenetrable autarchy but subsistence within an irreducible singularity" (190), since opacity "is that which cannot be reduced, which is the most perennial guarantee of participation and confluence" (191). Black feminist poethics insists on the right to opacity for everyone. A Black feminist poethics points us toward psychic genealogies where knowledge or "knowing is a reciprocal activity" (Whitt 2009, 51). This is why they wrote of healing as a laying-on of hands or an exchange of energy. Not unlike contemporary Black women theorists such as Sylvia Wynter, Hortense Spillers, M. Jacqui Alexander, and da Silva, who engage various philosophies of thought to address the delimitation of Black life, Collins turns to the fictional forms of writing to engage various nonmedical philosophies to better understand her illness and theorize herself out of both the biopolitical mandate of life and the sociological idea of Black life as social death.

Presenting the BOTA diary and the Nicholson interview first conveys this premise about a rhetoric of transformation and the search for new life in a reverse chronology to demonstrate that Collins was not simply out of time but out of space as well. That is, not only was there no cure for her cancer; there was no discourse and no narrative that could help her make sense of the empty definitions of life she had been saddled with in living and then in dying. She had to create it elsewhere. She would try . . . again . . . and again.

BEGIN THE BEGUINE: OUT OF PLACE

In Collins's personal papers, the cover page of *Begin the Beguine* includes the phrase "a quartet of one-act plays," which suggests that the plays may have been meant to be performed together and seen in one sitting. *Begin the Beguine* is comprised of the self-titled one-act play and three others: *Remembrance*, *The Reading*, and *The Healing*. The plays are published as separate works in the 2019 collection *Notes from a Black Woman's Diary: Selected Works of Kathleen Collins*. However, if one assumes from the cover page in the personal papers that these are one-act plays meant to be performed in one sitting, then the overall arch of their thesis on life and death, and the impact of gender and race on both, seems apparent.

The title symbolizes more than a connection to a Cole Porter song. The word *beguine* has several meanings and definitions: the first is a form of dance important in West African fertility rites; the second, a nineteenth-century genre of music that combined African drum/percussion and rhythms, both derived from Guadeloupe and Martinique; and the third, a religious order. Collins uses the Creole French spelling, a feminine form, and doing so might be her allusion to the third definition. The Beguine religious order was a Christian community or society, ascendant from the thirteenth to the sixteenth century, comprised of women who devoted themselves to emulating the life of Jesus Christ, without having to take lifetime vows as nuns, though some might practice chastity. Their informal spiritual practices garnered the women much scrutiny and suspicion despite the good works they performed.

The multiple meanings of the beguine are important and relevant to understanding how the set of one-act plays convey Collins's main concern about women finding new forms of life, which would also provide a platform for them and her to process reliance on or rejection of a singular biomedical meaning of life and therefore an approach to cancer diagnosis. For Collins, the literal and metaphorical beginnings of these beguines are modes to access whatever forms can get her/us out of the prison of the body while showcasing its marvels and ability to assist us in developing higher consciousness.

The quartet of plays examines women attempting to locate a form of life equivalent to the life that men lead, mistakenly represented as a life of freedom and liberation. As Collins once wrote, "The terror I feel in the face of a man's freedom, the boundless arbitrariness of it. How ruthless it can be in pursuit of itself. Men become themselves out of a refusal of certain kinds of limitations, women out of an acceptance of them" (Collins 2019, 47). The one-act play *Begin the Beguine* stands as an homage to African American writer Zora Neale Hurston, "a real vagabond for . . . dreams" (Collins 2019, 177). Collins uses the play to reinterpret the Christian origins of the Beguine order to account for the racialized experience of gender. Set in a park and centered on two characters, a twenty-five-year-old Black man and a fifty-five-year-old Black woman, the play depicts a conversation between the two, who may be son and mother, or life and death. The son reveals the woman to have a flighty and foreboding personality: "You're inside the goddamn things, you are the cloud" (Collins 2019, 174). The woman, an actor, tells the younger man, "I once played Zora Neale Hurston. . . . I'm convinced that somewhere in this universe there's a vagabond black spirit" (175). The dialogue hints that the woman abandoned the young man to pursue her own dreams. Hurston not only becomes an iconic figure to emulate but also serves as the foundation of a spiritual system that could release the woman from her bondage/gendered form.

Their dialogue contains a folktale from Hurston's *Mules and Men*, "Why the Waves Have Whitecaps," featuring the personified elements Mrs. Wind and Mrs. Water, both maternal figures with children. As the folktale reveals, a conflict between the two results in Mrs. Water drowning Mrs. Wind's children in the ocean. Though it is a significant folktale, it is not the only one the mother knows. The son reveals, as the two talk in the park, how she was an avid story-teller and often recounted tall tales before putting him to sleep. As the story moves forward, the audience learns that the woman became an actor because she comprehended that embodied performance in the secular/sacred space of theater would allow her to escape the dilemma of devoting her life to someone other than herself. We know this because she says, "When I was playing Zora, I called on parts of myself unwelcome in our household" (Collins 2019, 181). Domesticity requires maternal and wifely servitude in the care of family and home, factors that are starkly in opposition to a vagabond spirit. The son recalls, "Even when you read me stories, tucked me in . . . you were looking around for something" (184).

"Begin the Beguine" underscores that race and gender are social constructs foundationally sustained and advanced by biopolitics alongside religious or sacred beliefs. Collins understood these two operating systems as impacting her entire life. In one journal entry, she pessimistically proclaimed, "Women are bound. They must come to terms with a whole centrifugal force of taboos that they cannot violate without doing severe violence to themselves. We are in bondage to life. A woman's life is a terrible thing. Make no mistake about it. And I believe in liberation, but I don't believe it is at all the thing we think it is" (Collins 2019, 47). Collins would attempt, time and again, to write herself out of a woman's life, a Black woman's life, while also seeking to ascertain what liberation might look like in a new life. The quartet of one-act plays metaphorically suggests the recursiveness of this struggle to disengage from social and biological life.

In another of the one-act plays, *Remembrance*, Collins uses monologue to make evident the confinement of domesticity and its foreclosure of women's metaphysical being. Much like Ntozake Shange's *For Colored Girls*, the critique of the social life that evolved from the moral imperialism of colonial religion is obvious. *Remembrance*, however, is steeped in the quiet isolation of bourgeois capitalist domesticity that imprisons its female character. As the stage directions explain, "There should be no hint of madness. She is not mad, nor should she be played in a distracted fashion" (Collins 2019, 137). Rather than a Black woman character who is angry, mad, or distracted, Collins insists on "preoccupation" and "disjointment." Moreover, because the one-act play is a soliloquy presented as a one-sided conversation, the audience is meant to understand how disconnected this woman feels from her family and other women who may be exactly like her—women in search of something more. After a day of homemaking and a night of insomnia, she explains, "It's not easy to pin down the exact moment when I went looking for God" (140). I referenced Shange's play because its structure deliberately has Black women talk across time and space to demonstrate their metaphysical connection, even as they live very different lives. The salve and salvation in that play are themselves, Black culture, and each other. In Collins's unnamed narrator, we see a Black woman reaching for a god to solve and reconcile her sense of self, which seems out of sync with her everyday life.

Speaking from a bathroom that functions as an altar and a confessional, the character delivers her dialogue before an audience—but she is not speaking to the audience: "I wander into the bathroom to find God. . . . Who the hell is God. . . . And what God . . . Jehovah, Jesus, Baba, the Old Rugged Cross, the Fountain Filled with Blood, like you could open the Christian language and find God" (Collins 2019, 143). From then on, the conversation makes it clear that the rites and rituals (gospel music) of "a lot of colored churches" lead to deep emotional and spiritual reactions of weeping because "colored people remember something from somewhere, sometime, someplace, and cry because they know it and recognize it at the same time" (143).

As the woman continues recounting her experiences in the publics of Black churches and in the private spiritual space she creates within her home, stillness and movement, silence and noise, are juxtaposed. The struggle is to establish an internal rhythm that can save the woman. Whenever she can, the character constructs a temporary altar by lighting a candle and speaking with a higher power. Eventually, Collins conceptualizes spiritual practices as a psychic dance, as opposed to a religious order: "Out of my own holiness, I provoke You . . . with my breath I draw you from me . . . I forget You, then remember, forget, then remember . . . it's a dance, my dance . . . to forget You in order that I might remember You, it goes on forever, this dance" (Collins 2019, 145). Dance comes with rites and rituals, but it also emphasizes movement and shifting perspectives that might elicit change, adaptation, and evolution so that fixed and dogmatic ideas do not deaden us to one another's differences and needs. Unfortunately, for this character, there is no escape, and the temporary reprieve she seeks will be repeatedly intruded upon by the labor she must provide to a husband and two sons.

The structure of the play's ending signifies the irresolution of the woman's life. Whereas the play has been mostly soliloquy, it ends with the husband coming home early from work before she can finish her ritual. She tells the audience that her husband asks, "Are you alright?" As she attests to being fine and quickly shifts into caretaking mode, the play ends with, "He reached for me . . . I screamed . . . [with violence] Which world will it be" (Collins 2019, 146). There is no joy, no resolution, and certainly no laying-on of hands. There is no healing for the woman. Moving into another woman's life might reveal a possible resolution, even if there is no salvation.

In *The Reading: A Play in One Act*, Collins uses the waiting room of a psychic's office as a plot device to explore how two women in their forties, a Black woman named Marguerite Simpson and a white woman named Helen Mills, might reimagine change in themselves. Marguerite is a fashion designer and Helen a writer, and both are untethered to husbands or children. Collins's belief in extrasensory perception consistently influenced her artistic vision and personal life. In the play, these experiences become a layered meditation on race and gender. Meditation becomes a practice for visualization that is not accounted for in Western aesthetics and visual art. Specifically, Collins investigates how to move her Black woman character through light, space, and time. As Marguerite sits waiting to see Queenie, a Black psychic medium, a candle in the waiting room keeps going out. Marguerite stands up to relight it each time. The final time that she lights the candle, she chooses not to return to her seat but to settle in front of the candle. According to Collins's stage directions, Marguerite stares "defiantly at the candle as if daring it to go out. It stays lit" (Collins 2019, 148). When the candle goes out upon Helen's entrance into the waiting room, or because Marguerite stopped staring at it, Marguerite convinces Helen to adopt her strategy of staring at the candle to keep it lit.

The scene is a perfect metaphor for Collins's belief that the ability to move people through space and light is an art, but it might also be a practice of producing a new metaphysics of being. In one act, Collins provides alternatives to what kinds of movement are possible for Black people, whose movement is always curtailed by seen and unseen forces. For Marguerite, who says that she "believe[s] in the mind and the will . . . the darker mysteries of self" (Collins 2019, 149), the visit to the psychic's office is presented as an alternative to her Black social life, which is focused on the external. Yet it is a focus on the light that enables Marguerite to focus on interiority. It is movement less influenced by public notions of space and more aligned with world-making notions of space that refuse the public for something older, more ancient, and futuristic. As the two women discuss the reasons they are visiting Queenie, the audience learns about their marriages, their identities as women, and their past readings. The key to Collins's representation, however, is that none of those universals can be deracinated from lived experience.

Marguerite's description of her previous reading is especially relevant to what Collins proposed in her 1984 lecture at Howard University. Though her prior psychic reading sought to answer whether Marguerite might find a man or love, Marguerite tells Helen that Queenie's response was not about romantic love: "She warned me that I might miss it altogether because I was so strict with myself and suffered like most women of the race from feelings of unworthiness. . . . That's how she put . . . the race . . . like it was an affliction" (Collins 2019, 158).

During the Howard University lecture, Collins details how at the age of twenty-four she was introduced to Jean-Paul Sartre's *Saint Genet: Actor and Martyr*, his analysis of Jean Genet's *The Thief's Journal*. Collins explains that she was drawn to Genet's book because it captured the experience of what it means to be an outsider. Much later, at the end of the lecture, teary-eyed, she comments, "The pain of being outside never goes away" (Collins 1984). If the pain of being an outsider never goes away, then figuring out what to do with it needs to be addressed if rebellions and revolutions are to exist. Additionally, a reconsideration of temporality and spatiality might shift us from thinking of the pain of being an outsider to thinking of the exhilaration of being out of time and out of place. *The Reading* tends to the mechanisms that create boundaries, borders, and outsiders in the external world and replaces them with internal structures organized by perception. Helen recounts to Marguerite her first experience with Queenie: "I'd never been for a reading, I didn't know what one was, except to go hear other writers read from their work or reading from mine. . . . But after the first time, I thought, it's not so different, except I'm the book . . . she's reading me" (Collins 2019, 156).

Collins's play understands that stories and narratives construct identities, social and personal. Yet she also demonstrates a fundamental understanding of the role of intuition in interpreting or editing any type of text. Helen's words highlight the need for literacy about each of these acts. However, such literacy is impeded by unacknowledged narratives of white supremacy that privilege rationality to produce fictions of raced and gendered monstrosity. Later, when Helen accuses Marguerite of being difficult, Marguerite responds: "It must be some colored thing, passed down through the genes . . . refuse the white logic of things" (Collins 2019, 163). The white logic of things also becomes an issue when Queenie's assistant tells the two women that due to fatigue, Queenie will only be able to see one of them. Though Marguerite was there first and had an appointment, Helen argues that she should be prioritized because her reading qualifies as a medical emergency. She fears her doctor's appointment will be a diagnosis of cervical cancer, whereas Marguerite's appointment is a follow-up about her life and whether she has learned to navigate the race problem. Helen asks, "But is yours an emergency?" Marguerite responds, "In which case, crumbling breasts and vaginas have it all over me." Helen fires back, "You're not going to make this racial" (171).

Marguerite's refusal of white logics draws even more currency because she does so in a space that white logics refuse to acknowledge as medical, scientific, or religious. Helen's privileging of the biological over the psychic is rooted in white supremacy and the scientific colonization of other orders of knowledge. By the end of the play, when Marguerite does see Queenie, she hears these sage words: "Color, honey, that's all I see, ain't nothing but color left between you and me" (Collins 2019, 172). The construction of race and anti-Blackness leaves a tale so vivid that no psychic can ignore them. Collins persists in presenting being and living as a metaphysical dilemma.

Audre Lorde chose the personal essay, a public genre of writing foundationally vested in establishing a sense of intimacy and community, to address her first cancer diagnosis and fight to survive as well as to engage her terminal diagnosis and its resolution. In her essays, Lorde advocated for broad education about the disease, treatment, and possible causes, insisting, "We owe ourselves this information before we may have to use it" (Lorde 1980, 73). Still, Lorde's public battle with cancer and the corporate entities organized to cure it was hers and did not necessarily encompass everyone's experience, as she noted.

Though impacted by the same conditions of racism and sexism within the medical, research, and philanthropic industries, other Black women took alternative routes to surviving, living with, and dying from breast cancer. Collins's decision was to use playwriting and fictional characters to linger in the ambiguous choice between self-determination and responsibility to the greater community, family, or political world. Throughout the quartet of plays, she constructs characters that allow an audience to vacillate between challenging and finding comfort in the Western Judeo-Christian ideologies embedded in Western medicine's biopolitics, which govern and regulate the ways in which one could live with chronic illness or die. Becoming a filmmaker unveiled for Collins an entirely new dimension of psychic work that could be done, regardless of whether it was seen or understood as work in the white public sphere. Collins critiqued Western medicine's biopolitics, but she also critiqued Western empire's colonization of alternative spiritual practices.

Three of the one-act plays explicitly demonstrate psychic fracturing and illness for Black women, and their only depiction of physical illness comes in the form of countering white responses to cancer diagnoses that do not account for the experience of race. In the last one-act play, *The Healing*, Collins depicts the convergence of psychic well-being with physical well-being for a Black woman, Ellen, who, as a result of a terminal diagnosis, consults with an energy healer, a white man named Joe. The play is explicitly about cancer and the colonization of holistic healing traditions, and as in the other one-act plays, Collins refuses to provide a resolution for her audience.

While *The Reading* depicted a Black woman refusing the devaluation of her psychic illness (caused by racism) by a white woman who views her cancer as more pertinent, *The Healing* depicts Ellen attempting to make Joe understand the importance to her healing of the psychic toll racism takes on the body. The session of energy work reveals the layered ways in which colonization and racism are dismissed. First, Ellen asks questions related to morality and illness: "But sin must be there somewhere, sins against the body that we call disease" (Collins 2019, 191). Joe ignores her as he continues to "lay on hands" and insists that she "give in." As he continues working on her, she attempts to explain the way she feels: "It's as if I were in church, and the spirit got the better of me. . . . Do other black women react the same . . . shout, cry out?" (194). Ellen demonstrates a comprehension of both Western colonial religious practices and the racialized cultures that shape them, alongside the alternative spiritual traditions related to non-Western medicine that she reaches for in attempts to be healed. However, Joe insists on quieting her perspective: "Others react the same. . . . I don't know about their color, you're the first black woman to come to me. Be still . . . and just breathe" (194). As Jackey Stacy asserts in *Teratologies: A Cultural Study of Cancer*, "These self-health discourses . . . lose sight of any social, economic or environmental forces which affect health and offer instead an entirely individualistic world view which posits the patient and her/his will-power at the center of a manipulable universe" (Stacy 1997, 221). Collins's play presents the irony of racism and privilege in alternative healing communities, where alternative ways of knowing somehow still do not include knowing the impact of racial constructs and racism on the body.

In discussing the marketing of Native America as a form of biocolonialism, Whitt touches on some of the ways in which elements of Indigenous knowledge characterized as spirituality are commodified when it is profitable: "Whether peddled by white shamans, plastic medicine men and women, opportunistic academics, entrepreneurs, or enterprising New Agers, Indian spirituality—like Indian lands before it—is rapidly being reduced to the status of a commodity, seized, and sold. . . . A succession of born-again medicine people have—with greater or lesser subtlety—set themselves and their services up for hire, ready to sell their spiritual knowledge and power to anyone willing and able to meet their price" (Whitt 2009, 6). Though Whitt's scholarship is not specifically concerned with cancer cures and research, she lays out what Collins presents in her play and what complementary alternative medicine critics had discussed earlier (Nielsen 2018, 88).

Later in the play, when Ellen has tired of Joe's dismissals, she insists, "Somewhere inside that history are the *reasons* why my body's playing tricks on me."

Joe replies, "I'm not a psychiatrist, I don't try to make connections between things" (Collins 2019, 195). Collins uses the four one-act plays to make the point that she and other Black women *do* try to make connections, and that to do so remains a significant strategy and narrative in healing narratives and the search for new life. Though most African American literary critics who study Black women's narratives of healing understand this critique of Western medicine traditions, none categorize this as a pursuit and search for new life (see Wilentz 2000; T. Harris 2001; Mitchem 2007; Lee 1996). Collins's work makes this last evolution clear; *Begin the Beguine* stands as her description of a world in which any of the battles throughout Black women's living are also metaphysical, even when there exists biomedical rationalization for them.

ANOTHER FORM OF LIFE

Emperor of All Maladies provides a glimpse at the medicalization of cancer using the narrative approach of briefly presenting ancient figures of health and medicine who were not beholden to the biomedical and its sociality. The book notes that in the Egyptian, Greek, and modern Western eras, cancer was associated with a crab, a scarab, a tumor, and a zodiac sign. Nevertheless, the film and book continue to conceptualize cancer as a tumor, in the tradition of Western biosciences that fail to challenge the stories that Black women tell about cancer.

These stories are not only about illness and death but also about other forms of life less linked with the biological. Contemporary Western medicine undervalues the importance of Greek and Egyptian mythologies to disrupting the biomedical stories that dominate approaches to cancer. For example, in Greek mythology, "A giant crab (*karkinos*) came along to help the Hydra, and bit Herakles on the foot. For this he killed the crab" (Apollodorus 1975, 77–80). Favorably looked upon by Hera, the crab is placed among the stars in appreciation of the aid rendered. Alternatively, the Egyptian scarab, which resembles the crab in many visual renderings, is a sacred cultural symbol of immorality also linked with self-creation and the sun. In these mythological and astrological narratives, explicitly meant to explain the origins of a universe or world, the lessons presented to us matter: The cancer/scarab aids a greater being in a battle and for doing so is rewarded with escape from death. Is this cancer's metaphorical and biological refusal to die? Such storytelling is important for the cellular study of cancer and the social life of cancer, remembering, as poststructuralists would note, that the biological explanation is simply another narrative rooted in a culture of empiricism and rationality, as mythology and astrology are not.

Black women's refusal of the biological and biopolitical is not irrational; it is simply based in alternative ways of knowing, sometimes psychic and sometimes based on the experiences of colonization, settler colonization, Jim Crow, racism, and sexism. In *Simians, Cyborgs, and Women: The Reinvention of Nature*, Donna Haraway notes that "the power of biomedicine and biotechnology is constantly reproduced, or it would cease. This power is not a thing fixed and permanent, embedded in plastic and ready to section for microscopic observation by the historian or critic. The cultural and material authority of biomedicine's productions of bodies and selves is more vulnerable, more dynamic, more elusive, and more powerful than that" (Haraway 1991, 204). "Cancer Inc." is one of the nicer labels Audre Lorde assigned to the bioeconomy of cancer research, treatment, and advocacy (1980, 55)

In research on cancer, production of knowledge and ownership over research findings via patents have become major ethical issues about who owns both biological material and spiritual relationships to various life-forms. Scholars of Indigenous sciences have argued that "to convert life forms into intellectual property is to distort their value, to alter their contribution to the natural order. The commodification of both knowledge and genetic resources entailed by biocolonialism results in the abandonment of crucial moral responsibilities to future generations (Whitt 2009, 50). Certainly, the now-infamous case of Henrietta Lacks's cancer cells is one example, but there are others. Take, for example, what happened after University of California, Berkeley, scientific teams, led by Mary-Claire King, "discovered" the BRCA gene in 1990, a modern scientific breakthrough in devising a method to locate a gene associated with breast cancer. Four years later, an infamous example of capitalist greed occurred when Myriad Genetics followed up on the Berkeley team's research and began sequencing and patenting BRCA1 (and later BRCA2), cornering the market on diagnostic tools that could save women's lives. The company got away with charging upward of four thousand dollars for the test before more ethical members of the scientific community began challenging Myriad in 2010 and the Supreme Court overturned the patents in 2013 (Gold and Carbone 2010; Klusty and Weinmeyer 2015). Myriad Genetics, however, is not an outlier. Such moves happened in the early days of cancer research and affected the availability of ultrasounds, mammograms, and cosmetic surgery. These innovations in treatment and cure, based on rational modes of knowing, cannot be divorced from the white supremacist capitalist heteropatriarchy that produces them. What good is a cure in a world that does not allow all to access it? The transformation and search for new life can never be about repair and restructuring. Collins knew this in living and being.

From seeing herself in Hansberry, to her BOTA diary, to *Begin the Beguine: A Quartet of One-Act Plays*, Kathleen Collins left a guidebook that should be read as being about Indigenous and psychic knowledge that can complement and sometimes intervene on the biocolonialism of Western medicine. For the liberator, guerilla, freedom fighter, healer, and seventh-sighter, it seems impossible to imagine beating cancer by killing it, since it is an entity that has proven its ability to elude the bio-logics of life. We can imagine a mode of reciprocity, as Octavia Butler did in *Dawn*, or theorize the environmental factors that cause it, as Lorde did, or envision its possible transformation, as Collins did. Their approaches, even as they were dying, were the result of an entirely different worldview that is not produced or rehearsed through immersion in Indigenous knowledge systems coming from peoples or communities they were not a part of. It comes from what Indigenous knowledge systems see as real and valuable: psychic knowledge that unveils connections between life-forms. In Collins's case, writing and tarot were a spiritual practice of knowledge production. This is what I mean when I say she was in search of new life-forms. Collins was dedicated to developing this alternative schema of knowledge until her death: Death, then, does mark the end of living in one future. The writings she left are her other future/life.

Earlier chapters discussed Collins's search for new life as shaped by challenges to political and historical temporality as well as by a refusal of the dominant spatialization of Black public life, in which the public is prioritized over the private interior life. In this chapter, I assert that Collins was theorizing a type of anteriority in order to challenge and interrogate the biopolitics embedded in dominant Western rites and spiritual ideologies of living with chronic illness or dying of it. In the BOTA diary, she was exploring the psychic as a bridge for the exterior and interior, and in doing so, she makes a strong case for it as anterior to biopolitical life.

Collins's less-than-public experience of, at one point, surviving breast cancer in secret and, years later, discretely dying of it demonstrates her commitment to control and power over her definition of living. But Collins's narrative approach to her breast cancer diagnosis is also a final confirmation of her commitment to searching for new life through a Black feminist poet(h)ics. She distinguishes her cancer writings in form—they are a diary of psychic life as opposed to a journal of external life—and in how she approaches writing dying from cancer. Moving beyond a singular focus of writing about the toll cancer was taking on her body and life, Collins used the diary as a way of tracking and charting her spiritual journey. It is a diary about her spiritual ascension and development of higher consciousness during her last days on earth. Even in her transition, she remained squarely fixated on the interior. Rather than seeing herself as a survivor of cancer or a warrior, she saw herself as doing something else: providing evidence of a transformation that would reconcile her being out of time and out of place. The search for new life is neither an attempt to survive or to beat cancer but rather a means to being and becoming for the next life.

EPISTOLATING BLACK FEMINIST FUTURES (ANOTHER BEGINNING)

(To Nina, with Love)

Dear Nina,

Your mother's love of Lorraine Hansberry, Haile Gerima's insistence that she read Hansberry, and Hansberry's incorporation of Langston Hughes's line from "Harlem" make me believe that the recursiveness of black women's living and culture will always try to answer the opening line of the poem and the question that precedes "a raisin in the sun": "What happens to a dream deferred?" It was the question that immediately came to mind after I read her interview with David Nicholson, where she confides to him, "I had written a script called 'Women, Sisters and Friends,' and I had gone all round the country trying to raise money to do it. Nobody would give any money to a black woman to direct a film. This was in 1971.... And then I got so discouraged" (1988-89, 10). After reading her letters to you and her good friends, I wonder, if she had gotten to make the film based on her script "Women, Sisters, and Friends," how different her life might have been; how different your life might have been; how different the world of filmmaking would be. Even as she made two films, she was never able to make this film. Though we may never know or see her vision for the screenplay, I am writing to say thank you for allowing so many of us to dream alongside the Collins women—to dream of a world made by women, sisters, and friends. Though deferred, the dream has not dried up, festered, or exploded. It has blossomed, nourished, and expanded into whole other worlds.

CONCLUSION

DREAMS NO LONGER DEFERRED

NINA COLLINS, THE DAUGHTER OF filmmaker Kathleen Collins, was an elite literary scout and agent who built her own company, the Collins Literary Agency, from the ground up before walking away from it in 2008. She is now an accomplished author and founder of the online Woolfer community. Nina has made sure that two collections based on her mother's creative writings were published—*Whatever Happened to Interracial Love?* (2017) and *Notes from a Black Woman's Diary: Selected Works from Kathleen Collins* (2019). She has donated valuable materials to the Schomburg Center for Black Culture so that others might produce new studies of her mother's work. Nina is also completing her own memoir. I hope she realizes that these endeavors will be as important to Black feminist futures as her mother's films and writings are. In writing and reflecting on her own life, will she see, as her mother finally did, the many lives she made possible in writing herself into a larger narrative meant to seek out new life forms? As Kathleen Collins would write in a letter to her second husband, "There is a saying that goes 'your children are your soul.' And if it be so, then I could ask for no more clearer mirror, no more clarifying vision of who I am and what I have struggled to be."[1] But this closing is not simply about mothering as feminist method of genealogy; it is also about the connections made possible in a reconfiguration of the maternal and concepts of love. Kathleen Collins and Nina Collins wrote many letters to each other. These letters were kept, first by Kathleen and then by Nina. Their deliberate preservation of the letters signifies that love letters between Black women are a genre that should be heralded as an ancient technology still useful for Black feminist futures.

We have come to know more about Kathleen Collins because she left us with films, plays, and unproduced words, but mostly because she left behind a family who knew how important filmmaking was to her sense of being and to the many lives left to be lived. To know and care deeply about the dreams our mothers had for themselves is not something that is taught and learned in this society. Children, in youth and adulthood, can be selfish and self-absorbed, demanding blood and exacting sacrifices from their mothers in ways that they never would ask of, let alone demand from, their fathers. If and when they do come to care about the woman who was their mother, it is because some form of her life survived heteropatriarchal narratives of motherhood and maternal duty. It is because a seed was planted inside that child, rooted in the soil of familial love and fertilized by agape and platonic love. Like a chimeric cell, the dream survived the birthing and nurturing process, a testament to how important the dream was to the mother and the world she inhabited. We need to sit with our mothers' dreams, as Nina did, so that their lives can be valued.

I love Nina Collins. I love her for being fearless in speaking about the anger she felt at her mother for not revealing her cancer diagnosis, and for still loving her and holding on to her dreamworks despite the lack of closure caused by that decision. Nina's anger and the resolution of that anger shows that daughters cannot abdicate the dreams of their mothers for the myths of mothering.[2] I love her because she has done what many women wish they could do for their own mothers: ensure that their dreams are no longer deferred. I love her, because, unlike Alice Walker visiting the unmarked grave of Zora Neale Hurston, she allows us to begin with all the life, living, and lives that we have before us. I love her because she has opened up and laid bare the difficult, emotional, and personal nature of Black feminist recovery and its importance to life and living. Certainly, these are the lives that deserve to be rendered on-screen, onstage, and on the page, as Kathleen Collins knew. But will they be seen and appreciated and, if so, by whom?

Collins's life and work are certainly worthy of a biography, popular or critical, written by a film or literary historian who can bring mass attention to her writing and filmmaking in the way that all iconic figures receive. However, Collins also deserved something more than a biography—itself a form of writing that, I have argued, would undermine the purpose of her collective creative production. Her writing functioned as means to establishing a world order, a master narrative for the very existence of the person she was becoming: a fugitive from a life manifested and designed by someone else. Since Nina Collins has ensured that her mother's work will be accessible, I chose to imagine and theorize the possible futures that such accessibility can make happen. In lieu of biography, I offer instead this afterlife-writing because it is what I learned from my encounters with Collins's work: to attempt to tell the story of life in every form available to me. I cannot pretend to not know that Kathleen Collins was first, last, and always a polymathic storyteller. She told stories in fiction; onstage; on film; in classrooms; in philosophical, theoretical, and critical writings; in song; and in tarot readings. She told stories to her children that now provide a rebirth of her own writing and ideas.

Audre Lorde once wrote that matrilineal inheritance can become a recursive narrative of shared self-love: "the elegantly strong triad of grandmother, mother daughter, with the 'I' moving back and forth flowing in either or both directions as needed" (1984, 7). In ways that exceed nuclear family models of patriarchal archetypes and motifs, such a legacy has community-building potential if those stories are shared. In Hollywood, there are not enough love stories about Black mothers, daughters, or sisters. In the scholarly and archival tradition of mapping Black feminist genealogies, there are not enough love stories. There are race women and men with heroic ideals and missions of uplift. We have seen glimpses of Black mother-child love relationships in films such as *Soul Food*, *Crooklyn*, *Eve's Bayou*, *Claudine*, *A Raisin in the Sun*, and *Imitation of Life* as well as in television series such as *Half and Half* and *Living Single*. In recent years, Misha Green's writing of the televised neo-slave narrative *Underground*, incorporating the love story of the mother and daughter Ernestine and Rosalee, has provided a brief glimmer of the bond in times of resisting enslavement and settler colonialism. Black feminist thought needs the expansion of the relational genealogy of storytelling that Nina Collins offers. Black feminist thought can be filled with love, empathy, envy, frustration, criticism, and reflection, but what it needs to develop beyond a static "good" representation is space and time. This is also an alternative romance genre ripe for filmmaking in our current era, as seen in director Stella Meghie's 2020 film *The Photograph*.

Nina's preservation of her mother's work proves what many of us already know: that there are a lot more ways for us to love our mothers, if they love us and we love them, beyond the traditional caretaker/nurturer roles so privileged in patriarchal society. Nina's efforts show that we can literally love someone across time and space. Parents can leave children many material things, but to will them love that reflects, transcends, and endures into many generations and lives conveys an acceptance of ancestral obligation and burden. For parents to will children a love that will ensure, protect, and fulfill dreams that they themselves could not fulfill or finish in their own lifetime because time expired, without those dreams subsuming or replacing their children's own, denotes the difference between gendered narratives of romantic and familial love and the role revolution plays in the completion of divine love. I hope this examination of Collins has revealed why in the hell she wrote and made movies: to seek out and find new life . . . to begin living in any of her many possible afterlives.

NOTES

INTRODUCTION

1. Collins letter to Peggy Dammond, April 23, 1974, Kathleen Collins Papers, Sc MG938 Box b.3 f.8.

2. See Nina Collins's extensive general biography at http://kathleencollins.org/about/ and Mountain (2007) for an overview of Collins's awards, summaries of her work and its critical reception, and discussion of Lorraine Hansberry's aesthetic influence on Collins.

3. In chapter 2, my discussion of her screenplay about Bessie Coleman, *Only the Sky Is Free,* details the queer approach Collins took in her unproduced bio-pic.

4. According to family biography, Collins was born to Frank Conwell and Loretta Pierce Conwell. Her biological mother passed when she was a baby. See Plant (2007, 98) for details about Hurston's work as a technical advisor and writer for Paramount.

5. See Steven R. Carter's biographical entry in Andrews, Smith, and Foster (1997) and Elizabeth A. Hadley's "Eyes on the Prize" chapter in Klotman and Cutler (1991, 91–122).

6. During an acceptance speech during the Black Girls Rock award show, April 5, 2015, DuVernay acknowledged that some Black women filmmakers never received the recognition they should have, including "the trailblazers Kathleen Collins and Julie Dash." Since then DuVernay has acknowledged Collins's significance in multiple ways. In 2019, when Turner Classic Movies asked her to curate an "essential" film series, she included Collins's *Losing Ground;* she also highlighted that film in her ARRAY 360 film series (Morales 2019). For her own part, Dash told an interviewer from the *Stanford Daily,* "I knew Kathleen Collins! . . . I was in my twenties, and she had just graduated from the Sorbonne, was fluent in

French, had studied in French. And here I am, coming out of New York from the projects. And she's just here like [fanfare noise]" (Valladares 2016).

7. The excellence of minor releases such as Rodney Evan's *Brother to Brother* (afterlife-writing at its finest) and Dee Ree's amazing biopic *Bessie* highlights why the dearth of biopics on Black LGBTQ figures who have contributed so much to Black culture and politics is appalling.

8. For discussions of Hattie McDaniel's life, see du Lac (2010) and Watts (2005).

ANTERIOR LIFE

1. Perspective of Kathleen Collins's student, Susan Korda. Interview with author (November 19, 2012).

SHE LIKED WRITING

2. A writer in the film journal *Chamba Notes* provided information about the film location: "They will be shooting in Nassau with Kent Garrett producing" (Bourne 1972).

3. Terri Geis has discussed how "the history and culture of Haiti and Vodou held a central position within Breton's turn to myth and esotericism in the mid-1940s, and informed his creative projects on secret initiation and utopia as political tools of freedom and the imagination" (56). In addition, Breton was a collector of fifteen Hyppolite paintings; he used Hyppolite's painting *Ogoun Ferraille* for *L'Art Magique*; and in *Surrealism and Painting*, he included a chapter titled "Hector Hyppolite" (300–310). Breton also delivered lectures such as "Surrealism and Haiti" delivered in Port-au-Prince in 1945 and in Paris in 1947.

4. Four years after *Women, Sisters, and Friends*, Collins penned another script titled *The Story of Three Colored Ladies* (1975), whose settings include shooting locations on the island of Jamaica, and in New York and New Jersey. The two scripts share similar themes.

5. Collins letter to Bluette L. Dammond, September 13, 1968, Kathleen Collins Papers, Sc MG 938 b.3 f.6.

6. "On Surrealism in Haiti," Between Utopia and Reality (UNESCO, 1997). Reprinted in Kafou: Haiti, Art and Vodou, 95.

7. See Alice Walker to Kathleen Collins, December 22, 1975, Schomburg box 3. F12, as well as Toni Morrison to Kathleen Collins, March 22, 1977, Toni Morrison General Correspondence, Rare Book & Manuscript Library, Columbia University in the City of New York, Box 1528-Morrison's Random House files.

8. In "Why Black Cinema," Bambara (2009) speculates about a genealogy when she casually references a 1970 Black film retrospective arranged by Pearl Bowser as being the impetus for such action. As a film director, producer, archivist, scholar, and teacher in the 1970s, Bowser was credited with the rediscovery

of Oscar Michaeux's films and the founding of the archival project African Diaspora Images. Her efforts provide evidence of a tradition that those trained in predominantly white universities might have ignored or omitted.

9. Gerima has mentioned being influenced by Angela Davis and Hansberry. His film *Child of Resistance* (1973) details Davis's influence.

10. Based on several of Collins's diary entries and letters from the late 1960s to early 1970s, there is evidence that Collins's first husband, Douglass, produced and directed some adult films to make money during their life outside the United States.

11. See oral history interview with Carolyn Mazloomi, September 17–30, 2002. Archives of American Art, Smithsonian Institution. https://www.aaa.si.edu /collections/interviews/oral-history-interview-carolyn-mazloomi-11150.

LOVE, A CRISIS OF POSSESSION

1. Specifically, she declares, "Love—this is a word I would love to talk to you about so far does it lie outside my vocabulary of feelings. That is to say I love Douglas . . . when he inspires me emotions so torn that the word love seems inept, lifeless. ("Letter to Bluette L. Dammond," 1967, Kathleen Collins Papers, Sc MG938, b.3.f.6.)

2. Collins letter to Ellen Craft, September 24, 1973, Kathleen Collins Papers, Sc MG938, b3.f.7.

3. See Fischer-Hornung (2008) for a smart discussion of Hurston, Dunham, and Deren.

4. In an analysis of films by Larry Clark and Charles Burnett, Collins examines representations of women in Black independent cinema ("*A Place in Time* and *Killer of Sheep*: Two Radical Definitions of Adventure Minus Women," 7.)

5. Ibid.

6. Collins letter to Bluette L. Dammond, August 14, 1984, Kathleen Collins Papers, Sc MG938, b.3.f.6.

7. Collins letter to Peggy Dammond, date unknown, but the letter references life with Alfred [Prettyman], which places it in the early 1980s, Kathleen Collins Papers, Sc MG938, b.3.f.8.

8. Collins letter to Bluette L. Dammond, postmarked from Jamaica, date unknown but, given context about film work, 1970s, Kathleen Collins Papers, Sc MG938, b.3.f.6.

9. From the manuscript for "Losing Ground," Kathleen Collins Papers, Sc MG938, b.4.f.9.

10. Collins letter to Bluette L. Dammond, November 15, 1967, Kathleen Collins Papers, Sc MG938, b.3.f.6.

11. Collins to letter to Bluette L. Dammond, August 28, 1967, Kathleen Collins Papers, Sc MG938, b.3.f.6.

12. See Nina Collins's biography of Collins at http://kathleencollins.org /about/.

13. Phone interview with Alfred Prettyman. After her divorce from Doug Collins in 1974, Collins had relationships with Henry Roth, Ronald Gray, Carl Weathers, and others.

14. Collins to Bluette L. Dammond, August 28, 1967, Kathleen Collins Papers, Sc MG938, b.3.f.6.

15. Collins to Bluette L. Dammond, November 8, 1964, Kathleen Collins Papers, Sc MG938, b.3.f.6.

LIFE OF THE MIND

1. In adapting a science-fiction film scene, I have taken the words and tone from Collins's Howard University lecture (Collins 1984).

FIFTH DIMENSION CINEMA

2. Korda, a white Jewish editor, teacher, and filmmaker, has become quite well-known as an important feminist filmmaker. Her works include *One of Us* (1998) and *Salomea's Nose* (2014). Korda also taught editing at Columbia University.

3. See Nkiru Nzegwu's "African Art in Deep Time: De-race-ing Art and De-racializing Visual Art."

4. I am aware that a theory of a fifth dimension was taken up in physics by Theodor Kaluza and Oskar Klein during the 1920s, when they sought to add to Einstein's general theory of relativity and space-time. My own theory concerns the aesthetic and formal usage of dimension in artmaking.

5. In 1972, United Artists executive and CCNY alum Arnold Picker donated $100,000 to establish the Celia and David Picker Film Institute, a pilot program to train people of color for jobs in the film industry. It eventually became part of the Leonard David Center for the Performing Arts. ("C.C.N.Y. Gets $100,000 Gift To Establish Film Institute," *New York Times*. May 11, 1972, p. 58).

6. Collins to Bluette L. Dammond, 1971 (day and month illegible). Kathleen Collins Papers, Sc MG938, b.3.f.6.

7. Collins to Bluette L. Dammond, 1971 (day and month illegible). Kathleen Collins Papers, Sc MG938, b.3.f.6.

8. Ibid.

9. Letter to Lauretta Conwell, n.d., Kathleen Collins Papers, Sc MG938, b.3.f.5.

10. See historical summary of the report: https://current.org/2016/03/a -look-back-at-a-pivotal-moment-for-public-broadcasting/.

11. See *The Great American Dream Machine* five-DVD set (Smore Entertainment, 2015), which includes a four-page insert with background on the show written by National Public Radio TV critic David Bianculli.

12. Letter to Peggy Dammond (October 12, 1976), Kathleen Collins Papers, Sc MG938, b.3.f.8.

13. Rebecca Williams, interview with the author (December 9, 2012). Williams met Collins in 1979 when she was an eighteen-year-old aspiring filmmaker. She is currently an Essex County College professor of English and politician in New Jersey.

14. Susan Korda, interview with the author (November 19, 2012).

15. In her conversation with me, Williams goes on to say that Collins was also very supportive and giving of time: students were often invited into her home, had her phone number, and that her cohort with Collins felt "very much like a family."

16. For a discussion of this phrase as attributed to Lumière, see James Nare-more's "Introduction" in *An Invention without a Future: Essays on Cinema*, 1–12. University of California Press, 2014.

17. Korda actually indicated, "she had her favorites . . . Kevin Baguette and Joe Vasquez" (November 19, 2012).

18. Vasquez completed other minor movies while dealing with mental illness. He died in 1995 from AIDS-related complications.

CINEMATIC MARRONAGE

1. I use Gregson Davis's solid translation of the poem (Césaire 1997, 18–19).

2. See Rustin (2003) for discussions of nonviolence and civil disobedience strategies during the Civil Rights movement.

3. Michelle Alexander's *The New Jim Crow* attests that "the seeds of the new system of control—mass incarceration were planted during the Civil Rights Movement itself, when it became clear that the old caste system was crumbling" (2010, 22).

4. In 2017, reports leaked that *Game of Throne* creators were developing an HBO show, *Confederate,* based on the premise of an alternative reality in which the South won the Civil War. That such a show is imagined as being worth devel-opment, specifically during a time when the threat of racial violence and white supremacy remains an active threat, demonstrates the conditions that make challenges to a carceral imagination difficult.

5. These range from the historically detrimental cases of Carolyn Bryant (Emmet Till), the Scottsboro Boys, and the Kissing Case to contemporary nui-sance calls that have spawned Karen memes. They can also become weaponized, as Amy Cooper's attempt to call the police on a Black man birdwatching threat-ened to be.

6. Later, Collins would tell Franklin, after another question about whether her films were Black enough, "If Black or Third World filmmakers only accept extro-verted art as reality, then they're denying that there are as many psychological

types among Black people as among other races of people. Based on the type of personality one naturally has . . . that's where one's art has to come from" (Franklin 2015, 34).

7. In the film, Grant attempts to tape the arrest before cops order him to put his phone away.

KARKINOS LIFE

1. Taken from a letter republished in one of the posthumous edited collections of Collins's writings, this sentence takes the declarative form in the letter and was presumably written before Collins's cancer diagnosis. The letter provides a context for the words as being about the suicide of a close friend's husband. She marks the phrase to distinguish between the finality of death and other losses in life (divorce or brief absence) where some sense of future possibility remains. I have added the question mark to preview a possible shift in the finality of this statement brought on by Collins's cancer diagnosis and her response to it (Collins 2019, 43).

BLACK FEMINIST POETHICS AND CANCER

2. BOTA Diary Entry, January 4, 1988, Kathleen Collins Papers, Sc MG938, b.9.f.2.

3. Collins letter to Peggy Dammond (7/26/80), Kathleen Collins Papers, Sc MG938, b.3.f.8.

DREAMS NO LONGER DEFERRED

1. Collins to Alfred Prettyman, August 6, 1986, Collins Papers.

2. Nina has discussed this in *Elle*, *Vogue*, and *The Guardian* as well as in several talks and interviews (see Collins 2013, 2016; Kellaway 2017).

REFERENCES

Adesokan, Akinwumi. 2011. *Postcolonial Artists and Global Aesthetics*. Bloomington: Indiana University Press.

Akomfrah, John. 2012. "De-Westernizing as a Double Move: An Interview with John Akomfrah." In *De-Westernizing Film Studies*, edited by Saër Maty Bâ and Will Higbe, 257–75. London: Routledge.

Alexander, Elizabeth. 1994. "Can You Be Black and Look at This? Reading the Rodney King Video(s)." *Public Culture* 7, no. 1 (January): 77–79.

Alexander, Michelle. 2010. *The New Jim Crow: Mass Incarceration in the Age of Colorblindness*. New York: New Press.

Alvarez, Carlos. 2014. "For Colombia 1971: Militancy and Cinema." In *Film Manifestos and Global Cinema Cultures: A Critical Anthology*, edited by Scott MacKenzie, 258–64. Berkeley: University of California Press.

American Cancer Society. 2019. *Cancer Facts and Figures for African Americans, 2019–2021*. Atlanta: American Cancer Society.

Anderson, Benedict. 2006. *Imagined Communities: Reflections on the Origin and Spread of Nationalism*. Rev. ed. London: Verso.

Andrews, William L., Frances Smith Foster, and Trudier Harris, eds. 1997. *The Oxford Companion to African American Literature*. New York: Oxford University Press.

Apollodorus. 1975. *The Library of Greek Mythology*. Translated by Keith Aldrich. Lawrence, KS: Coronado.

Bâ, Saër Maty, and Will Higbee, eds. 2012. *De-Westernizing Film Studies*. London: Routledge.

Baldwin, James. 1976. *The Devil Finds Work: An Essay*. New York: Dial.

Bambara, Toni Cade. 1996. *Deep Sightings and Rescue Missions: Fiction, Essays, and Conversations*. Edited and with a preface by Toni Morrison. New York: Pantheon Books.

———. 2009. "Why Black Cinema?" In *Savoring the Salt: The Legacy of Toni Cade Bambara*, edited by Linda J. Holmes and Cheryl Wall, 199–206. Philadelphia: Temple University Press.

Barclay, Barry. 2003. "Celebrating Fourth Cinema." *Illusions* 35 (Winter):7-11

Barlet, Olivier. 2000. *African Cinemas: Decolonizing the Gaze*. Chicago: University of Chicago Press.

Benjamin, Ruha. 2016. "Catching Our Breath: Critical Race STS and the Carceral Imagination." *Engaging Science, Technology, and Society* 2 (2016): 145–56.

Bentley, Arthur F. 1954. *Inquiry into Inquiries: Essays in Social Theory*. Boston: Beacon Press.

Berger, Doris. 2014. *Projected Art History: Biopics, Celebrity Culture, and the Popularizing of American Art*. New York: Bloomsbury.

Bingham, Dennis. 2010. *Whose Lives Are They Anyway? The Biopic as Contemporary Film Genre*. New Brunswick, NJ: Rutgers University Press.

Boggs, Grace Lee. 2012. "Reimagine Everything: From a Speech by Grace Lee Boggs." *Reimagine* 19, no. 2. Excerpt from "On Revolution: A Conversation between Grace Lee Boggs and Angela Davis." March 2, 2012, University of California, Berkeley. http://www.reimaginerpe.org/19-2/boggs.

Bourne, St. Clair. 1972. *Chamba Notes* 1 (Fall): 1–4. Edited by Dolores Elliott. Chamba Productions. Brooklyn, NY.

Brakhage, Stan. 2014. "Metaphors on Vision." In *Film Manifestos and Global Cinema Cultures: A Critical Anthology*, edited by Scott Mackenzie, 62–69. Berkeley: University of California Press.

Brodber, Erna. 1997. *Louisiana: A Novel*. Jackson: University Press of Mississippi.

Brown, Tom, and Belén Vidal, eds. 2013. *The Biopic in Contemporary Film Culture*. AFI Film Readers. New York: Routledge.

Browne, Simone. 2015. *Dark Matters: On the Surveillance of Blackness*. Durham, NC: Duke University Press.

Buckland, Warren. 2008. "Film and Media Studies Pedagogy." In *The Oxford Handbook of Film and Media Studies*, edited by Robert Phillip Kolker, 527–56. Oxford: Oxford University Press.

Burnett, Charles, dir. 1994. *The Glass Shield*. Miramax Home Entertainment. DVD.

———. 2016. "The Glass Shield Q&A." Film at Lincoln Center, New York, September 10, 2016. Video, 27:02, https://www.youtube.com/watch?time_continue=4&v=gz0e24lKfsg&feature=emb_logo.

———. 2017. "Director Charles Burnett Talks in Depth about 'The Glass Shield'—His Most Explicitly Political Film." *Shadow and Act*, April 20, 2017. https://shadowandact.com/director-charles-burnett-talks-in-depth-about-the-glass-shield-his-most-explicitly-political-film/.

Butler, Octavia E. 1988. *Dawn: Xenogenesis*. Popular Library ed. New York: Popular Library.

Campbell, Loretta. 1983. "Reinventing Our Image: Eleven Black Women Filmmakers." *Heresies* 4, no. 4: 58–62.

Carby, Hazel. 2019. "Where Are We Going (and Why)?" Paper presented at the Black Women Writers at Work: From Slavery to Freedom Lab. Duke University Franklin Humanities Institute. Livestreamed September 6, 2019, 3:43:50–3:45:09. https://www.youtube.com/watch?v=C3pffnapdNE.

Carnegie Commission on Educational Television. 1967. *Public Television, a Program for Action: The Report and Recommendations of the Carnegie Commission on Educational Television.* New York: Harper & Row.

Carnegie Commission on Public Broadcasting. 1979. *A Public Trust: The Report of the Carnegie Commission on Public Broadcasting.* New York: Bantam Books.

Cartwright, Lisa. 1995. *Screening the Body: Tracing Medicine's Visual Culture.* Minneapolis: University of Minnesota Press.

Césaire, Aimé. 1997. *Aimé Césaire.* Translated by Gregson Davis. Cambridge: Cambridge University Press.

Christie, Ian. 2002. "A Life on Film." In *Mapping Lives: The Uses of Biography,* edited by Peter France and William St. Clair, 283–301. New York: Oxford University Press.

Clark, VèVè A. 2009. "Developing Diaspora Literacy and Marasa Consciousness." *Theatre Survey* 50, no. 1: 9–18.

Collins, Kathleen. Begin the Beguine, Kathleen Collins Papers, Sc MG938, b.8.f.5-6.

———. BOTA Diary, Kathleen Collins Papers, Sc MG938, b.9.f.2.

———. 1982 *The Brothers.* Reprint, Alexandria, VA: Alexander Street Press, 2002.

———. *But Then She's Madame Flor,* Kathleen Collins Papers, Sc MG938, b.10.f.7.

———, dir. 1980. *The Cruz Brothers and Miss Malloy.* Milestone Film and Video. 2016. DVD.

———. 1984. "Kathleen Collins Master Class, 1984." Lecture at Howard University. Milestone Film and Video. https://vimeo.com/203379245.

———. Kathleen Collins Papers, SC MG 938, Schomburg Center for Research in Black Culture, Manuscripts, Archives and Rare Books Division, NYPL.

———. 1981. In the Midnight Hour. B9f7.

———. 1993–94. "Lollie: A Suburban Tale." *Drumvoices Revue: A Confluence of Literary, Cultural and Vision Arts* 3, no. 1–2: 109–19.

———, dir. 1982. *Losing Ground.* Milestone Film and Video, 2016. DVD.

———. 2019. *Notes from a Black Woman's Diary: Selected Works of Kathleen Collins.* New York: HarperCollins.

———. 1985. *Only the Sky Is Free.* Reprint, Alexandria, VA: Alexander Street Press, 2002.

———. "*A Place in Time* and *Killer of Sheep*: Two Radical Definitions of Adventure Minus Women," In *Color: 60 Years of Minority Women in Film, 1921–1981* (New York: Third World Newsreel, n.d.) 7.

———. 2017. *Whatever Happened to Interracial Love?* London: Granta Books.

Collins, Nina. 2013. "The Fighter: Domestic Violence against Men." *Elle*, March 24, 2013. https://www.elle.com/life-love/sex-relationships/advice/a11650/the-fighter-562842/.

———. 2016. "How Kathleen Collins's Daughter Kept Her Late Mother's Career Alive." *Vogue*, September 5, 2016. https://www.vogue.com/article/kathleen-collins-filmmaker-career-daughter-nina-lorez-collins.

Coogler, Ryan, dir. 2013. *Fruitvale Station*. Weinstein Company, Significant Productions, Anchor Bay Entertainment. DVD.

Custen, George Frederic. 1992. *Bio/Pics: How Hollywood Constructed Public History*. New Brunswick, NJ: Rutgers University Press.

da Silva, Denise Ferreira. 2014a. "Toward a Black Feminist Poethics: The Quest(ion) of Blackness toward the End of the World." *Black Scholar* 44, no. 2: 81–97.

———. 2014b. "'Transversing' the Circuit of Dispossession." *Eighteenth Century* 55, no. 2/3: 283–88.

Daniels, Lee. dir. 2021 *The United States vs. Billie Holiday*. Lee Daniels Entertainment. Film.

Docterman, Eliana. 2017. "Filmmaker Gina Prince-Blythewood Wants *Shots Fired* to Speak to Everyone." *Time*, March 9, 2017. http://time.com/collection-post/4696466/gina-prince-bythewood-filmmaker/.

Du Bois, W. E. B. 1898. "The Study of Negro Problems." *Annals of the American Academy of Political and Social Science* 11 (January): 1–23.

———. (1902) 1996. *The Souls of Black Folk*. New York: Penguin.

du Lac, J. Freedom. 2010. "And Hattie McDaniel's Oscar Went to . . . ? 1940 Prize, Howard U. Play Roles in Mystery." *Washington Post*, May 26, 2010. https://www.washingtonpost.com/wpdyn/content/article/2010/05/25/AR2010052501844.html.

Ehrenreich, Barbara. 2001. "Welcome to Cancerland." *Harper's*, November. 43–53.

Engelman, Ralph. 1996. *Public Radio and Television in America: A Political History*. Thousand Oaks, CA: Sage.

Epstein, William H. 2011. "Introduction: Biopics and American National Identity." *a/b: Auto/Biography Studies* 26, no. 1: 1–33.

———, and R. Barton Palmer. 2017. *Invented Lives, Imagined Communities: The Biopic and American National Identity*. Albany: State University of New York Press.

Ernst, Max. 1959. "Interview." In *Le Monologue du peintre*, edited by Georges Charbonnier, 33–40. Paris, Julliard.

Fauset, Jessie Redmon. 1921. "Impressions of the Second Pan African Congress." *The Crisis* 23, no. 1 (November):12–18. Harlem, NY.

———.1921. "What Europe Thought of the Pan-African Congress" *The Crisis* 33 (December), 60.

Field, Allyson, Jan-Christopher Horak, and Najuma Stewart, eds. 2015. *L.A. Rebellion: Creating a New Black Cinema*. Berkeley: University of California Press.

Fischer-Hornung, Dorothea. 2008. "'Keep Alive the Powers of Africa': Katherine Dunham, Zora Neale Hurston, Maya Deren, and the Circum-Caribbean Culture of Vodoun." *Atlantic Studies: Literary, Cultural and Historical Perspectives on Europe, Africa, and the Americas* 5, no. 3: 347–62.

Fleetwood, Nicole. 2010. *Troubling Vision: Performance, Visuality, and Blackness.* Chicago: University of Chicago Press.

Ford, James Edward II, ed. 2015. "Close-Up: Fugitivity and the Filmic Imagination." Special issue, *Black Camera: An International Film Journal* 7, no. 1. 110–114

Francis, Terri. 2018. *Framing Media Podcast,* Episode #109 (10/17) on Cinephiliacs. net. http://www.thecinephiliacs.net/2018/10/episode-109-terri-francis-losing -ground.html.

Franklin, Oliver. 2015. "Interview with Kathleen Collins." *Losing Ground* Press Kit. Milestone Film and Video. 33–35.

Gates, Henry L., and Nellie Y. McKay. 2004. *Norton Anthology of African American Literature.* New York: W. W. Norton.

Gates, Racquel J. 2018. *Double Negative: The Black Image and Popular Culture.* Durham, NC: Duke University Press.

Gerima, Haile, dir. 1993. *Child of Resistance.* Mypheduh Films.

Gibson-Hudson, Gloria J. 1991. "African American Literary Criticism as a Model for the Analysis of Film by African American Women." *Wide Angle* 13, no. 3–4: 52.

Gillespie, Michael Boyce. 2016. *Film Blackness: American Cinema and the Idea of Black Film.* Durham, NC: Duke University Press.

Gilmore, Ruth Wilson. 1998–99. "Globalisation and US Prison Growth." *Race and Class* 40, no. 2–3. 171–88.

———. 2007. *Golden Gulag: Prisons, Surplus, Crisis, and Opposition in Globalizing California.* Berkeley: University of California Press.

Givanni, June. 2004. "A Curator's Conundrum: Programming 'Black Film' in 1980s–1990s Britain." *Moving Image* 4, no. 1: 60–75.

Gold, Richard E., and Julia Carbone. 2010. "Myriad Genetics: In the Eye of the Policy Storm." *Genetics in Medicine* 12, no. 4: 39–70.

Goodman, Barak, dir. 2015. *Cancer: The Emperor of All Maladies.* Presented by Ken Burns. Aired on March 30, 2015, on PBS.

Gordon-Reed, Annette. 2014. "Writing Early American Lives as Biography." *William and Mary Quarterly* 71, no. 4: 491–516.

Graulich, Melody, and Mara Witzling. 1994. "The Freedom to Say What She Pleases: A Conversation with Faith Ringgold." *NWSA Journal,* 6:1 (Spring): 1–27.

Greaves, William, dir. (1968) 2006. *Symbiopsychotaxiplasm: Two Takes.* Criterion Collection.

———. 1970. "100 Madison Avenues Will Be of No Help." *New York Times,* August 9, 1970.

———. 1998. "William Greaves: Filmmaker." *Film Quarterly* 52, no. 1: 61.

Griffin, Ada Gay, and Michelle Parkerson, dirs. 1996. *A Litany for Survival: The Life and Work of Audre Lorde.* Third World Newsreel.

Griffiths, Alison. 2016. *Carceral Fantasies: Cinema and Prison in Early Twentieth-Century America.* New York: Columbia University Press.

Grupenhoff, Richard. 1988. "The Rediscovery of Oscar Micheaux, Black Film Pioneer." *Journal of Film and Video* 40, no. 1: 40–48.

Hanahan, Douglas, and Robert A. Weinberg. 2000. "The Hallmarks of Cancer." *Cell* 100, no. 1: 57–70.

Haraway, Donna. 1991. *Simians, Cyborgs, and Women: The Reinvention of Nature.* London: Free Association.

Harris, Keith. 2006. *Boys, Boyz, Bois: An Ethics of Black Masculinity in Film and Popular Media.* New York: Routledge.

———, ed. 2016. "Close-Up: Black Film and Black Visual Culture." Special issue, *Black Camera: An International Film Journal* 8, no. 1.

Harris, Mark. 1991. "Hanging Out with Joseph B. Vasquez." *Entertainment Weekly*, June 7, 1991. https://ew.com/article/1991/06/07/hanging-out-joseph-b-vasquez/.

Harris, Trudier. 2001. *Saints, Sinners, and Saviors: Strong Black Women in African American Literature.* London: Palgrave.

Hartman, Saidiya. 2008. "Venus in Two Acts." *Small Axe: A Caribbean Journal of Criticism* 26, no. 3: 1–14.

Holloway, Karla F. C. 2002. *Passed On: African American Mourning Stories: A Memorial.* Durham, NC: Duke University Press.

Holmes, Linda Janet, and Cheryl A. Wall, eds. 2007. *Savoring the Salt: The Legacy of Toni Cade Bambara.* Philadelphia: Temple University Press.

Hudlin, Warrington, and George P. Cunningham. 1978. "Black Filmmakers, Black Audiences, and Public Television: An Examination of Issues and Options for the Future." Experimental Television Center Archives. New York: Black Filmmaker Foundation. http://experimentaltvcenter.org/sites/default/files/history/pdf/Hudlinblackfilmmakers_1736.pdf.

Hunter, James Davison. 1991. *Culture Wars: The Struggle to Define America.* New York: Basic Books.

"Jersey City NAACP Rally Told of Southern Violence." 1962. *Hudson Dispatch*, September 25, 1962.

Jones, Gayl. 1986. *Corregidora.* Boston: Beacon.

Jones, Peter. 2006. *Teaching Black Cinema.* London: British Film Institute.

Kasper, Anne S., and Susan J. Ferguson, eds. 2000. *Breast Cancer: Society Shapes an Epidemic.* New York: St. Martin's.

Kellaway, Kate. 2017. "Nina Collins: 'Much of My Adult Pain Came from My Mother's Betrayal.'" *The Guardian*, February 5, 2017. https://www.theguardian.com/books/2017/feb/05/nina-collins-kathleen-collins-bad-decision-mothers-part-interracial-love.

King, Rosamond S. 2019. "Radical Interdisciplinarity." *Meridians* (Middletown, Conn.) 18, no. 2: 445–56.

Klawiter, Maren. 2008. *The Biopolitics of Breast Cancer: Changing Cultures of Disease and Activism*. Minneapolis: University of Minnesota Press.

Klotman, Phyllis. 1984. "Interview with Kathleen Collins." April 10, 1984. Black Film Center/Archive, Indiana University Bloomington. Video.

———, ed. 1991. *Screenplays of the African American Experience*. Bloomington: Indiana University Press.

Klotman, Phyllis Rauch, and Janet K. Cutler. 1999. *Struggles for Representation: African American Documentary Film and Video*. Bloomington: Indiana University Press.

Klusty, Tobin, and Richard Weinmeyer. "Supreme Court to Myriad Genetics." *AMA Journal of Ethics* 17, no. 9: 849–53.

Knee, Adam, and Charles Musser. 1992. "William Greaves, Documentary Film-Making, and the African-American Experience." *Film Quarterly* 45, no. 3: 13–25.

Lawal, Babatunde. 2001. "Àwòrán: Representing the Self and Its Metaphysical Other in Yoruba Art." *Art Bulletin* 83, no. 3: 498–526.

Lindsay, Dan, and T. J. Martin. Dirs. 2021. *Tina*. HBO Documentary Films. Film.

Lorde, Audre. 1980. *The Cancer Journals*. San Francisco: Aunt Lute.

———. 1984. *Sister Outsider: Essays and Speeches*. Trumansburg, NY: Crossing.

———. 1988. *A Burst of Light: Essays*. Ithaca, NY: Firebrand.

MacDonald, Scott, ed. 1995. "Williams Greaves Interview." In *Screen Writings: Scripts and Texts by Independent Filmmakers*, 31–48. Berkeley: University of California Press.

Mars, Louis B. 1977. *Crisis of Possession in Voodoo*. Translated by Kathleen Collins. N.p.: Reed, Cannon, and Johnson.

Martin, Kameelah L. 2016. *Envisioning Black Feminist Voodoo Aesthetics: African Spirituality in American Cinema*. Lanham, MD: Lexington Books.

Master, Samantha. 2016. "*13th* and the Invisibleness of Black Women." *The Root*, October 12, 2016. https://www.theroot.com/13th-and-the-invisibleness-of-black-women-1790857199.

Mazloomi, Carolyn. 2002. "Oral history interview with Carolyn Mazloomi," September 17–30. Archives of American Art, Smithsonian Institution.

Merleau-Ponty, Maurice. 1968. *The Visible and the Invisible*. Edited by Claude Lefort. Translated by Alphonso Lingis. Evanston, IL: Northwestern University Press.

Mitchell, Faith. 1978. *Hoodoo Medicine: Sea Islands Herbal Remedies*. Berkeley, CA: Reed, Cannon & Johnson.

Mitchell, Koritha. 2016. "What I Learned about Police Brutality Videos from Studying Lynching Photos." *VOX*, July 28, 2016. https://www.vox.com/2016/7/28/12241082/police-brutality-lynchings-self-care.

Mitchem, Stephanie. 2007. *African American Folk Healing*. New York: New York University Press.

Morales, Wilson. 2019. "Ava DuVernay Announces ARRAY 360 Film Series Launching Sept 27." *Black Film*, September 13, 2019. https://www.blackfilm.com/read/2019/09/ava-duvernay-announces-array-360-film-series-launching-sept-27/.

Mountain, Chandra Tyler. 2007. "Kathleen Conwell Collins (1942–1988)." In *Encyclopedia of African American Women Writers*. Vol. 1, edited by Yolanda Williams, 106–11. Westport, CT: Greenwood.

Mukherjee, Siddhartha. 2010. *Emperor of All Maladies: A Biography of Cancer*. New York: Scribner.

Mulvey, Laura. 1975. "Visual Pleasure and Narrative Cinema." *Screen* 16, no. 3 (October 1): 6–18.

Naremore, James. 2014. "Introduction." In *An Invention without a Future: Essays on Cinema*, 1–12. Berkeley: University of California Press

Nash, Jennifer C. 2014. *The Black Body in Ecstasy: Reading Race, Reading Pornography*. Durham, NC: Duke University Press.

Nicholson, David. 1988–89. "A Commitment to Writing: A Conversation with Kathleen Collins Prettyman." *Black Film Review* 5, no. 1: 6–14.

Nielsen, Emilia. 2018. *Disrupting Breast Cancer Narratives: Stories of Rage and Repair*. Toronto: University of Toronto Press.

Nzegwu, Nkiru. 2019. "African Art in Deep Time: De-race-ing Art and De-racializing Visual Art." In *The Journal of Aesthetics and Art Criticism*, 77(4): 367–378.

O'Malley, Hayley. 2019. "Art on Her Mind: The Making of Kathleen Collins's Cinema of Interiority." *Black Camera* 10, no. 2 (April 1): 80–103.

Ongiri, Amy Abugo. 2009. *Spectacular Blackness: The Cultural Politics of the Black Power Movement and the Search for a Black Aesthetic*. Charlottesville: University of Virginia Press.

Petty, Miriam J. 2016. *Stealing the Show: African American Performers and Audiences in 1930s Hollywood*. Oakland: University of California Press.

Plant, Deborah G. 2007. *Zora Neale Hurston: A Biography of the Spirit*. Westport, CT: Greenwood.

Poe, Edgar Allan. 1966. Letter to Charles Anthon. In *Letters of Edgar Allan Poe*. Vol. 1, edited by John Ward Ostrom, 168. New York: Gordian.

Prettyman, Alfred. Interview, conducted by L. H. Stallings December 15, 2012.

Quashie, Kevin Everod. 2021. *Black Aliveness, or a Poetics of Being*. Durham, NC: Duke University Press.

———. 2012. *The Sovereignty of Quiet: Beyond Resistance in Black Culture*. New Brunswick, NJ: Rutgers University Press.

Ramanathan, Geetha. 2006. *Feminist Auteurs: Reading Women's Film*. London: Wallflower.

———. *Kathleen Collins: The Black Essai Film*. Edinburgh: Edinburgh University Press, 2020.

Redmond, Shana. 2017. "A Family Like Mine." *Abolition Journal*, December 13, 2017. https://abolitionjournal.org/family-like-mine/.

Reid, Mark. 1997. *PostNegritude Visual and Literary Culture*. Albany: State University of New York Press.

Roberts, Neil. 2015. *Freedom as Marronage*. Chicago: University of Chicago Press.

Rojas, Paula X. 2007. "Are the Cops in Our Heads and Hearts?" In *The Revolution Will Not Be Funded: Beyond the Non-Profit Industrial Complex*, edited by INCITE!, 197–214. Boston: South End.

Rolando, Gloria, dir. 1997. *The Eyes of the Rainbow: A Documentary Film with Assata Shakur*.

Roth, Henry H. 1989. *The Cruz Chronicle: A Novel*. New Brunswick, NJ: Rutgers University Press.

Rush, Dana. 2010. "Ephemerality and the 'Unfinished' in Vodun Aesthetics." *African Arts*, 43(1): 60–75.

Rustin, Bayard. 2003. *Time on Two Crosses: The Collected Writings of Bayard Rustin*. Edited by Devon W. Carbado and Donald Weise. San Francisco: Cleis.

Sanjinés, Jorges. 1976. "Problems of Form and Content in Revolutionary Cinema." In *Film Manifestos and Global Cinema Cultures: A Critical Anthology*, 2014. Edited by Scott MacKenzie, 286–94. Berkeley: University of California Press.

Scofield, Martin. 2006. *The Cambridge Introduction to the American Short Story*. Cambridge: Cambridge University Press.

Sembène, Ousmane. (1960) 1995. *God's Bits of Wood*. London: Longman.

Sered, Susan, and Amy Agigian. 2008. "Holistic Sickening: Breast Cancer and the Discursive Worlds of Complementary and Alternative Practitioners." *Sociology of Health and Illness* 30: 616–31.

Sexton, Jared. 2009. "The Ruse of Engagement: Black Masculinity and the Cinema of Policing." *American Quarterly* 61, no. 1: 39–63.

Shakur, Assata. 1987. *Assata: An Autobiography*. New York: Lawrence Hill.

Sharpley-Whiting, T. Denean. 2015. *Bricktop Paris: African American Women in Paris between the Two World Wars*. Albany: State University of New York Press.

Smith, Caleb. 2008. "Detention without Subjects: Prisons and the Poetics of Living Death." *Texas Studies in Literature and Language* 50, no. 3: 243–67.

———. 2009. *The Prison and the American Imagination*. New Haven, CT: Yale University Press.

Smith-Shomade, Beretta E., Racquel Gates, and Miriam J. Petty. 2014. "Introduction: When and Where We Enter." *Cinema Journal* 53(4): 121–27.

Solanas, Fernando, and Octavio Getino. 2014. "Toward a Third Cinema." In *Film Manifestos and Global Cinema Cultures: A Critical Anthology*, edited by Scott MacKenzie, 230–50. Berkeley: University of California Press.

Stacy, Jackey. 1997. *Teratologies: A Cultural Study of Cancer*. London: Psychology Press.

Stallings, L. H. 2011. "'Redemptive Softness': Interiority, Intellect, and Black Women's Ecstasy in Kathleen Collins's *Losing Ground*." *Black Camera* 2, no. 2: 47–62.

Stewart, Jacqueline N. 2005. *Migrating to the Movies: Cinema and Black Urban Modernity*. Berkeley: University of California Press.

Stork, Benedict. 2016. "Aesthetics, Politics, and the Police Hermeneutic: Online Videos of Police Violence beyond the Evidentiary Function." *Film Criticism* 40, no. 2. https://doi.org/10.3998/fc.13761232.0040.210.

Tate, Claudia, ed. 1983. *Black Women Writers at Work*. New York: Continuum.

Tinsley, Omise'eke Natasha. 2018. *Ezili's Mirrors*. Durham, NC: Duke University Press.

Tocqueville, Alexis de. 1968. *Democracy in America*. Vol. 2. London: Collins.

Trottier, David. 2019. *The Screenwriter's Bible: A Complete Guide to Writing, Formatting, and Selling Your Script*. (7th ed.), expanded and updated. Los Angeles: Silman-James Press.

Valladares, Carlos. 2016. "'Daughters of the Dust' Director Julie Dash Talks Filmmaking, Shaping the Black Female Image." *Stanford Daily*, November 21, 2016. https://www.stanforddaily.com/2016/11/20/julie-dash-interview/.

Vasquez, Joseph B. 1991. "Director Joseph Vasquez on His Latest Film about the South Bronx." Interview with Terry Gross. *Fresh Air*. Aired June 17, 1991, on WHYY. https://freshairarchive.org/segments/director-joseph-vasquez-his-latest-film-about-south-bronx.

——, dir. 1991. *Hangin' with the Homeboys*. New Line Cinema/Triumph Home Video. VHS.

Vogel, Susan Mullin. 1997. "Baule: African Art Western Eyes." *African Arts* 30(4): 64–95.

Warren, Kenneth W. 2011. *What Was African American Literature?* Cambridge, MA: Harvard University Press.

Watts, Jill. 2005. *Hattie McDaniel: Black Ambition, White Hollywood*. New York: Amistad.

White, Hayden. 1988. "Historiography and Historiophoty." *American Historical Review* 93, no. 5: 1193–99.

Whitt, Laurelyn. 2009. *Science, Colonialism, and Indigenous Peoples: The Cultural Politics of Law and Knowledge*. Cambridge: Cambridge University Press.

Wilderson, Frank B. III. 2010. *Red, White, and Black: Cinema and the Structure of U.S. Antagonisms*. Durham, NC: Duke University Press.

Wilentz, Gay. 2000. *Healing Narratives: Women Writers Curing Cultural Dis-ease*. New Brunswick, NJ: Rutgers University Press.

Williams, Linda. 2004. "Skin Flicks on the Racial Border: Pornography, Exploitation, and Interracial Lust." In *Porn Studies*, edited by Linda Williams, 271–308. Durham, NC: Duke University Press.

——. 2008. *Screening Sex*. Durham, NC: Duke University Press.

Willis, Deborah, and Barbara Krauthamer. 2013. *Envisioning Emancipation: Black Americans and the End of Slavery*. Philadelphia: Temple University Press.

Willis, Deborah, and Carla Williams. 2002. *The Black Female Body: A Photographic History*. Philadelphia: Temple University Press.

Wilson, Franklin T., and Howard Henderson. 2015. "Hollywood, the Police, and Ourselves: A Shared Responsibility for a Better Future." *Huffington Post*, April 13, 2015. Updated December 6, 2017. https://www.huffingtonpost.com/franklin-t-wilson/hollywood-the-police-and-ourselves_b_7013688.html.

Worrell, William. 1962. "Jersey City Girl Went to Jail for Praying." *Jersey Journal*, September 1962.

Wynter, Sylvia. 1971. "Novel and History, Plot and Plantation." *Savacou*, no. 5 (June): 95–102.

———. 1994. *No Humans Involved: An Open Letter to My Colleagues*. Forum N.H.I.: Knowledge in the 21st Century. Vol 1.1 (Fall). Moor's Head: Stanford, CA: 42–74.

L. H. Stallings is Professor in the Department of African American Studies at Georgetown University. She is author of *A Dirty South Manifesto: Sexual Resistance and Imagination in the New South*; *Funk the Erotic: Transaesthetics and Black Sexual Cultures*; and *Mutha' Is Half a Word: Intersections of Folklore, Vernacular, Myth, and Queerness in Black Vernacular Culture*.

CPSIA information can be obtained
at www.ICGtesting.com
Printed in the USA
LVHW031043031022
729820LV00002B/87